TOUR BOOK
For Antique Car Buffs
4th Edition

by Richard E. Osborne

Riebel-Roque Publishing
Indianapolis, Indiana
www.riebel-roque.com

ISBN 0-9628324-7-2

Published and printed in the U. S. A.
Second printing with revisions, 2007
Third printing with revisions, 2007

RIEBEL-ROQUE PUBLISHING COMPANY

6027 CASTLEBAR CIR.

INDIANAPOLIS, IN 46220

Phone: 317-849-3680

www.riebel-roque.com

Cover Photo By: ROBERT SBARGE,
President, Auburn-Cord-Duesenberg Museum
Auburn, IN

Distributed by:
CASEMATE PUBLISHERS & BOOK DISTRIBUTORS, LLC.
2114 DARBY ROAD
HAVERTOWN, PA 19083

INTRODUCTION

The purpose of this book is to provide a directory that can be used to identify and find the many places of interest to the traveling antique car buff in the United States and Canada. Included here are antique car museums, dealers, salvage yards, historic sites, libraries, restaurants and other business and public organizations specializing in displaying and marketing antique vehicles, and preserving their history.

I have sought to locate and list only those organizations that welcome visitors, have permanent facilities, staff workers and regular hours. I am well aware that some organizations might have been overlooked and I welcome information from readers and interested parties regarding those organizations for future listing. There is no charge for being listed in this book.

Listings in this book are in alphabetical order by states (provinces for Canada), and cities within those states and provinces.

—Richard E. Osborne

TOUR BOOK FOR ANTIQUE CAR BUFFS

IMPORTANT NOTE—Please Respect Businesses

While "tourists" are welcome at museums, restaurants and historic sites, this is not always the case at salvage yards and antique car dealerships. These are businesses that exist to make a profit and time is important to them. Please use good judgement in this regard.

FINDING PLACES

Whenever possible, the street address has been given for the listings in this book to make it as easy as possible to find the places you seek. In large cities that is not always easy. Please be reminded, however, that detailed city maps are usually available at most convenience stores. And then, there's MapQuest.

NOTE TO CORVETTE ENTHUSIASTS

Corvettes are one of the most popular collector cars and sports cars in the world. While Corvette museums are listed in this book, Corvette dealers are not. There are simply too many of them. Corvette dealers can be found on the web at www.vettescape.com/retainers/Retailersv.htm. At the time of the printing of this book there were 23 pages of Corvette dealers on this website.

Additional copies of this book may be ordered from:
Riebel-Roque Publishing Co.
Phone: 317-849-3680
6027 Castlebar Cir.
www.riebel-roque.com
Indianapolis, IN 46220

CONTENTS BY STATE AND PROVINCE

THE UNITED STATES

CANADA

ALABAMA

BARBER VINTAGE MOTORSPORTS MUSEUM
512 28th Street South
BIRMINGHAM, AL 35233
Phone: 205-699-7275
www.barbermuseum.org
Hours: W–F 9–11 and 1–3, closed holidays. Admission charged.

There are more than 325 motorcycles on display at this impressive museum making it the largest motorcycle museum in America. The oldest motorcycle is a 1904 Shaw, and others represent almost all US-made motorcycles and many makes from around the world. You'll see street bikes, race bikes, military motorcycles, side cars and specialty bikes, all in restored condition and most in running condition. Barber's has its own restoration shop and a gift shop. Barber's sponsor an antique motorcycle racing team. Museum founded in 1995.

AUTO INVESTORS (Dealer)
634 S. Shady Lane
DOTHAN, AL 36301
(Southeastern corner of the state)
Phone: 334-793-1658 or
334-793-9510
www.auto-n-vest.com
Hours: M–Sat. 8–6

You will find a nice selection of antique and classic cars in this dealer's showroom. Most of the vehicles are American-made. The company takes trades, sells on consignment, helps with financing and shipping. As the company name implies, they specialize in vehicles that will appreciate in value. If you need gas, they have a couple antique gas pumps in front of their store that still do their thing.

VINTAGE AUTO, INC. (Dealer)
1860 I-65 Service Rd.
MILLBROOK, AL 36054 (5 miles north of Montgomery at exit 179)
Phone: 334-285-3000
www.vintageautosinc.com
Hours: M–F 9–5

Vintage Autos, Inc. is a family-owned business that has been at the same location since 1989 and in business since 1962, so they know the antique car business very well. The company specializes in high-performance muscle cars but also offers classic and collectable cars. They can all be viewed in their modern 6,000 sq. ft. showroom. Vintage Autos takes trades, buys vehicles outright, gives appraisals and helps with shipping and financing. Car clubs are welcome.

INTERNATIONAL MOTORSPORTS HALL OF FAME AND MUSEUM
4000 Speedway Blvd.
(Off I-20, exit 173 or 168)
TALLADEGA, AL 35160
(40 miles east of Birmingham)
Phone: 256-362-5002

7

The Mercedes-Benz Visitor Center, *Tuscaloosa, AL.*

www.motorsportshalloffame.com
Hours: Daily 8–5, closed holidays.
Admission charged.

This is a five-building museum adjacent to the Talladega Superspeedway. The museum displays over 100 race cars in mint condition. Included in the collection is the famous Budweiser Rocket Car that broke the speed of sound in 1979. Also displayed are cars driven by many famous race drivers. Other displays include pace cars, go-karts, drag racers, stock cars, and memorabilia associated with famous drivers, inventors and racing events. Tickets to speedway events are available. There is an extensive research library and a gift shop. Guided tours are available.

MERCEDES-BENZ VISITOR CENTER
(Factory visitor center and museum)
    I-59 at Exit 89 (East of Tuscaloosa)
    TUSCALOOSA, AL 35403
    (50 miles southwest of
    Birmingham on I-59
    Phone: 205-507-2266 or
    888-286-8762
    www.bamabenz.com

Hours: M–F 9–5, first Saturday of each month 10–3. Closed major holidays. Admission to the Visitor Center is free.

There is a large visitor center and museum attached to the huge Daimler-Benz manufacturing complex outside Tuscaloosa. It is the only such Mercedes-Benz facility in North America. Displays in the center follow a self-guided tour that traces the history and current operations of the Daimler-Benz Corporation. There is a theater showing some of the company's worldwide advertisements and other films pertaining to the company and its history in racing from the early 1920s to the present.

Of interest to antique car buffs is the display of old Mercedes-Benz automobiles. There is also a replica of the world's first motorcycle.

A tour of the factory can be arranged at the museum. Reservations are required for the factory tour and no sandals, open-toe shoes or shorts are allowed. There is a charge for the factory tour.

ALASKA

MILLER SALVAGE, INC.
1307 30th Av. PO Box 82509
FAIRBANKS, AK 99708
Phone: 800-451-7279 (orders only
please) and 907-452-2695
Hours: M–F 8:30–6, Sat. 9:30–1:30

If you go north to Alaska you'll find
this very interesting salvage yard here
in Fairbanks. Miller has some 1,500
vehicles available dating back to the
1950s, and even to World War II. The
WW II vehicles are very unique in that
some of them were used to construct the
ALCAN (Alaska-Canadian) Highway
from Montana to Alaska during the
war. These vehicles are on display in a
museum-like setting. Millers has a large
collection of license plates and is open
all year. In business since the 1950s.

MUSEUM OF ALASKA
TRANSPORTATION AND INDUSTRY
Milepost 46.7 Parks Highway
(near the Wasilla Airport)

P.O. Box 99687
WASILLA, AK 99687
(28 miles north of Anchorage)
Phone: 907-376-1211
www.museumofalaska.org and
www.aero-web.org/museums/ak/
mati.htm
Hours: *Memorial Day through
Labor Day,* Tues.–Sun. 10–5.
Rest of year Sat. 9–5. Admission charged.

Alaska's transportation and industrial
history is amply preserved in this museum for the educational and scientific
benefit of current and future generations. On the museum's grounds and inside the spacious museum building
are displays of trains, aircraft, mining
equipment, fire trucks, ambulances,
farm equipment, a sheepherder's wagon,
construction equipment, boats, dog
sleds, snow removal machines, and
antique cars. The museum has a gift
shop and a picnic area.

ARIZONA

Arizona has been in the forefront of preserving sections of the famous old highway U.S. 66 and many of the sites along its way. Sites of interest will be found in the following cities (recorded here from east to west): *HOLBROOK, WINSLOW, FLAGSTAFF, WILLIAMS, ASH FORK, SELIGMAN, TRUXTON, HACKBERRY, KINGMAN,* and *OATMAN.*

A unique night's rest awaits you at Shady Dell.

SHADY DELL RV PARK

1 Douglas Rd.
BISBEE, AZ 85603 (Southeastern part of the state on SR 80, 23 miles west of Douglas)
Phone: 520-432-3567
www.theshadydell.com
Check-in: anytime after 2:00 p.m.
Check out: 11:00 a.m.

Want to spend the night in a 1949 aluminum travel trailer? This is the place where you can do it. Shady Dell RV Park has a number of antique travel trailers available for overnight guests or for weekly rental. All trailers are equipped with modern-day conveniences. There are also hookups for your travel trailers or RVs, and all the necessities for camping, including laundry services, are available. On the grounds is a 1957 Valentine ten-stool diner serving home-cooked meals.

Children under ten not allowed in the antique trailers because they are not child-proofed. Smoking and pets not permitted.

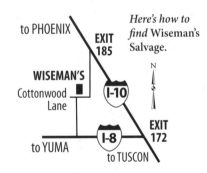

Here's how to find Wiseman's Salvage.

WISEMAN'S AUTO SALVAGE

900 W. Cottonwood Ln.
CASA GRANDE, AZ 85222

(45 miles southeast of Phoenix off I-8 and I-10)
Phone: 800-798-2465 and 520-836-7960
www.wisemansalvage.com
Hours: M–F 8–5, Sat. 9–1.

This is a large salvage yard containing 3,000 rust-free vehicles. Wiseman's also specializes in antique vehicles awaiting restoration and can supply parts for custom rods and late model vehicles. Towing service available. Browsers welcome.

▶ PHOENIX AREA

ANTHEM MOTORS (dealer)
21242 N. Black Canyon Hwy.
NORTH PHOENIX, AZ 85027
Hours: daily 9–9
Phone: 623-879-0930 and 319-329-2069
www.anthemmotors.com

This is a dealer of antique vehicles associated with the famous Duffy's Collectible Cars of Cedar Rapids, IA. Sports cars and muscle cars are a specialty here. Anthem can provide car histories, insurance and assists in shipping. They also buy cars, take trades and sell on consignment.

BARRETT-JACKSON
(Auctioneers and dealer)
3020 N. Scottsdale Rd.
SCOTTSDALE, AZ 85251-9865
Showroom hours: M–F 9–5.
Phone: 480-421-6694
www.barrett-jackson.com

Barrett-Jackson is one of the country's largest auction houses specializing in antique vehicles, muscle machines and classics. It is housed in a former Rolls-Royce dealership and has a museum-like showroom that accommodates from 50 to 70 vehicles. The company takes cars on consignment and provides appraisals and

a locator service. Browsers welcome.

DESERT VALLEY AUTO PARTS
(Salvage)
2227 W. Happy Valley Rd.
PHOENIX, AZ 85027
Phone: 623-780-8024 or 800-905-8024 (toll free)
www.dvap.com
Hours: M–F 8–5, Sat. 8–2.
Directions: Leave I-17 at Exit 218 north of Phoenix, go east ½ mile to 23rd Av. At 23rd Av. and Happy Valley Rd. go south. The road will curve to the left and lead you to Desert Valley Auto Parts.

It's not often one sees some 5,000+ vintage vehicles in one place, but that's what you will see here. This yard has some 40 acres-worth of 1940s, 1950s, 1960s, 1970s and 1980s vehicles. The yard is exceptionally clean with many of the cars resting on concrete slabs. The vehicles are of mixed makes although there is a large number of Chevrolets. There is a large selection of restorable vehicles, mostly rust-free, which will save the restorer from some unpleasant surprises. Desert Valley Auto Parts has a towing service and can provide repair services. Customers may browse the yard. In business since 1991.

ARIZONA

LEO GEPHART, INC. (Dealer)
7360 E. Acoma Dr. Suite 14
SCOTTSDALE, AZ 85260
Phone: 480-948-2286
www.gephartclassics.com
Hours: M–F 9–5, Sat. 9–noon

You will find beautiful machines here in Gephart's spacious showroom. They specialize in fine quality American-made classics and often have in inventory such cars as Duesenbergs, Pierce-Arrows, Packards, Cadillacs and the like. They carry about 45 cars in inventory and can provide an inventory list. Gephart's take trades, arranges financing and transportation, will search for specific vehicles and sells on consignment. Leo Gephart, the owner, says car clubs are always welcome.

GRAND TOURING CARS
(dealer and restorer)
14722 N. 78th Way
SCOTTSDALE, AZ 85260
Phone: 480-991-5320
www.GTC-mirage.com
Hours: M–F 8–5

If you love to gaze upon vintage Ferraris, Maseratis, Jaguars, Alfas, Porsches and the like, you'll love this place—and you can buy one or more of them. This dealer has some of the most exotic machines in the country and also restores vehicles like these on the premises. If you are looking for a certain make and model, Grand Touring Cars will help you find it. They also arrange shipping.

PENSKE RACING MUSEUM
7125 E. Chauncey Ln.
PHOENIX, AZ 85054-6145
Phone: 480-538-4444
www.penskeracingmuseum.com
Hours: M–closed, Tues.–Sat. 8–4,
Sun. noon–4
Directions: Exit Loop-101 south onto North Scottsdale Rd. Go south on North Scottsdale Rd. about ¼ mile to Chauncey Ln. Turn right (west) onto Chauncey Ln. to the museum. Adjacent to Princess Resort.

Vrooom… This is a large new museum created by the famous Penske racing team celebrating some 40 years of winning racing tradition. On display is an amazing collection of vintage race cars, trophies and racing memorabilia. Eleven of Penske's 13 race cars that won at the Indy 500 are on display. There are also NASCAR vehicles, pace cars, off-road vehicles and a display honoring some of the famous personalities in racing. The museum has a cafe, a test track, and sponsors events throughout the year.

End of Phoenix Area ◄

H. H. FRANKLIN FOUNDATION MUSEUM
1405 E. Kleindale Rd.
TUCSON, AZ 85719
Phone: 520-326-8038
www.franklincar.org
Hours: *Open October to Memo-* *rial Day* W–F 10–4. Other times by appointment. Admission free, donations accepted.

One of the largest collections of Franklin automobiles in the country is on display at this museum. The museum

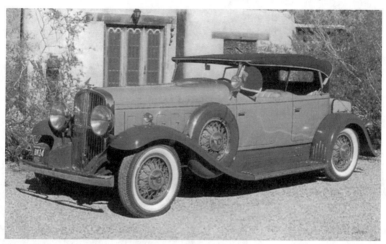

One of the beautifully-restored Franklins on display at the H. H. Franklin Foundation Museum *in Tucson, AZ*

currently has Franklins ranging from 1910 to 1934 and is constantly looking for additional models. The Franklins were unique in that they had air-cooled engines and were constructed for light weight. Aluminum was used extensively in their manufacture. Antique cars of other marques can also be seen in the museum as well as historic items and literature relating to the Franklin automobile. The museum has its own library and a newsletter is available. This is a non-profit corporation founded by the late Tom Hubbard, a well-known collector and restorer of automobiles, and is run primarily by volunteers.

ARKANSAS

The Last Precinct Police Museum, *Eureka Springs, AR.*

THE LAST PRECINCT POLICE MUSEUM (Museum)
15677 Highway US 62 West
(5.3 Mi. west of Jct. US 62 and SR 23)
EUREKA SPRINGS, AR 72632
(Northwest corner of the state)
Phone: 479-253-4948
Hours: Tues.–Sat. 10–6.
Admission charged.

Over 150 years of law enforcement history is on display at this museum including one of the largest collection of police cars in the country. One of the cars is a 1979 Camaro Z-28, one of only twelve, built especially for the California Highway Patrol. Also to be seen are motorcycles, uniforms, weapons, badges, police toys and more. Displays are arranged in chronological order with the first display being that of a sheriff's office of the 1880s. Confiscated weapons are shown and there is information on such famous law enforcement agencies as the Royal Canadian Mounted Police, Texas Rangers, New York City Police Department and others. The museum has a gift shop with a wide array of police and fire department collectibles.

► FORT SMITH AREA
(West-central part of the state on the Texas state line)

RANDY BLYTHE'S FINE CAR CENTER
(Dealer)
> 4210 Towson Av.
> **FORT SMITH**, AR 72901
> Phone: 479-646-6351
> www.Randyblythe.com
> Hours: M–F 8:30–6:30, Sat. 9–5.

Randy and his friends specialize in muscle cars and will have between 50 and 60 of them in their showroom to offer you at any one time. They also work on a few classics, special interest cars and other collectibles periodically. An inventory list is available. The company takes trades, does appraisals and helps arrange financing and shipping. Randy Blythe's has been in business since 1977.

CARDINAL MOTORS
(Dealer and restorer)
> 5610 Towson Av.
> **FORT SMITH**, AR 72901
> Phone: 479-646-2302
> Hours: M–Sat. 8–6,
> *Winter* M–Sat. 8–6:30.

This dealer has a showroom and lot with additional storage facilities elsewhere and offers, on average, 15 vintage cars for sale at all times. Cardinal does restoration work, repairs, arranges financing, sells on consignment and takes trades. Car clubs welcome.

End of Fort Smith Area ◄

GOOD OLD DAYS VINTAGE MOTORCAR MUSEUM
> Main St. (US 62/412)
> **HARDY**, AR 72542 (North-central part of state on US 62 and US 412)
> Phone: 870-856-4884
> Hours: *March 1 through Nov. 31* M–F 10–4, Sat. 9:30–4:30, Sun. noon–4. *Rest of year* Sat.–Sun. 10–4. Admission charged.

This museum has a very nice array of vintage cars from 1903 to 1977. Most of the cars, however, are from the 1920s to the 1950s. There are some 60 vehicles in all and some of them are for sale. There is a fine gift shop selling memorabilia, souvenirs, models, etc. Car clubs are always welcome. The owner of the museum is Ernest Sutherland and he started it in 1996. Michael Reed is the manager.

THE MUSEUM OF AUTOMOBILES
> State Rd. 154 near *Petit Jean Mountain State Park* (16 miles southwest of Morrilton)
> **MORRILTON**, AR 72110
> (Northwest of Little Rock)
> Phone: 501-727-5427

ARKANSAS

The Museum of Automobiles *in Morrilton was founded by late Arkansas Governor Winthrop Rockefeller and houses some of his collection.*

www.museumofautos.com
Hours: *daily* 10–5. Closed
Christmas. Admission charged.

This is an outstanding museum founded by the late Arkansas Governor Winthrop Rockefeller in 1964 containing some 50 antique cars including several from Rockefeller's personal collection. About half cars on display are part of the museum's permanent collection and the other half are on loan from private collectors and change regularly. Included in the collection is a 1923 Arkansas-built Climber Automobile. Also on display are motorcycles, guns, antique gas pumps, engines, signs and antique arcade machines. Also available is a unique gift shop. The museum is the headquarters of the *Mid-America Old Time Automobile Association (www.motaa.com)*. Annual swap meets are held each June and September at which some of the museum's cars are offered for sale.

CALIFORNIA

A stretch of old U.S. 66, now known as the "Old National Trail Highway", *is maintained in southeastern California.*

ROUTE 66

California has made determined efforts to preserve sections of historic roads within the state. A section of old U.S. 66 has been preserved in the desert country of southeastern California from *LUDLOW* to an interchange 21 miles west of *NEEDLES*. It is known as the **"Old National Trail Highway"** and still serves the local communities along its route. The road is well maintained and many old buildings and businesses can be seen along its length. Other sections of U.S. 66 are also preserved. Along old Route 66 are several Route 66 museums that preserve the history, artifacts and memory of this famous road.

Sections of the **Lincoln Highway**, which connected New York City and San Francisco, still exist and are being preserved. The Lincoln Highway parallels much of I-80 between Reno, NV and Sacramento.

In the southeastern corner of the state along I-8, 15 miles west of Yuma, AZ, sections of an old plank road can still be seen from the interstate highway. The plank road was built in 1914–15 across the shifting sands of *ALGODONES DUNES*. It was 6 miles long, a single lane and built of wooden sections laid end-to-end and then covered over with asphalt. There were turnouts along the road where one vehicle could pass another. Travellers often traveled this route in caravans carrying extra tires, water, tools and food. In 1926 the road was replaced by a conventional asphalt highway.

CALIFORNIA

ROUTE 66 "MOTHER ROAD" MUSEUM

Harvey House
681 N. First Av.
(northern edge of town)
BARSTOW, CA 92311
(Southern part of the state
in the Mojave Desert at the
intersection of I-15 and I-40)
Phone: 760-255-1890
http://barstow66museum.itgo.com
Hours: F–Sun. 11–4. Free.

Route 66 was an important road to desert communities such as Barstow because it provided a secure line of communications with neighboring communities which tended to be far apart and otherwise isolated. The importance of Route 66 is remembered in this museum which is an old hotel, built by the Santa Fe Railroad, when the railroad was the town's main communication with the outside world. The museum is filled with displays, artifacts and memorabilia related to the road and the surrounding area. Experienced docents are available to walk visitors through the museum, and the museum is used extensively for local events. There is a large gift shop with many items related to Route 66.

▶ THE FRESNO AREA

CENTRAL VALLEY CLASSICS (Dealer)

3180 S. Parkway Dr.
(Parallels SR 99)
FRESNO, CA 93724
Phone: 559-252-7742 or
888-285-7355 (toll free)
www.classicshowroom.com
Hours: Tues.–Thurs.
10–6, F–Sat. 10–3

This dealer proudly boasts that he has the largest vintage auto showroom in the San Joaquin Valley—so plan to stay a while. The company specializes in classic cars, muscle cars and street rods. They also offer an impressive array of automotive books and memorabilia. Central Valley Classics can provide certified appraisals, takes trades, sells on consignment and will arrange shipping and financing. Vincent Mathia is the owner and has many year's experience in the vintage auto business.

ROMO AUTO WRECKING (Salvage)

4625 N. Golden State Blvd.
FRESNO, CA 94722
Phone: 209-275-4823
www.world-parts.com
Hours: Tues.–Sat. 8–5, Sun. 9–4

Romo's is one of the oldest auto salvagers in California. Located on a 10-acre site outside Fresno, the lot has more than 1,500 vehicles, including trucks, from the 1930s to the 1980s. Muscle cars are also to be found here. Employees remove all parts to ensure that quality is maintained. The company was founded in the 1920s and manager Ron Romo is the third generation of the family to run the place.

TURNER'S AUTO WRECKING (Salvage)

4248 S. Willow Av.
(Old highway 99)
FRESNO, CA 93725
Phone: 559-237-0918 and

18

888-212-0918
www.turnersautowrecking.com
Hours: Tues.–Sat. 8–5

This is a large salvage yard of about 100 acres covered with cars dating back to the 1920s. This is one of the oldest salvage yards in California and has some 10,000 vehicles including trucks, commercial vehicles and a few hearses

and ambulances
orphan cars, such
Hudsons, Kaisers, e
at Turner's. Turner b
a year and scraps c
many. Yard personne
In business since the 1⁊ɔus. Jerry Turner is the manager and has a large personal collection of antique cars. Car clubs are welcome.

End of Fresno area ◄

▶ THE LOS ANGELES/LONG BEACH AREA

Now you're in *HOLLYWOOD*! There are some very fine automobiles running around on the streets here—be on the lookout for them. If you see a *Duesenberg* its driver might be **Clark Gable, Gary Cooper, Mae West** or **Greta Garbo**. They all own **Duesenbergs**! **Jean Harlow** drives a gorgeous **Packard** and **Mary Pickford** drives a **Rolls-Royce**. If you see a **Voisin** or an **Isotta-Fraschini**, **Rudolph Valentino** might be at the wheel. **Clara Bow** also likes Italian cars. She has a **Lancia**. **Al Jolson** drives a **Mercedes-Benz** and **Fatty Arbuckle** has a **McFarlan**. If you see a cowboy hat behind the wheel of a **Rolls-Royce** it could be **Tom Mix**.

Keep your eyes open!

ALL CADILLACS OF THE FORTIES AND FIFTIES (Auto display and parts dealer)

12811 Foothill Blvd.
SYLMAR, CA 91342-5316
(Northern end of San Fernando Valley)
Phone: 818-361-1147,
orders 800-808-1147
www.wayhome.com
Hours: M–F 8–4:30

As the name implies, this company

sells professionally restored and original Cadillacs and parts for Cadillacs from the 1940s through the 1950s. Engines, transmissions and major body parts are available as well as smaller parts and chrome. They also have a buy now and pay later program. Inside All Cadillacs' spacious building is one of the finest collection of 1940s and 1950s Cadillacs in the country. It is the private collection of the Ed Cholakian family and is available for viewing by customers and interested parties. In business since 1979.

19

WITH CLASS (Dealer)
1115 Wilshire Blvd.
SANTA MONICA, CA 90401
Phone: 310-656-3444
www.carsclassic.com
Hours: M–F 9–6, Sat. 11–4

You'll find between 40 to 45 affordable collector cars at this dealership. Cars With Class offers a general line of vehicles including muscle cars and hot rods in their attractive indoor showroom which was once a Cadillac dealership. They can arrange financing, do appraisals, sell on consignment, take trades, publish an inventory list and will search other dealers for specific vehicles. Car clubs are welcome. Cars With Class is owned and operated by Grant Woods, a native of New Zealand.

CHECQUERED FLAG INTERNATIONAL, INC. (Dealer)
4128 Lincoln Blvd.
MARINA DEL REY, CA 90292
Phone: 310-827-8665
www.checqueredflag.com
Hours: M–F 9–7, Sun. 10–6

You'll see a lot of British cars here as well as other European makes and some American cars—some 120 in all. Checquered Flag has an active export business and sells cars worldwide. Visitors often arrive at the Los Angeles International Airport which is only three miles away. The company will help arrange nearby hotel accommodations. Checquered Flag will search for specific vehicles and can help arrange financing. They provide an inventory list, lease cars, sell on consignment, take trades and do appraisals. Car clubs welcome.

CLASSIC AUTO GALLERY (Dealer)
146 N. Glendora Av.
GLENDORA, CA 91741
(Western suburb of Los Angeles)
Phone: 626-335-0985 and
877-335-2818 (toll free)
www.classicautogallery.com
Hours: Sun. noon–2, M–Tues. closed, W–Thurs. 10–5, F 10–9, Sat. 10–5

How about a 1938 Ford roadster, or a 1929 Packard or a 1957 Chevy, or a bright red hot rod? You can see cars like this in Classic Auto Gallery's large showroom. The company's experienced personnel can tell you all about them. Ask for Fred or Lois. The company helps with shipping and financing, takes trades, sells on consignment, offers appraisals and more. Car clubs drop by once in a while and are always welcome. You'll like Glendora too. It's a nice town.

EUROPEAN COLLECTIBLES (Dealer)
1974 Placentia Av.
COSTA MESA, CA 92627
(35 miles south of Los Angeles on the Pacific Ocean)
Phone: 949-650-4718
www.europeancollectibles.com
Hours: M–F 9–5, Sat. 10–2

You will find a nice selection of Europe's finest automobiles in this dealer's showroom. Some vehicles are restored while others are nice originals. The company does restoration work and sells parts. European Collectibles, which has been operating since 1994, takes trades, sells on consignment, searches for specific vehicles, provides references and can aid in financing and shipping. Costa Mesa is a vacation town and European Collectibles is less than two miles from the beach. They will help you make hotel reservations if you would like to stay for a while.

HERITAGE CLASSIC MOTORCARS
(Dealer and book store)
8980 Santa Monica Blvd.
WEST HOLLYWOOD, CA 90069
Phone: 310-657-9699 (dealership),
310-657-5278 (book store)
www.heritageclassics.com
Hours: M–F 9–5, Sat. 9–3

When you walk into Heritage Classic Motorcars, you are entering the largest classic car dealer in Los Angeles. You'll see top-of-the-line classics and sports cars as well as affordable antique vehicles you can drive around the neighborhood to show off. Heritage has a well-tuned car locator service and will search the world over for the car of your dreams. They buy cars, sell on consignment, take trades and help with financing and shipping.

There's another business here too, Heritage Classic Motorbooks, which provides an unparalleled selection of fine books, magazines and prints with an automotive flair. You'll have fun at Heritage Classics.

HIGH-LINE MOTORSPORTS (Dealer)
1240-A Pioneer St.
BREA, CA 92821 (Western suburb of Los Angeles)
Phone: 714-278-0696
www.hilineonline.com
Hours: 7 days a week

This progressive dealer offers vintage classic cars and sportscars—Aston Martins, Cadillacs, Jaguars, Panteras, Porsches, Studebakers, Volvos and a lot more in their spacious showroom. They also sell hot rods. High-Line offers warranties, sells on consignment, takes trades, and helps with financing and shipping. You'll like what you see here at High-Line Motorsports.

JUSTICE BROTHERS RACING MUSEUM
2734 E. Huntington Dr.
DUARTE, CA 91010
(Eastern suburb of Los Angeles)
Phone: 626-359-9174
www.justicebrothers.com
Hours: M–F 8–5. Free.

This museum is a part of Justice Brothers, Inc., manufacturers and distributors of automotive products worldwide. In the museum one can trace the evolution of motorsports. There is a fine collection of race cars, street rods, Indy cars, dragsters, midget racers, motorcycles, ice-racers, as well as several restored classic automobiles. Some of the vehicles have been used in movies. There are also displays of automobilia and a Pitts acrobatic biplane is hanging from the ceiling. The museum was founded in 1985.

MARCONI AUTOMOTIVE MUSEUM
1302 Industrial Dr.
TUSTIN, CA 92780
(20 miles southeast of downtown Long Beach)
Phone: 714-258-3001
www.marconimuseum.org
Hours: M–F 9–4:30. Tours given.
(It would be best to phone this museum before you visit because

21

they have many corporate events, banquets, conferences, etc. at which time the museum is closed to the public.) Donations suggested.

This is the personal collection of industrialist Dick Marconi, who has a special liking for Ferraris. There are some 70 vehicles in the collection and makes, other than Ferrari, can be seen. Some of the vehicles have been restored in Marconi's own restoration shop while others have connections with well-known celebrities. Car clubs are welcome. Profits from the museum are passed on to the Marconi family's charitable foundation for the benefit of children. The museum was founded in 1994.

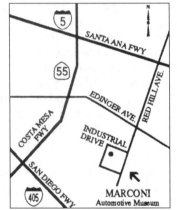

Here's where you find **Marconi Automotive Museum.**

METROPOLITAN HISTORICAL COLLECTION (Museum and parts dealer)

5330 Laurel Canyon Blvd.
NORTH HOLLYWOOD, CA 91607 (Eastern end of San Fernando Valley)
Phone: 818-769-1515 and 800-677-5519
www.metpitstop.com

Hours: M–F 10–6
Please phone first. Free.

This is a collection of 8 Nash Metropolitans. Included in the collection is the world's only Metropolitan station wagon and the "Astra-Gnome", a dream car built on a Metropolitan body for the 1956 International Auto Show in New York to preview what Metropolitans would be like in the next millennium. There is a Metropolitan fire truck, a right-hand drive Met, one of the very first Mets with all original equipment and one of the last Mets made which was a show car named "The Westerner" exhibited at all of the West Coast auto shows in 1961-62. This company is also a supplier of all Nash Metropolitan parts. Car clubs welcome. In business since 1975.

NATIONAL HOT ROD ASSOCIATION MOTORSPORTS MUSEUM

Pomona Fairplex
(County Fair Grounds, gate 1)
1101 W. McKinley Av.
POMONA, CA 91768 (Eastern edge of metropolitan Los Angeles)
Phone: 909-622-2133
www.nhra.com
Hours: W–Sun. 10–5.
Admission charged.

This is a very large museum with some 28,000 sq. ft. of floor space. There are about 50 vintage vehicles at this museum and as the name implies, they are hot rods, street rods, drag racers, dry-lake racers and vehicles run on the Bonneville Salt Flats. There are also Indy cars and midget racers. On display, too, are trophies, fire suits, helmets, photos, art and other memorabilia. The museum has an interesting gift shop, a research library, an

The NHRA Motorsports Museum*, Pomona, Ca. The very roots of hot-rodding come alive with the cars and memories inside this museum.*

art gallery and multi-media classroom. The museum opened in April 1998 and is available for private parties, weddings, meetings and other events. Group tours are provided upon request.

THE NETHERCUTT COLLECTION
15151 and 15200 Bledsoe St.
SYLMAR, CA 91342
Phone: 818-364-6464 for museum;
818-367-2251 for tours
www.nethercuttcollection.org
Hours: Tues.–Sat. 10–1:30. *Shown*

by guided tour only. Tour length approximately 2 hours. *Children under 12 not allowed*. Parking available. Admission free.

The Nethercutt collection is a world-class treasure house—all 60,000 sq. ft. of it—of prize-winning automobiles, automobilia, and antique furniture. The auto collection consists of some 200 exquisitely restored vehicles of American and foreign manufacture dating from 1898 to 1982. Most of them are luxury

23

CALIFORNIA

cars. Not all are on display at one time, so the collection rotates. The museum has its own restoration shop, a library, a large collection of musical instruments, pocket watches and one of the world's largest Wurlitzer pipe organs. The museum is the product of J. B. Nethercutt, co-founder of the Merle Norman cosmetics empire.

RICHARD NIXON PRESIDENTIAL LIBRARY AND BIRTHPLACE

18001 Yorba Linda Blvd.
YORBA LINDA, CA
(40 miles southeast of
downtown Los Angeles)
Phone: 714-993-5075
www.nixonlibrary.org
Hours: M–Sat. 10–5, Sun. 11–5.
Admission charged.

This is a memorial complex dedicated to the life and career of President Richard Nixon. There is a museum, gardens, the house in which Nixon was born as well as the gravesite of Former President Nixon and his wife, Pat. Many items relating to the Nixon family and presidency are on display including two automobiles of interest. One of the vehicles is Nixon's bullet-proof 1967 Lincoln limousine. This vehicle was made for presidential use and has many built-in and sophisticated safety and communication devices as well as fold down bumpers and hand rails for Secret Service agents. Presidents Ford, Carter and Reagan also used the car and many world leaders were passengers.

The second vehicle on display is a 1949 Mercury woody station wagon which is a replica of the vehicle Nixon used during his 1950 senatorial campaign. Throughout the museum are many photographs showing Nixon and the automobiles he used.

PETER'S MARINA MOTORS (Dealer)

800 Lincoln Blvd.
VENICE BEACH, CA 90291
(On the ocean west of
downtown Los Angeles)
Phone: 310-399-8313
www.englishcars.com
Hours: M–F 9–5

You will find a wide variety of English cars here on Peter's lot and in the showroom. Some are restored and some not. Peter, the owner, is a master mechanic and has personally restored some of the vehicles. That tells you he knows English cars in and out. He will personally give you an accurate description of any of his vehicles. The company sells parts for English cars, takes trades, and helps with shipping and financing. They also have a place where you can store your surf board while you look around.

PETERSEN AUTOMOTIVE MUSEUM

6060 Wilshire Blvd. (In the "Miracle Mile" District of Los Angeles)
LOS ANGELES, CA 90036
Phone: 323-930-2277
www.petersen.org
Hours: Tues.–Sun. and Mon. holidays 10–6. Discovery Center closes Tues.–F at 4, Sat.–Sun. and Mon. holidays at 5. Admission and parking charged.

This excellent museum is one of the largest automotive museums in the country and is located in one of Los Angeles' most colorful areas. Scattered throughout the museum's 300,000 square feet of floor space is a very large collection of antique automobiles, many of them quite unique. Included in the collection are many luxury cars, hot rods, muscle

Prestige Thunderbird *is the world's largest restorer of 1955-56-57 Thunderbirds and can offer restored Thunderbirds ready to drive.*

cars and cars owned by famous people and cars used in movies. The Petersen Museum has additional cars in storage, so the cars on display rotate. There is a hands-on exhibit known as the Discovery Center which is designed as a learning center for both children and adults. In the penthouse is an all-glass conference center for special events that can hold up to 600 people. The museum has a large book store and gift shop. Profits generated by the museum are passed on to a charitable foundation. The museum was founded by Robert and Margie Petersen and others in 1994.

PRESTIGE THUNDERBIRD
(Restorer and dealer)
　　10215 Greenleaf Av.
　　SANTA FE SPRINGS, CA 90670
　　(12 miles southeast of downtown
　　Los Angeles)
　　Phone: 562-944-6237 or
　　800-423-4751 for orders
　　www.prestigethunderbird.com
　　Hours: M–F 8–5:30, Sat. 8:30–4.

This is the world's largest restorer of 1955-56-57 Thunderbirds. Prestige will restore your Thunderbird, or you may buy one restored from their showroom floor. There are between 40 and 50 cars in inventory at all times in various stages of restoration. Many of their cars have been show winners. The company can arrange financing and transportation. They also do appraisals, have a service department and sell NOS, new and used parts. Parts catalog available.

VINTAGE COACH
(restorer and museum)
　　16593 Arrow Blvd.
　　FONTANA, CA 92335
　　(46 miles east of Los Angeles,
　　5 miles west of San Bernardino)
　　Phone: 909-823-9168
　　Email: albrighthudsons@msn.com
　　Hours: M–Sat. 9–5

This company restores, displays and sells Hudsons, specializing in the "Stepdown" models of the late 1930s through the 1950s. Vintage has about 70 vehicles, with some being on display and some in the process of restoration. Included in the collection are pre-war Hudsons and Hudson pickup trucks. The company

CALIFORNIA

does service work on Hudsons and the museum is decorated with Hudson dealership and service signs. The owner, William Albright, has a personal collection of about 20 restored Hudsons, most of which are usually on display. Albright calls his establishment "The last Hudson dealership in America." Car clubs are welcome. Founded in 1971.

WEST COAST CLASSIC RESTORATIONS
(Dealer and restorer)
1002 E. Walnut Av.
FULLERTON, CA 92831 (An eastern suburb of Long Beach)
Phone: 714-871-1322

www.classicvws.com
Hours: M–F 9–5

Volkswagens—all kinds of Volkswagens—that's what they do here! West Coast Classic Restorations restores VWs partially or from the ground up and offers them for sale in their 6,400 sq. ft. "One stop shop" showroom. Usually there are about 10-12 vehicles on their floor for sale. All facets of the restoration work are done in house—upholstery, painting, mechanical work... The company will also restore customers' VWs with the same care they give their own. Lenny Copp is the man behind this interesting operation which he started in 1990.

End of Los Angeles/Long Beach area ◀

EXOTIC MOTOR CARS (Dealer)
4525 E. Ramon Rd.
PALM SPRINGS, CA 92255
Phone: 760-778-5444
www.exoticmotorcars.com
Hours: M–Sat. 9–5

Here's where they keep the really good stuff—Rolls-Royces—Mercedes—Cadillacs—etc. Most of Exotic Motor Cars' 100–125-car inventory consists of fully restored vehicles. And, if they don't have it, they'll try to find it. The company takes trades, sells on consignment, provides appraisals, helps with financing, insurance and world-wide shipping. Car clubs are always welcome. Marv Sholl, the owner, says come by for a free cold drink—which tastes pretty good here in the desert. In business since 1978.

PEARSON'S (Salvage)
236 Pearson Rd.
PEARSONVILLE, CA 93527
(In the Mojave Desert 74 miles east northeast of Bakersfield on US 395)
Phone: 760-377-4585
www.classicautoinc.com
Hours: M–Sat. 8:30–5

"Hubcap Lucy" they call her. That's Lucille Pearson. She got the name because she handles the yard's vast collection of wheel covers and knows just about everything there is to know about hubcaps. Husband Andy and their two boys handle the rest of the 30-acre lot and some 3,000 vehicles. Most of the vehicles are post-war sedans, wagons and pickups of all makes. There are other yards in Lancaster and Ridge Crest, but the older stuff is here. They also own the Pearsonville Raceway, a dirt track, site of the locally famous "Turkey Classic" race, which is run each Thanksgiving. Escorted tours of the lot are available.

PLACERVILLE, CA (35 miles east of Sacramento on U.S. 50):

One of the heros of this town is John M. "Wheelbarrow Johnny" Studebaker, one of the famous brothers of the Studebaker Corp. of South Bend, IN. As a young man, John Studebaker came west to this gold mining area to seek his fortune and found it, not in gold, but in wheelbarrows. Studebaker was a blacksmith and wheelwright and soon discovered that there was a tremendous need for wheelbarrows in the gold fields. He established a shop at 534 Main St. in Placerville and produced wheelbarrows from 1853 to 1858. Studebaker eventually sold out and returned to Indiana where he went into business with his brothers making wagons and eventually automobiles. The money he made in Placerville helped finance the Studebaker Corporation.

The Placerville Town Hall now rests on the site of Studebaker's wheelbarrow shop and a bronze plaque commemorates Studebaker and his enterprise. Every year at the county fair Studebaker is remembered in a unique way when they hold the "Johnny Studebaker Wheelbarrow Races". The El Dorado County Museum, 100 Placerville Dr. has displays and exhibits on "Wheelbarrow Johnny".

PLAY TOYS (Dealer)
　　32300 Outer Highway 10
　　REDLANDS, CA 92373 (East of
　　the Los Angeles area on I-10)
　　Phone: 909-797-1111
　　www.playtoys.com
　　Hours: Tues.– Sat. 10–7
　　Location: Exit I-10 at the Oak
　　Glen/Live Oak Canyon Rd. Seek
　　and ye shall find.

Play Toys is just what the name implies. This dealer has about 125 toys for big boys

The **Placerville Town Hall** *now rests on the site of "Wheelbarrow Johnny" Studebaker's wheelbarrow shop in downtown Placerville. A bronze plaque on the wall (behind the fire plug) commemorates Studebaker and his Wheelbarrow shop.*

and girls in their showroom at all times. They include vintage cars, motorcycles, trucks and some SUVs and water craft. An inventory list is on the web. Play Toys sells on consignment, takes trades, does appraisals, and offers shipping, financing and auto insurance. In business since 1986. Ask for Tom, Nancy or Terry Greve.

TOWE AUTO MUSEUM OF AUTOMOTIVE HISTORY
2200 Front St. (just off Broadway)
SACRAMENTO, CA 95818
Phone: 916-442-6802
www.toweautomuseum.org
Hours: Daily 10–6. Closed Dec. 25, Thanksgiving and Jan 1.
Admission charged. Free parking.

This area of Sacramento is called "museum row" and right in the middle of it is this fine auto museum. Displays in the museum are based on "dream themes" with many of the museum's 160 vehicles worked into the displays. The themes are *"Dream of Mobility"*, *"Dream of Luxury"*, *"Dream of Independence"*, *"Dream of a Rich Harvest"*, *"Dream of Speed"* and *"Dream of Cool"*. Other museum themes include displays entitled *"Down Memory Lane"* and *"Hall of Technology"*. Some of the vehicles had been associated with famous people. A highlight of the museum's auto collection is some 30 antique Fords.

Other displays include period costumes, tools, equipment, license plates and miscellaneous artifacts. The museum has a fine gift shop and a growing automotive library. Numerous events such as swap meets, antique toy sales, organ concerts, dances, musical shows, etc. are held at the museum. Phone for information on these events. Founded May 1987.

▶ SAN DIEGO AREA

CALIFORNIA CLASSICS AND COLLECTIBLES, INC. (dealer)
2244 S. Santa Fe #C14
VISTA, CA 92084
(Eastern suburb of San Diego)
Phone: 760-598-9667
www.fordmustangsales.com
Hours: M–F 8–6, Sat. 9–5

If you are a lover of Fords and Mustangs, you will want to know about this dealership. That's their specialty, and they carry about 20 to 30 vehicles at all times. On occasion, they will have other makes in the showroom and there is a nice selection of automobilia for sale. The company takes trades in other classics only, and can help arrange financing and transportation. Scott Andrews is the owner.

J. A. COOLEY MUSEUM
4233 Park Blvd. (One of the streets leading to Balboa Park)
SAN DIEGO, CA 92103
Phone: 619-296-3112 or
619-295-1611
http://emporium.turnpike.net/
-walk/mg-world/Museums/
museums.htm
Hours: M–F 10–5:30, Sat. 10–5, Sun. noon–4. Small admission charge.

Here is one of the most unique car museums in the country—it's full of old, old stuff. There are about 24 vehicles on display which are rotated from time-to-time from the museum's larger collection. The oldest car is an 1886 ¾ hp Benz and the second oldest is an 1895 Benz Velo, and then an 1899 Mobile Steamer. Many of the other vehicles are pre-World War I. The museum has a restoration shop but endeavors, whenever possible, to preserve the car's original components such as mechanical parts, upholstery, tires, etc. Occasionally, some of the cars are for sale and there are several motorcycles in the collection. J. A. Cooley, the museum's founder and owner, is a man of many interests. He has collected many other antique items such as early phonograph machines (with the big horns), early phonograph records, cameras, business machines, toys, spittoons, cuckoo clocks, license plates, World War I posters, and more. Examples of these collections are on display in the museum.

Associated with the museum is an antique toy train shop which buys, sells and displays antique toy trains. They have the largest inventory of Lionel train cars west of the Mississippi. Mr. & Mrs. Cooley speak Spanish and they opened the museum in 1997. The museum is just a few blocks north of Balboa Park so it is easy to get to for a tourist. This is a place you'll long remember after your visit. It's also a great place for a car club to visit.

DEER PARK AUTO MUSEUM

29013 Champagne Blvd.
(Parallels I-15 on the east side of the road, north of Escondido)
ESCONDIDO, CA 92026
(Northern suburb of San Diego)
Phone: 760-749-1666
www.caohwy.com
Hours: Thurs.–M 10–5. Closed Thanksgiving and Dec. 25.
Admission charged.

This museum is part of a large winery which has a tasting room, a wine shop, a market/deli and a gift shop. The auto collection of over 100 cars consists primarily of convertibles, retractables and early open cars. Most of the cars are American-made and are housed in three buildings along with a very interesting collection of automobilia. There are also collections of other items to be seen, such as Barbie dolls, TVs, appliances and wine-making equipment. There are many activities at this establishment such as weddings, car shows, wine-tasting dinners and parties, etc.

GRAND PRIX CLASSICS (Dealer)

7456 La Jolla Blvd.
LaJOLLA, CA 92037
Phone: 858-459-3500
www.grandprixclassics.com
Hours: M–F 9–5

For sale in this company's showroom are from 15 to 20 historic cars ranging from pre-war Alfa Romeos and Bugattis to the great post-war sports and racing cars from both Europe and the United States. Not only are beautiful machines available here, but also invaluable advice for those interested in world-wide racing events, auto tours and Concouers de Elegance. The owners of this dealership, who are multilingual, have had years of first hand experience in these events and can provide information on what cars have eligibility and are best suited for such events. Their opinions on collector cars of these high standards have been quoted in *USA Today* and *Forbes Magazine*. The company also has a collection of rare automotive posters, a book and video library and a photo archive. Grand Prix Classics takes trades, sells on consignment, provides appraisals, and helps with shipping and financing. The company was started in Frankfurt, Germany in 1977 and moved to La Jolla in 1980.

CALIFORNIA

HORSELESS CARRIAGE FOUNDATION AUTOMOTIVE RESEARCH LIBRARY

8186 Center St. Suite F
LA MESA, CA 91942
(10 miles east of San Diego off I-8)
Phone: 619-464-0301,
Fax 619-464-0361
www.hcfi.org E-mail: hcfi@aol.com
Hours: Tues.–F 10–4, Sat. 9–2

The Horseless Carriage Foundation Library, founded in 1995, is a must for hobbyists seeking information on restoration projects. Here is one of the finest publicly accessible collections of original factory literature in the U.S. The Library features a pleasant reading room, research service center, climate-controlled archival storage and warehouse. A librarian will assist on-site patrons in self-directed research at no charge. Phone, Fax, E-mail or mail requests for research by Library staff are accommodated for a modest charge.

The Horseless Carriage Foundation Library has a working relationship with other automotive libraries around the country including the Smithsonian Institute. They also work with legal firms, the media and the IRS. On occasion they sell surplus automotive literature.

SAN DIEGO AUTOMOTIVE MUSEUM

2080 Pan American Plaza
in Balboa Park
SAN DIEGO, CA 92101-1636
Phone: 619-231-2886
www.sdautomuseum.org
Hours: *Daily in the summer* 10–5
with last admission at 4:30, Closed

Jan. 1, Thanksgiving, Dec. 25.
Admission charged.

This is a publicly-owned museum with a large collection of vintage vehicles and motorcycles. On display are classics, historically significant vehicles, horseless carriages, muscle cars and concept cars. There is an automotive library, an art gallery, ongoing programs of various sorts, and the museum publishes a quarterly publication called *"Auto Museum News"*. There is a fine gift shop offering automotive literature, souvenirs and automobilia. The museum sells some of its cars from time-to-time. A list of cars for sale is on the web.

VIP CLASSICS (Dealer)

861 5th Av.
SAN DIEGO, CA, 92101
Phone: 619-232-6864
www.vipclassics.com
Hours: M–Sat. 10–10

Interested in buying a new Porsche Speedster Replica off the floor? Or how about a CAV GT Replica or a new, and genuine, Shelby? You can do it here. They carry them in stock. There are also about 100 classic and vintage cars available of European and American make. They include affordable, as well as top-of-the-line, vehicles. VIP takes trades, sells on consignment, offers appraisals, locates specific vehicles for customers and assists in financing and shipping. Car clubs are welcome. The owner is Roy Sayles and he's been in the business since 1979.

End of San Diego area

▶ SAN FRANCISCO BAY AREA

BLACKHAWK AUTOMOTIVE MUSEUM

3700 Blackhawk Plaza Circle (at the intersection of Crow Canyon Rd., Camino Tassajara, and Blackhawk Rd. in Danville) **DANVILLE**, CA 94506 (On I-680 east of Oakland)
Phone: 925-736-2280 and 925-736-2277 (recording)
www.blackhawkauto.org
Hours: W–Sun. 10–5. Open most major holidays except Christmas and New Years Day. Admission charged.

Here is one of the most magnificent collection of classic and historic automobiles in the world. The Blackhawk Automotive Museum presents and displays historically-significant and artistically-inspired automobiles, automotive art and related artifacts from the very earliest to the contemporary for public enjoyment and educational enrichment.

The 100,000 square foot multi-level glass and granite architectural masterpiece showcases an ever-changing exhibition of over 100 of the world's greatest autos dating from the 1890s.

The Blackhawk Automotive Museum *is one of the finest automotive museums in the world and has an oustanding collection of meticulously restored vehicles.*

Included are luxury cars, grand prix race cars, and numerous vehicles owned by famous people.

The Automotive Art wing features automotive art and highlights the history of the automobile from its inception to the present day.

The Museum's Shop and Bookstore is open during museum hours and has a large selection of automotive books, posters, die-cast models and kits in plastic and metal of varied skill levels.

The Museum and its facilities are totally wheelchair-accessible. Conducted tours are available. Visitors will not be disappointed with this museum.

CARS DAWYDIAK (Dealer)
1450 Franklin St.
SAN FRANCISCO, CA 94109
Phone: 415-928-CARS (2277)
www.carsauto.com
Hours: M–F 10–7, Sat. 10–5
& Sun. 10–4.

This is a dealer of classic, sports and antique luxury vehicles in downtown San Francisco. Cars Dawydiak carries anywhere from 35 to 55 restored or fine original cars in inventory at all times and specialize in Porsches. An inventory list is available. All of their cars are rust-free California cars. They have their own restoration facility and also do service and repair work. Company

personnel will help arrange financing and world-wide transportation, search for specific vehicles and make appraisals. Cars are sold on consignment, leased and the company takes trades. There is a gift store and car clubs are welcome. The owner is Walter Dawydiak.

FANTASY JUNCTION (Dealer)
1145 Park Av.
EMERYVILLE, CA 94608
(a northern suburb of Oakland)
Phone: 510-653-7555
www.fantasyjunction.com
Hours: M–Sat. 9:30–5:30
Directions: From the intersection of W. MacArthur Blvd. and San Pablo Av., proceed north on San Pablo Av., two blocks, to Park Av. Turn left (west) onto Park and look for Fantasy Junction on a corner location.

This dealer specializes in post-war European sports cars and carries about 50 cars in inventory at all times in their indoor showroom. Race cars are also available at times. Fantasy Junction sells cars on consignment, will search for specific vehicles, does appraisals and can

Fantasy Junction *of Emeryville, CA specializes in the sale of post-war European sports cars.*

provide an inventory list. Car clubs are most welcome.

KASSABIAN MOTORS (Dealer)
6080 Dublin Blvd.
DUBLIN, CA 94568 (At the junction of I-580 and I-680)
Phone: 925-829-2825
www.californiaclassics.com
Hours: M–F 10–7, Sat. and Sun. 10–6

There's 24,000 sq. ft. of beautiful cars here in Kassabian's showroom—some 125 in all. You'll be able to select from the highest quality of high performance, classic muscle, modern European and Hot Rod cars. Kassabian Motors takes trades, sells on consignment and is always on the lookout for cars to buy. They have many satisfied and repeat customers, and you might want to get on their mailing list. Dee and Brad Kassabian are the owners/operators who say the business is a lot of fun. They've been having fun since 1968.

OAKLAND MUSEUM OF CALIFORNIA
1000 Oak St.
OAKLAND, CA 94607
Phone: 510-238-2200
www.museumca.org
Hours: W–Sat. 10–5. Sun. noon–5. First Friday of each month, open until 9:00 p.m. Closed holidays. Admission and parking charged.

This is a beautiful terraced museum designed to reflect California's ecol-ogy, history and art. One of its many exhibits honors the life and works of Henry J. Kaiser, co-founder of the post-World War II Kaiser-Frazer Corporation. Two of the company's automobiles are on display and the museum's events are centered around the Kaiser Events Center. Kaiser is buried in the mausoleum at Oakland's Mountain View Cemetery on Piedmont Av.

O'CONNOR CLASSIC AUTOS (dealer)
2569 Scott Blvd.
SANTA CLARA, CA 95050
(a northern suburb of San Jose)
Phone: 408-727-0430 or 888-346-3647
www.oconnorclassics.com
Hours: M–F 9–5, Sat. 9–noon

This dealer specializes in British sports cars, primarily MGs, Triumphs and Austin-Healeys from the 1940s through the 1970s. They normally carry a large inventory of affordable cars in their showroom. O'Connor sells on consignment, offers appraisals, takes trades and can assist with restorations. They also sell parts and accessories, and offer technical advice, a catalog and a newsletter. Car clubs are welcome at O'Connor's.

O'Connor Classic Autos *of Santa Clara specializes in MGs.*

CALIFORNIA

SHOWROOM AUTO SALES
(Dealer & restorer)
960 S. Bascomb Av.
SAN JOSE, CA 95128 (At the
southern end of San Francisco Bay)
Phone: 408-279-0944
www.showroomcars.com
Hours: M–F noon–7, Sat. noon–4.

This company specializes in the restoration and sales of Mercedes-Benz automobiles and other high-end and classic automobiles. At any time they will have 75 or more vehicles in their showroom. The company sells cars on consignment, takes trades, offers leases, does appraisals, will search for specific vehicles and arranges financing and transportation. Car clubs are welcome. Ron Perry is the owner of the company.

CAR SCENE (Dealer)
8 California Av.
PLEASANTON, CA 94566
Phone: 925-426-1969
www.carscene.net
Hours: M–Sat. 11–6

This dealer has an interesting mix of vintage vehicles from preceding decades. Some are in pristine condition and some are drive-to-the office and drive-to-the store types. Some of the cars are on consignment. Car Scene takes trades, provides an inventory list, helps with financing and shipping and has convenient showroom hours. You will enjoy your visit to Car Scene.

SPECIALTY SALES (Dealer)
4321 First St.
PLEASANTON, CA 94566
Phone: 925-484-2262 or
800-600-2262
Hours: M–F 10–7, Sat. 10–6,
Sun. 11–5

Here is a large dealer of antique, classic, muscle and special interest cars, most of which are sold on consignment. Specialty Sales has a 14,000 sq. ft. showroom and carries an average inventory of 70 vehicles. About 80% of the vehicles are in the "affordable" range and an inventory list is available. The company helps arrange financing and transportation, does appraisals, takes trades, offers leases and searches for specific vehicles. Car clubs are welcome at Specialty Sales.

SOLVANG VINTAGE MOTORCYCLE MUSEUM
320 Alisal Rd. (In the former
Solvang Designer Outlet Center)
SOLVANG, CA 93463 (115 miles
northwest of downtown Los
Angeles on US 101)
Phone: 805-682-9522
www.motosolvang.com
Hours: Sat.–Sun. 11–5; weekdays,
check at the office and the museum
will be opened for your visit.
Admission charged.

This is the private motorcycle collection of Dr. Virgil Elings and it consists of a broad selection of vintage motorcycles. The emphasis is on racing bikes, both road racing and motocross. Several of the motorcycles are pre-World War I and many of them have been used in vintage motorcycle racing events. The motorcycles on display in the museum

Packard Alley, *Vallejo, CA.*

are constantly changing, so this is a museum one can see often. Solvang is a beautiful little town in a popular tourist area which caters to Los Angeles day-trippers. Plan to spend some time here.

VALLEJO (On the east shore of San Pablo Bay which is the northern extension of San Francisco Bay)

When this town was laid out in the early 1900s the city planners named the town's alleys after popular automobiles of the day. They were named in alphabetical order from "*A*" through "*T*", with "*T*" being the last of the original alleys because they had no more. Over the years, Alleys "*A*" through "*C*" have disappeared due to urban renewal, but the others remain. From south to north they are; *Dodge, Everett, Ford, Garford, Hudson, Indian* (the motorcycle), *Jeffry, Kissel, Lozier, Maxwell, National, Overland, Packard, Quincy, REO, Stutz* and *Templar.*

End of San Francisco Bay area ◀

FAMILY CLASSIC CARS (Dealer)
26181 Avenida Aeropuerto
SAN JUAN CAPISTRANO, CA 92675
Phone: 949-496-3000
www.familyclassiccars.com
Hours: M–F 9–5

When you come to San Juan Capistrano to see the famous mission, stop for a few minutes at Family Classic Cars. Here, in their attractive showroom, you will find a nice selection of muscle cars, classics, sports cars, convertibles, collector cars and more. This dealer takes trade-ins, assists with shipping and financing and provides appraisals. Marc Spizzirri is the man behind it all. He started the business in 2001.

Almeida's Classic Cars *of Turlock, CA.*

ALMEIDA'S CLASSIC CARS (Dealer)

551 N. Tully Rd.
TURLOCK, CA 95380
(Midway between Merced and
Modesto on SR 99)
Phone: 209-667-7828
www.almeidaclassiccars.com
Hours: Tues.–Sat. 10–5.
Directions: From the intersection of
SR 99 and W. Main Av. (also known
as county highway J17), turn east
on W. Main Av. Go one block, to
Tully Rd. and turn left (north) onto
Tully Rd. Almeida's will be on the
west side of the street.

This dealer carries an average inventory
of between 30 and 35 antique and classic
vehicles for sale in an indoor showroom.
They buy vehicles and sell on consignment. Almeida's also offers appraisals,
detailing and can arrange domestic and
export shipping. In business more than
10 years. Car clubs are welcome.

CALIFORNIA ROUTE 66 MUSEUM

On U.S. 66 in downtown (Old
Town) Victorville, PO Box 2151
VICTORVILLE, CA 92392
(28 miles north of San Bernardino
on I-15)
Phone: 760-951-0436
www.califrt66museum.org
Hours: Thurs.–M 10–4. Free.
Location: On US 66 (D St.) between
5th and 6th streets on the south
side of the street.

Route 66 museums have sprung
up in various places all along the old
historic Route 66 and this is one of the
biggest and best. The California Route
66 Museum is located in the heart
of Victorville in an old (1918) bank
building and, as the name implies,
has numerous displays on the historic
Route 66. Displays rotate regularly, so
you'll see new things the next time you
visit. There's an art gallery, exhibits on

other great roads and Indian trails. More exhibits provide information on books and movies which involved Route 66 including John Steinbeck's "Grapes of Wrath" and, of course, the famous TV series. A gift shop offers items of interest including the newest maps showing where the old road might still be found. A library contains old literature about Route 66 and has a copy of every book published on the road. The museum was founded in 1995.

HEIDRICK AG HISTORY CENTER (Two museums)

1962 Hays Ln.
Heidrick Ag History Center
WOODLAND, CA 95776
(18 miles northwest of Sacramento)
Phone: 530-666-9700
www.aghistory.org
Hours: M–F 10–5, Sun. 10–6.
Admission charged.
Directions: *Approaching Woodland from the south* on I-5, exit onto County Rd. 102. At the top of the ramp (signal) drive straight ahead into Hays Lane. Museum is on the left. *Approaching Woodland from the north* on I-5, exit onto County Rd. 102, Turn left at the top of the ramp crossing over I-5. Take the first left onto Hays Lane and proceed to museum.

You can see two museums at this location: the Hays Antique Truck Museum and the Fred C. Heidrick Antique Ag Collection. The Hays Antique Truck Museum was founded in 1982 by A. Wayne "Pop" Hays and is dedicated to the procurement, care and display of antique trucks and truck-related artifacts. There is also an archive and library specializing in literature related to trucks. On display are some 100 trucks, representing many manufacturers and dating from 1903. The Museum provides evidence of the industry's effort to meet the needs of the drivers and the demands of the builders, the providers and the consumers to deliver bigger loads more efficiently. Changes in the design and engineering of the cabs, bodies, wheels and tires can be seen.

The History Center operates a gift shop, has a 300-seat conference center, is wheelchair accessible and provides guided tours.

COLORADO

L & M USED AUTO PARTS (Salvage)
8425 County Rd. 8 South
ALAMOSA, CO 81101
(South-central part of the state)
Phone: 719-589-9205 or
866-589-9205 (toll free)
Hours: M–F 8–5, Sat. 8–noon

You are not far from New Mexico when you visit L & M. It is high and dry here and that means very little rust in old cars. L & M has some 1400 vehicles on the lot of mixed makes and many years. There are also trucks. If L & M does not have it they will try to find it. Customers may browse the yard. Car clubs are welcome. L & M started in 1963 and is owned by Leroy Martinez.

SHELBY AMERICAN COLLECTION
(museum)
5020 Chaparral Ct.
BOULDER, CO 80308-2228
Phone: 303-516-9565
www.shelbyamericancollection.org
Hours: Sat. 10–4. Call for special arrangements for groups and clubs. Admission charged.

Here's 10,000 sq. ft. of Shelbys. Some 50 famous Shelby sports cars are on display including Shelby Cobra AC Roadsters, Ford GT 40s and Mustang GT 350s. Some of the cars are on loan from individual owners so the display changes from time-to-time. Some of the

cars have impressive racing records from the past. There is also a large display of Shelby memorabilia from the 1960s which were heydays for this marque. The memorabilia is very detailed, displaying racing programs, trophies, tools, telling what the racing teams ate, where they stayed and who bunked together. There is a museum store offering Shelby-related souvenirs and merchandise. The museum was founded in 1996.

ROCKY MOUNTAIN MOTORCYCLE MUSEUM AND HALL OF FAME
308 E. Arvada
COLORADO SPRINGS, CO 80906
Phone: 719-633-6329
www.travelassist.com
Hours: M–Sat. 10–7. Free.

Indians, Harley-Davidsons, Excelsiors, Tornax, Vincents, Ariels are the names of just a few of the motorcycles that are to be seen in this fine museum. The museum has over 50 of them, all restored. There is also a library and a large collection of motorcycle memorabilia, photos, art, literature, patches, trophies, clothing, accessories, sidecars, dealer signs and more.

The Hall of Fame is somewhat different from other halls of fame in that it focuses on everyday people—the people who have dedicated their lives to motorcycling behind the scenes. The famous and the pioneers are here as well to make the display complete. The museum has a highly-acclaimed antique motorcycle restoration facility and offers its services to selected customer. Group tours are available. The staff says don't come by on Sunday, they're out ridin'.

▶ DENVER AREA

FORNEY MUSEUM OF TRANSPORTATION
4303 Brighton Blvd.
DENVER, CO 80216
Phone: 303-297-1113
www.forneymuseum.com
Hours: M–Sat. 9–5, Sun. 11–5.
Closed Jan. 1, Thanksgiving,
Dec. 25, New Years Day and Easter.
Admission charged.
Location: Just north of downtown Denver across the street from the Denver Coliseum.

This museum is a biggie with 140,000 sq. ft. of floor space. On display is a wide range of transportation equipment including the world's largest locomotive. There are airplanes, carriages, sleighs, motorcycles and about 150 classic and antique autos. In the auto collection is Amelia Earhart's 1923 Kissel and a 1923 six-wheel Hispano-Suiza which was used in the movies. The museum offers storage for privately-owned vehicles and can be rented for parties, meetings and other functions. There is an interesting gift shop carrying many automotive related items. The museum is run and operated by the Forney family. Founded in 1961.

The Forney Museum of Transportation *near downtown Denver.*

COLORADO

MARK VII CLASSIC CARS (Dealer)

1260 S. Havana
AURORA, CO 80012
(Eastern suburb of Denver on I-70)
Phone: 303-750-3363
www.markviiclassiccars.com
Hours: M–F 9–5

There's a saying in the old car business—*"you can either show them or drive them but you can't do both."* This dealer covers both ends of the spectrum and specializes in American-made vehicles. They have full frame-off restored vehicles and others that you can drive to the grocery store. Their vehicles range in age from 1900 to 1975. Not surprisingly, there are more grocery store cars around than frame-off beauties so you will find a nice selection of affordable vehicles here at Mark VII Classic Cars. They also have fixer-uppers now and then. The company takes trades, buys cars, sells on consignment, provides warranties and references, offers rentals, and can help with shipping and financing. You will be happy you stopped here.

THE MATHEWS COLLECTION & VINTAGE SALES, L.L.C.

(Dealer and restorer)
5889 Lamar St.
ARVADA, CO 80003 (A western suburb of Denver at the junction of I-70/I-270 and SR 121)
Phone: 303-456-0041
www.mathewscollection.com
Hours: M–F 9–5

Remember the famous McLaren race cars of the 1960s-70s? This company sure does. They have taken upon themselves the task of keeping McLaren cars available to the public through buying, selling, restoring and racing these historic vehicles—the "keepers of the flame"—as they put it. Their 3-acre site consists of two buildings, one for the restoration and maintenance shop and administration, and the other a showroom. There are usually about 50 vehicles in the showroom which, of course, included restored McLarens as well as sports cars, single-seat formula cars, hot rods and special-interest cars. On the walls of the museum are neat photographs and cool posters of the cars they handle. There is also a 1950s diner. The Mathews Collection is one of the few sources around for hard-to-find McLaren parts and they can provide technical and historical information about their cars. If you're into auto racing, you should know about this place.

TWO SHEAS MOTOR CO. (Dealer)

3232 S. Broadway
ENGLEWOOD, CO 80110
(Southern suburb of Denver)
Phone: 303-733-7883 and
866-311-3232
www.twosheasmotorco.com
Hours: M–F 8–8, Sat. 9–6

This cleverly-named antique car dealer specializes in unique and specialty cars and has them displayed in their spacious showroom. Before a car is sold it goes through a 55-point inspection and is fully detailed and ready for your garage. The company takes trades, will locate specific vehicles, and helps with shipping, financing and insurance—*touché!*

End of Denver area

The famous Stanley Hotel and Conference Center in Estes Park, CO. It was built by F. O. Stanley, inventor of the Stanley Steamer automobile.

THE STANLEY HOTEL AND CONFERENCE CENTER
333 Wonderview Av.
ESTES PARK, CO 80517
(55 miles northwest of Denver)
www.stanleyhotel.com
Phone: 800-976-1377 or
970-586-3371

This famous hotel was built in 1909 by F. O. Stanley, inventor of the Stanley Steamer Automobiles. Stanley's idea was to provide a fine hotel to house summertime tourists to the fabulous Rocky Mountain region and to carry those tourists into the mountains and to and from the rail heads in Stanley Steamer motor coaches. One of those old coaches can be seen in the Dougherty Museum Collection in Longmont, CO.

The hotel has a vintage Stanley Steamer automobile in the lobby, 138 guest rooms with refurbished antiques, down comforters, new bedding, and much more. Additionally, the Stanley Hotel is the site of the Stanley Museum, built in conjunction with the Stanley Museum in Kingfield, Maine, and displays items of interest regarding Stanley automobiles. The hotel is often used for meetings, weddings, reunions, etc., and of course, antique car meets.

The Estes Park Area Historical Museum, 200 4th St., has further information on the Stanley family.

▶ GREELEY AREA (50 miles north of Denver on US 85)

CLASSICAL GAS (Dealer and museum)
245 E. Collins
EATON, CO 80615
(8 miles north of Greeley on US 85)

Phone: 800-453-7955 or
907-454-1365
www.classicalgasstation.com
Hours: M–F 9–5, Sat. 9–2

COLORADO

This is a large antique vehicle dealer with a 14,000 sq. ft. showroom and a museum. They carry as many as 350 vehicles in inventory of all makes and models. Classical Gas sells on consignment, takes trades, provides an inventory list and does minor repairs and service work. They will search for a specific vehicle and can help with financing. The company also sells antique auto-related memorabilia such as signs and pedal cars.

DOWNTOWN DEALS ON WHEELS
(Dealer)
1320 8th Av.
GREELEY, CO 80631
Phone: 970-356-9232 or
888-801-7370 (toll free)
www.puremuscle.com
Hours: M–Sat. 8–8

This is northern Colorado's largest muscle car and antique car dealer, and they usually carry between 25 to 30 fine cars in inventory. Downtown Deals on Wheels takes trades, sells on consignment, does appraisals, helps arrange financing and transportation and will search for specific vehicles for customers. An inventory list is available and car clubs are welcome. The company's owner is Dean Juhl. Founded in 1993.

ROCKY MOUNTAIN CLASSICS
(Dealer)
245 5th St.
GREELEY, CO 80631
Phone: 970-352-44
www.rockymountainclassics.com
Hours; Tues.–Thurs. 9–2, F and Sat. by appointment.

Unrestored originals and fixer-uppers, that's Rocky Mountain Classics' specialty. If you like to restore 'em as you drive 'em or want to build a hot rod you will enjoy stopping here. Most vehicles are under $5,000 and some as low as $1,500. The company will search for specific vehicles and help with financing and shipping. An inventory list of their vehicles, with photos, is on their web site.

End of Greeley area

WOLLER AUTO PARTS, INC. (Salvage)
8227 Road SS
LAMAR, CO 81052
(Southeastern corner of the state)
Phone: 719-336-2108 or
800-825-0210
http://wollerclassicautoparts.com
Hours: M–F 8–5

Here's a large salvage yard with about 5,000 vehicles of all makes & models, mostly domestic, from 1955 to the mid-1980s. Their slogan is *"5,000 Beautiful Wrecks and Glamorous Bodies."* Many pickups are available and Woller's can provide glass and painting services. They will search for parts from other sources, and car clubs are welcome. In business since 1969.

DOUGHERTY MUSEUM COLLECTION
One mile south of Longmont
on US 287
LONGMONT, CO 80504 (30 miles north of downtown Denver)
Phone: 303-776-2520 or

The Dougherty antique car collection *is open to the public on weekends only and is south of Longmont, CO. on US 287.*

303-684-0366
Hours: F–Sun. 10–4.
Admission charged.

Here is a privately-owned museum displaying some 35 vehicles ranging in age from 1902-1937. They include a 1902 Mobile Steamer, a 1908 Packard 30 Runabout, a 1910 Lozier Type I Briarcliff, a 1913 Lozier Type 72 Riverside, a 1915 Stanley Mountain Wagon and a 1920 Pierce-Arrow Type 48 five-passenger touring car. Another item of interest is a fully restored Wells-Fargo stage coach like the ones you see in western movies. There are displays of carriages, steam engines, and the museum has a music room full of antique musical instruments including a large Wurlitzer pipe organ. The museum is owned and operated by the Dougherty family and car clubs are welcome. Founded in 1977.

COOL CARS ONLY (dealer)
320 N. Railroad Av.
LOVELAND, CO 80537
Phone: 800-290-0679 and
970-669-9550, call anytime.
www.coolcarsonly.com
Hours: Anytime

Here is one of the country's largest antique car dealers. They carry a large inventory of vintage vehicles of all makes, models, types and years. Cool Cars Only does appraisals, sells on consignment, can provide an inventory list, arranges transportation and can help with financing. They are always on the lookout for vehicles to purchase and will buy entire collections. These are good people to check with if you are looking for that specific vehicle.

WEST 29th AUTO, INC. (Salvage)
3200 W. 29th St.
PUEBLO, CO 81003
Phone: 719-543-4247 or
719-543-4249
Hours: Tues.–Sat. 8–5

This is an 80-acre salvage yard with approximately 4,000 vehicles of all makes and models of cars, domestic and imports, accumulated over 30 years. Employees remove all parts and the company welcomes mail orders. Some new parts are available. In business since 1957.

CONNECTICUT

▶ BRIDGEPORT AREA

DRAGONE CLASSIC MOTORCARS, INC. (Dealer & restorer)
1797 Main St.
BRIDGEPORT, CT 06604
Phone: 203-335-4643
www.dragoneclassics.com
Hours: M–F 8–6, Sat. 9–3

Here you will find a large dealer and restorer of vintage automobiles specializing in exotic vehicles and convertibles from the 1950s and older. Between 35 and 50 cars are in their 15,000 sq. ft. showroom which is a restored 1880s stable. Dragone does full restorations, repairs and service work on antique cars. They can arrange financing, offer leases, do appraisals, take trades and provide an inventory list. They will also search for specific vehicles. On the last Saturday of each month Dragone's holds an open house for friends and customers. Visitors and car clubs are welcome at any time. There is an automobilia gallery on the second floor offering for sale such items as period oil painting, toys, books and a wide variety of collectibles. The owners are George and Manny Dragone. In business for over 50 years.

THE NEW ENGLAND CLASSIC CAR COMPANY (Dealer)
1483 Stratford Av.

STRATFORD, CT 06615
(Eastern suburb of Bridgeport on US 1 and I-95 exit 31)
Phone: 203-377-6746
www.newenglandclassics.com
Hours: M–F 9–5

This very interesting dealership has three showrooms and about 60 cars in inventory. They specialize in vintage sports car for road use, vintage and historic racing cars and dual purpose road and race cars. The owners of this establishment pride themselves in the fact that they can make auto racing an affordable sport for people other than millionaires. Prices for their cars range from $15,000 to $60,000 with a few over and a few under. Their showrooms are tastefully decorated with vintage photographs, posters and other racing and automotive memorabilia. The New England Classic Car Company has some of the most experienced and finest auto mechanics in the business in their service department and the company can offer race car preparation, transport and track-side services. The company sells cars on consignment and can pick up and deliver cars in their own trucks. This is also a good source for hard-to-find parts.

End of Bridgeport area ◀

MANCHESTER MOTOR CAR CO.
(Restorer and dealer)
> 319 Main St. (SR 83)
> *MANCHESTER*, CT 06040
> Phone: 860-643-5874
> www.manchestermotorcar.com
> Hours: M, Tues., W, and F 9–5;
> Thurs. 9–9; Sat. 9–3.

This company restores 'em and sells 'em. So, you can make your dreams come true here. There's a nice selection of vehicles for sale in the showroom and you can tour the restoration area. You can also bring in your old vehicle and have Manchester Motors fix it up the way you want it. They sell cars on consignment, help with financing, insurance and shipping and carry many old car parts in stock. There is also an interesting automobilia display.

THE GOLDEN AGE OF TRUCKING MUSEUM
> 1101 Southford Rd.
> *MIDDLEBURY*, CT 06762
> Phone: 203-577-2181
> www.goldenagetruckmuseum.com
> Hours: Thurs.-Sat. 10–4, Sun. noon–4. Admission charged.
> *Directions*: Exit I-84 at Exit 16 onto northbound SR-188. Museum is less than a mile distant.

If you like trucks, you'll like this museum. There are between 40 and 50 antique trucks here, most of them big ones. Historical emphasis is on the 1950s era. A list of the trucks on display is available and the museum publishes a newsletter. The museum hosts special business and social events and there is a gift shop and a library. The museum was founded in 1998 by the late Richard Guerrera, Sr.

DELAWARE

MESSICK AGRICULTURAL MUSEUM

Walt Messick Rd.
HARRINGTON, DE 19952
Phone: 302-398-3729
Hours: M–F 7:30–5. Free.
Directions: 1.2 miles west of
Jct. US 31 and SR 14W on
Walt Messick Rd.

The farmers had to get to town, you know, so some of their old automobiles are shown here along with their tractors, wagons, plows, manure spreaders and other necessities of life on the farm. Also to be seen is a 20th-century kitchen and smokehouse furnished in the period. Can't you just smell the country ham?

HAGLEY MUSEUM AND LIBRARY

298 Buck Rd.
WILMINGTON, DE 19807
Hours: *Jan. 1–Mar. 14*, Sat.–Sun.
9:30–4:30. *Mar. 15–Dec.* daily
9:30-4:30. Admission charged.
Phone: 302-658-2400
www.hagley.lib
Directions: *From Wilmington*,
take SR 52 (Pennsylvania Av.) north
to SR 100 North, then to SR 141
North. Hagley is located on SR 141.
From US 202 (Concord Pike) take
SR 141 South.

The Hagley Museum encompassed outdoor exhibits, dams, an antique ma-chine shop, water-powered and steam-powered mills and related buildings which are now used to display exhibits. This 230-acre complex was part of the factory established by the E. I. duPont de Nemours Company in 1802 to produce black powder explosives. Also on the grounds is a charming Georgian-style mansion known as Eleutherean Mills, which was the first home of the duPont family in America. Of interest to antique car buffs is a fine collection of antique vehicles including some that were made specifically for the duPont family. There is a gift shop, lunch and snack facilities, a picnic area, and internal transportation around the complex is provided. Guided tours are available.

NEMOURS MANSION AND GARDENS (Historic home)

1600 Rockland Rd. (3.5 miles
NW on Rockland Rd between
US 202 & SR 141)
WILMINGTON, DE 19803
Phone: 302-651-6912 or
800-651-6912
www.nemoursmansion.org
Hours: *May through Oct.* Tues.–Sat.
9–3, Sun. 1–3. Admission charged.
Visitors are conducted through the
mansion by tours.

This is the 300-acre estate, home and gardens of Alfred I. duPont. The 102-room mansion is lavishly furnished in fine examples of antique furniture, tapestries, rare rugs and works of art. Included in the tour of the estate is a display of several antique automobiles located in the Chauffeur's Quarters and Garage. The automobiles belonged to the duPont family and include a 1924 Cadillac limousine, a Renault limousine, a 1951 Rolls-Royce Silver Wraith and a 1960 Rolls-Royce Phantom V, of which only 10 were built. There is also a 1933 Buick Sport Coupe, with rumble seat, which was used at the duPont's estate in Jacksonville, FL.

DISTRICT OF COLUMBIA

NATIONAL MUSEUM OF AMERICAN HISTORY

On Constitution Av. between
12th & 14 Sts. N.W.
WASHINGTON, DC 20560
Phone: 202-357-2700
www.si.edu
Hours: Daily 10–5:30.
Admission free.

This museum is one of several in the large and magnificent Smithsonian museum complex along the Mall in our nation's capital. The Museum of American History depicts the cultural, technological, scientific and political development of the United States. For the antique car buff, there is a display of some 20 antique automobiles, as well as motorcycles, trucks, tractors, race cars and buses. The automotive display includes an 1869 Roper steam velocipede and other vehicles from some of America's earliest automobile makers. The museum owns additional cars, including a Tucker, so the automobile displays rotate. There is a cafeteria, a restaurant and three gift shops.

FLORIDA

BRADENTON (see Sarasota/Bradenton area)

▶ DAYTONA BEACH AREA

DAYTONA USA (Museum)
Daytona International Speedway
1801 W. International Speedway
Blvd. (U.S. 92 just east of its
junction with I-95)
DAYTONA BEACH, FL 32114-1243
Phone: 386-947-6800
http://dbserver.iscmotorsports.com
Hours: Daily 9–7 with extended
hours during peak seasons.

They call it *"The Ultimate Motorsport Attraction"*. This fine museum on the grounds of the Daytona International Speedway is a one-of-kind interactive motorsports attraction which features hands-on activities. One such interactive display puts the visitor in the driver's seat of a race car going over 200 m.p.h. complete with visual and audio aids. Visitors enter the museum through twin tunnels which are replicas of the famous twin tunnels at the Speedway through which millions of fans have passed as they entered the infield. Once through the tunnels the world of racing opens up in a fascinating array of displays, race cars, race car drivers, racing events, great moments in racing and much more. The museum's gift shop offers NASCAR-related merchandise, clothing, postcards, books and a wide variety of collectibles. Tours of the Speedway's track are available through the museum.

The Twin-tunnel entrance to the Daytona USA museum at the Daytona International Speedway.

49

FLORIDA

MARK MARTIN'S KLASSIX AUTO MUSEUM

2909 W. International Speedway Blvd. (1 mile west of Daytona Speedway)
DAYTONA BEACH, FL 32124
Phone: 386-252-3800 and 800-881-8975 (toll free)
www.klassixauto.com
Hours: Daily 9–9.
Admission charged.

There's a magnificent mix of vintage machines in this museum including muscle cars, classics, sports cars, motorcycles and celebrity cars. The emphasis is on speed. There are about 120 cars and 40 motorcycles, many of which are Indians. Some of the vehicles are for sale. Displays of individual cars are highlighted by elaborate period-accented backdrops and manikins, and the museum has video presentations. The museum's large gift shop is filled with interesting souvenirs for the car enthusiast. You can also enjoy a chocolate soda or a lemon fizz at the museum's 1950s ice cream parlor.

End of Daytona Beach area ◀

▶ FORT LAUDERDALE AREA

BERLINER CLASSIC MOTORCARS, INC.
(Dealer)

1975 Stiring Rd.
DANIA BEACH, FL 33004
(Southern suburb of Ft. Lauderdale)
Phone: 954-923-7271
www.berlinerclassiccars.com
Hours: M-F 9–5, Sat. 10–1

This is an antique auto dealer that not only offers vintage cars but also a lot of other antique items. Regarding the cars, they carry a wide variety of fine quality automobiles and motorcycles. Berliner takes trades, sells on consignment, assists in financing and shipping, and searches for specific vehicles. The other antique items include vintage watercraft, jukeboxes, old cash registers, gas pumps, radios, phonographs, slot machines, bicycles, barber chairs, Coke machines, carousel horses, auto couches, scales and more. The facilities are available for corporate or private functions. Berliner's is a fun place to visit.

FORT LAUDERDALE ANTIQUE CAR MUSEUM

1527 S.W. 1st Av. (Packard Avenue)
FT. LAUDERDALE, FL 33315
Phone: 954-779-7300
www.antiquecarmuseum.org
Hours: M–F 9–3. Sat. & Sun. call for hours.

PACKARDS, PACKARDS everywhere, and they all run. This fine museum has more than 20 Packards on display, some of them very rare models. Their vintages run from the 1900s to the 1940s. The museum is a reproduction of a pre-war Packard showroom complete with a picture of President Franklin D. Roosevelt. In fact, there's an entire gallery devoted to FDR. Also on display is a wide range of automobilia related to

Packard and other makes. Included are old dashboards, hood ornaments, rare carburetors, side lamps, headlights, road signs, parking meters, horns, chauffeur badges, car whisky decanters—and the list goes on. The museum was created by Arthur and Shirley Stone and the curator is Russ Gagliano, Jr. All three hang out here a lot and are happy to see visitors like you drop in.

End of Fort Lauderdale area ◄

► FORT MYERS AREA

Henry Ford's winter home, "Mangoes", in Ft. Myers, FL. To the right is a bust of Henry Ford.

HENRY FORD AND THOMAS EDISON WINTER ESTATES (Historic homes)
2350 McGregor Blvd. (SR 867)
FORT MYERS, FL 33901 (in the southwest part of the Florida peninsula near the coast and on I-75)
Phone: 239-334-3614
Hours: Admission by guided tour only, M–Sat. 9–4, Sun. noon–4. Admission charged, covers both estates.

These are the winter homes of two famous Americans, Henry Ford and Thomas Edison who, as close friends, built their vacation homes side-by-side in this beautiful resort town. Ford's home is known as "Mangoes" and Edison's as "Seminole Lodge". Both homes are open to the public. Edison's extensive botanical garden and laboratory are preserved much as they were at the time of his death in 1931. On display in an adjoining

51

museum are many artifacts and personal belongings of both men as well as several antique automobiles. One of the vehicles is a Model T Ford given to Edison by Ford.

SOUTHWEST MOTORSPORTS, INC.
(Dealer)
17683 Summerlin Rd.
FORT MYERS, FL 33907
Phone: 239-415-1967
www.southwest-motorsports.com
Hours: M–F 9–5

As the company name indicates, this is the place to look for sports cars. They also carry selected classic cars along with motorcycles, trucks and special interest vehicles. Southwest prides itself in giving truthful and accurate descriptions of their vehicles and will take trades, search for specific vehicles, provide appraisals and help with shipping and financing. This is a family-owned company in business for many years.

End of Fort Myers area ◄

BANTER'S ANTIQUE AUTO AND TRUCK PARTS (salvage yard)
14322 Mayer Av.
HUDSON, FL 34669 (on the Gulf 30 miles north of the Tampa area off U.S. 19)
Phone: 727-863-6120
Hours: Tues.–Sat. 9:30–6

Howard Banter is a Chevrolet and General Motors man. There's no Fords and imports here. As the company name implies, there are lots of truck parts too, and a few buses around. Banter's has several buildings full of parts from vehicles that have long ago been sent to the crusher. The company can provide manuals, weatherstripping, interior parts, rubber parts, accessories, emblems, glass and other hard-to-find items. NOS and repro parts are also available. In business since 1970.

OLYMPIA MOTOR CARS (Dealer)
2727 St. Johns Bluff Rd. S.
JACKSONVILLE, FL 32246
Phone: 904-642-2277
www.olympiamotorcars.com

Hours: M–F 10–6, Sat. 11–3

When you enter Olympia's showroom, you will see British, German, French, Swedish and other national flags hanging from the wall. The flags tell you that this is a dealer specializing in vintage imports. But, they speak English. The company does lots of appraising, takes trades, aids in financing and shipping and will search for that special vehicle you're looking for. After your day at the beach, come by and take a look.

SUNRISE AUTO SALES AND SALVAGE
Academic Av.
LAKE CITY, FL 32025
(Northern Florida at the junction of I-10 and I-75)
Phone: 904-755-1810
Hours: M–F 8–5:30, Sat. 8–1

This yard has over 1,000 cars and trucks ranging from the 1930s and up. They specialize in vehicles from the 1940s through early 1970s with the highest concentration of cars being from the 1950s and 1960s. Most are domestic. Customers may browse the lot and car clubs are welcome. Sunrise has a brisk

mail-order business. In business since 1989. Ask for Bill, the owner.

▶ MIAMI AREA

One of the booths in the restaurant of the Dezerland Surfside Beach Hotel.

DEZERLAND BEACH RESORT AND SPA

8701 Collins Av. (on the ocean)
MIAMI BEACH, FL 33154
Phone: 305-865-6661 and
800-695-8284 (reservations—
toll free)
www.dezerlandhotelmiamibeach.
com
Hours: *Check in time—3:00,
check out time—12:00 noon.
Restaurant—*daily 7 am–10 pm.

This is a unique beach-front hotel decorated throughout in a 1950s motif. There are antique cars from that era tastefully placed around the hotel. Most of the cars are kept in running order and are used from time-to-time in events throughout the country. Many of the hotel's rooms are named after auto-

mobiles and in the restaurant there are booths made from vintage car bodies. Car clubs are welcome and are offered discounts. There is a large gift shop filled with items of interest to antique car buffs. The hotel has 225 rooms and all the amenities of a luxury hotel. It is close to other Miami attractions and has shuttle service to several locations.

TED VERNON SPECIALTY AUTOMOBILES, INC. (Dealer)

471 N.E. 79th St.
MIAMI, FL 33138
Phone: 305-754-2323
www.tedvernon.com
Hours: M–F 9–5, Sat. 9–4

Ted Vernon's is a no-frills, wholesale operation working out of a garage-type indoor showroom and an adjacent lot.

FLORIDA

They carry about 160 antique, classic and collectible cars available for sale. Vehicles range from $1,000 fixer-uppers to $100,000 ready-to-go Rolls-Royces. Limousines are something of a specialty here and up to 40 might be on hand at any one time. The company takes trades, can provide appraisals and helps arrange financing and transportation. Car clubs are welcome. The owners are Ted and Robin Vernon. In business since 1971.

End of Miami Area ◀

▶ OCALA AREA (35 miles south of Gainesville on I-75)

FLORIDA'S SILVER SPRINGS
(Theme park)
> 5656 E. Silver Springs Blvd.
> (SR 40 east)
> **SILVER SPRINGS**, FL 34488
> (An eastern suburb of Ocala)
> Phone: 352-236-2121
> www.silversprings.com
> Hours: Daily 10–5.
> Admission charged.

This is a large theme and wildlife park built around the world's largest fresh water springs area. Among the many activities and displays in the park is a collection of some two dozen antique and classic cars. Many movies and TV shows have been filmed at Silver Springs and the area was used for jungle warfare training during World War II.

DON GARLITS' MUSEUMS
> 13700 S.W. 16th Av.
> **OCALA**, FL 34473
> Phone: 352-245-8661 and
> 877-271-3278 (toll free)
> www.garlits.com

Hours: Daily 9–5.
Admission charged. Free parking and tractor trailers welcome.
Directions: Exit I-75 at Exit 341, just south of Ocala, onto CR 484. Proceed ¹/₄ mile east to CR 475A, then ¹/₄ mile south to the museums.

When you buy a ticket here, its a "twofer," that is, two museums for the price of one. Don "Big Daddy" Garlits is a famous drag racer who has put together two museums side by side. One is devoted to his sport of drag racing and the other is loaded with vintage vehicles. You'll want to see both. Some of the cars are on loan through special arrangements with the Ford Foundation. Garlits liked Fords for drag racing. Many of the drag racers are associated with other famous drag race drivers, and some of the vintage vehicles have connections to famous people of all walks of life. Two attractive gift shops offer a large selection of racing and antique car memorabilia and souvenirs. You'll have fun here.

End of Ocala Area ◀

▶ ORLANDO AREA

LATE GREAT CHEVY ASSOCIATION
(Salvage yard)

2166 Orange Blossom Hwy., US 41,
(just north of downtown Orlando)
ORLANDO, FL 32860
Phone: 407-886-1963
Hours: M–F 8–5

Can you guess? This salvage yard specializes in Chevrolets. Fords need not apply. Parts are available here for all the different types of Chevrolets, mostly post-war, up to 1972. New and reproduction parts are also available. The yard is owned and operated by Danny Howell and Robert Snowden, two guys who never outgrew cars. They got serious about it in 1980 and opened this yard.

MOUNT DORA MUSEUM OF SPEED

206 N. Highland St.
MOUNT DORA, FL 32757 (a northwestern suburb of Orlando)
Phone: 352-385-1945
www.classicdreamcars.com

Hours: Tues.–Sat. 10–5. By appointment. Admission charged, but free to large groups. Children under 14 not allowed in the Museum. Free parking.

Ever been to Mt. Dora? It's a delightful place with old restored homes, antique shops, fine restaurants, nice inns and bed & breakfasts, many lakes and lots of activities. It has been rated as one of the five best places in the US to retire.

In the midst of all this is the Mount Dora Museum of Speed. This museum specializes in ultra-low mileage, and restored classic muscle cars. There are about 15 cars on permanent display, some of them associated with famous people, and another 12–20 for sale. You'll see lots of other things of interest here too; vintage road signs, quarter midget race cars, pedal cars, an actual vintage Texaco gas station, jukeboxes, vintage gas pumps, old Coke machines, and more. There is also a fine gift shop. The museum opened in August 2001.

End of Orlando area ◀

▶ SARASOTA/BRADENTON AREA

SARASOTA CLASSIC CAR MUSEUM

5500 N. Tamiami Trail
(Just south of the airport)
SARASOTA, FL 34234
Phone: 941-355-6228
www.sarasotacarmuseum.org
Hours: Daily 9–6. Admission charged.

Here's a biggie. This is a 60,000 sq. ft. museum that used to be a World War II military installation. The museum has over 100 cars on display along with many other items of interest. The inventory of autos changes frequently, so multiple visits are recommended. Some of the cars are associated with famous people or of historic significance. Other enjoyments here are an antique camera and photography display and an antique game arcade with old time machines that still work. You can play a game here for a nickel. There is a large gift shop offering a wide variety of interesting items. The museum has a large atrium in the center of the building which is used for banquets, meetings, dances, etc. This can be a swinging place after hours. Founded in 1953 and still going strong.

THOROUGHBRED MOTORS
(Cars & Parts)
3935 N. Washington Blvd.
SARASOTA, FL 34234
Phone: 941-955-5960 or
941-359-2277
www.thoroughbred-motors.com
Hours: M–F 9–7, Sat. 9–5

A dealer specializing in vintage European cars; Jaguars, Rolls-Royces, Aston Martins, Austin Healeys, MGs, Triumphs, etc. Some cars are in their original state and are offered as rebuildable automobiles. Normally there are some 30 cars on display. Thoroughbred

Motors does appraisals, takes trades, makes repairs, publishes an inventory list and can arrange shipping. They also carry a large inventory of Jaguar parts. Car clubs are welcome. The owner is Rodney Dessberg.

VINTAGE MOTORS OF SARASOTA, INC. (Dealer)
2836 N. Tamiami Trail
SARASOTA, FL 34234
Phone: 941-355-6500
www.vintagemotorssarasota.com
Hours: M–F 9–5, Sat. 10–4

This is a large dealership with a wide variety of cars ranging from week-end run-abouts to chairman-of-the-board Rolls-Royces. They carry between 70 and 100 cars in inventory with about 30 of them on display in their showroom. Some of their inventory is held at the Sarasota Classic Car Museum, a mile and a half up the road. An inventory list is available. Vintage Motors also does appraisals, helps arrange financing and shipping, sells on consignment, takes trades and will search for that very special vehicle you've always wanted. Car clubs are welcome.

End of Sarasota Area

ELLIOTT MUSEUM
825 N.E. Ocean Blvd. (SR A1A)
STUART, FL 34996 (30 miles north of West Palm Beach)
Phone: 772-225-1961
www.elliottmuseumfl.org
Hours: M–Sat. 10–4, Sun. 1–4.
Admission charged.

Here is a large and diversified museum showing displays of Americana from 1835 to 1930. One wing of the museum has on display some 30 vintage autos, plus motorcycles and bicycles. There are also displays of the many industrial inventions of Sterling Elliott, the father of Harmon Parker Elliott, museum founder. Museum founded in 1960.

The **Elliott Museum** *of Stuart, FL.*

THE TALLAHASSEE
ANTIQUE CAR MUSEUM
   3550A Maham Dr. (U.S. 90 East)
   TALLAHASSEE, FL 32308
   Phone: 850-942-0137
   www.tacm.com
   Hours: M–Sat. 10–5, Sun. noon–5.
   Admission charged.

There's over 80 of them here—vintage cars, that is. Some of the cars have interesting histories and there are a few military vehicles and a very special horse-drawn carriage. It's the one that served as Abraham Lincoln's hearse. Your admission charge also gets you into the Museum of Arts & Crafts which displays a wide selection of items including sports memorabilia, over 100 pedal cars, outboard motors dating back to 1908, a baby bottle collection, cash registers, a large train display and antique and imported furniture, some of which is for sale. Here, too, is one of the largest collections of Indian (native American—not motorcycle) artifacts in the world. The museum also has banquet facilities for seminars, meetings, parties, dances, etc.

▶ TAMPA BAY AREA

BOB'S CLASSICS, INC. (Dealer)
   13111 93rd St. N.
   LARGO, FL 33773 (½ hour
   south of Tampa Airport)
   Phone: 727-581-9406
   www.bobsclassics.com
   Hours: M–Sat. 8–5

Wouldn't you like to own a shiney red Allard J2X or a bright yellow Auburn boat-tail speedster? You can get them here at Bob's for reasonable prices because Bob's specializes in selling turnkey replicas. Bob's also sells neo-classics, special interest cars and replica kits. The company does not assemble, however. All of the vehicles are indoor and under one roof. Bob's also sells an item you won't find many places—car-replica golf carts! These fun vehicles carry an interesting array of gadgets designed to spook your opponent on the golf course. You can turn up the sound on your in-dash TV set, or sound a siren or beep animal sounds! Bob's in run by Bob Simpson and his beautiful wife, Marcelle, who have been in the business since 1991.

RP CUSTOM (Dealer)
   8143 Winerton Rd.
   LARGO, FL 33773 ($1/2$ hour
   south of Tampa Airport)
   Phone: 727-535-7559
   www.rpcustom.com
   Hours: M–F 9–5

Sitting in this company's showroom, on their black and white checker-board tile floor, are some of the finest vintage cars you will find anywhere. Most cars are American-made, but there is a smattering of imports and a generous assortment of muscle cars. RP takes trades, offers appraisals and helps with shipping and financing. You'll have fun shopping here.

**CLASSIC CORVETTES
& COLLECTIBLES, INC.**
(Dealer, museum, restorer)
   304 S. Pinellas Av.
   TARPON SPRINGS, FL 34689
   (On the Gulf just north of
   Tampa area on US 19)
   Phone: 727-945-1500
   www.classiccorvettes.com
   Hours: M–F 9–6, Sat. 10–5

Here is a feast for the eyes of any antique car buff. This is the largest antique car showroom in the US southeast—over 32,000 sq. ft. Some 150 high-quality Corvettes, muscle cars, classics and street rods are on display and for sale. About a third of the collection are Corvettes. Most of the vehicles are of show and museum quality. This is due, in part, to the fact that Al Wiseman, the owner of the museum, is also a partner in a full restoration shop and takes a hand in much of the work done there. The restoration facility, Classic Car Restoration & Service Center, is just down the street at 440 S. Pinellas Av. A few vehicles from Wiseman's personal car collection are there. Classic Corvettes & Collectibles can arrange shipping and financing and they are always on the lookout to purchase fine quality cars.

LINCOLN LAND, INC. (Dealer)
   2925 Gulf to Bay Blvd. (Showroom)
   CLEARWATER, FL 33765
   Phone: 727-443-3646 (showroom),
   727-531-5351 (parts and service)
   www.lincolnlandinc.com
   Hours: M–F 8–5

If Lincolns are your thing, this is a place you should know about. They sell vintage Lincolns, Lincoln parts and do service work. You'll find a nice selection of Lincoln automobiles in their spacious showroom along with memorabilia, auto literature and automotive books. The parts and service department is at a nearby location. The company takes trades, offers appraisals, helps with financing and shipping and has a road rescue service. In business since 1979 and se habla Espanol.

P.J.'S AUTO WORLD CLASSIC, EXOTIC AND SPORTS CARS (Dealer)

(One of two locations)
1370 Cleveland St.
CLEARWATER, FL 33755
Phone: 727-461-4900 and
800-288-6386 (toll free)
www.pjautoworld.com
Hours: Normal daytime hours.
(Second of two locations)
151 Gulf to Bay Blvd.
CLEARWATER, FL 33755
Phone: 727-446-9999

When you step into P.J.'s, you ain't seen it all because there are two locations, both a short distance apart. Nevertheless, you will find a large selection of fascinating classics, exotic and sports vehicles. There are also a few vintage trucks and some late-model cars. All told, P.J.'s carries up to 300 vehicles at their two locations. They take trades, will search for cars, and help with shipping. In business since 1982.

End of Tampa Bay area ◀

WIRE WHEELS CLASSIC SPORTSCARS, INC. (Dealer)

995 36th St. Court S.W.
VERO BEACH, FL 32968
(on US 1, 60 miles north of
West Palm Beach)
Phone: 772-299-9788
www.wirewheel.com
Hours: M–F 9–5

Tallyho! When you visit this dealer, you're in Old England and you'll see nothing but beautiful and shiny British sports cars and race cars. There will be about 45 of them on display in their modern showroom. If you have a British car and are in the mood to sell, Wire Wheels is interested in talking. If you have a friend who's interested in selling a nice British-made sports car, they are interested in talking to him, and the company will pay you a "finder's fee" if they cut a deal. Wire Wheels takes trades, does appraisals and helps with shipping and financing. Car clubs are welcome. The business was started by Hayes H. Harris and his lovely wife, Charlotte, in the early 1990s.

THE MUSEUM AT RAGTOPS MOTORCARS (Museum and dealer)

2119 S. Dixie Hwy. (US 1)
WEST PALM BEACH, FL 33401-7701
Phone: 561-655-2836
www.ragtopsmotorcars.com
Hours: M–Sat. 10–5. Admission charged.

You can buy 'em here or just look at 'em. This is a big place offering multiple services for the antique car buff. There are three buildings on two entire city blocks. The main office and showroom is located in an ornate old building that was originally designed for a Hudson dealer. Ragtops offers over 90 classic, luxury and sports vehicles at all times. Customers may find the vehicle of their dreams parked in a simulated drive-in theater, a gas station, a barn, an old-fashioned main street, a car-as-art gallery, a working soda bar or in a beach scene with real sand. Ragtops helps arrange financing, offers leasing, storage and sells cars on consignment. There is a gift shop offering automotive memorabilia and Ragtops has an interesting

This is the multi-story facility of Ragtops Motorcars of West Palm Beach. FL.

display of memorabilia from decades past. Ragtops' owner is Ty Houck.

HOLDER'S AUTO SALVAGE
12404 Highway 231
YOUNGSTOWN, FL 32466
(In the Florida Panhandle 20 miles northeast of Panama City)
Phone: 850-722-4993
Hours: Tues.–Sat. 8–5

This salvage lot specializes in pre-1975 cars and trucks with some cars dating back to the 1920s. Most of the vehicles are American-made. The owner's brother operates a wheel cover and hub cap business on the same site with thousands of wheel covers from 1934 up. Visitors may browse the yard with permission. Car clubs welcome. The owner is Carlos Holder, formerly of Toledo, Ohio. In business since 1984.

GEORGIA

▶ ATLANTA AREA

BRANDON HOME FURNISHING/ CLASSIC CAR MUSEUM AND SHOWROOM

1990 Defoor Av. N.W.
ATLANTA, GA 30318
Phone: 404-350-0558 and
866-297-2331 (toll free)
www.brandonclassics.com
Hours: Daily 9–5. Museum free.

Here's a very unique and interesting car museum and dealership. It's inside Brandon's Furniture Store. The wife can shop for furniture and the husband can look at the cars. Brandon's carries a general line of vintage autos, trucks and motorcycles and has about 35 to 55 vehicles in the showroom at all times with many of them for sale. Brandon's is a big seller of vintage vehicles on-line. Most of their car business is done that way. Brandon's does appraisals, helps with financing and shipping and will search for specific vehicles. Car clubs are very welcome and the company will provide space, free of charge, for car club meetings and activities.

FRASER DANTE LTD (Dealer)

900 Sun Valley Dr. Building #10
ROSWELL, GA 30076
(Just north of Atlanta on U.S 19)
Phone: 770-641-8354
www.fraserdante.com
Hours: M–F 9–6, Sat. 10–4:30

You'll see antique vehicles here from the 1930s through the 1970s. One of Fraser Dante's specialties is 1969 and 1970 Pace Car Convertibles and they also sell brand-new muscle machines such as Vipers, Ram SRTs, Mercedes and Corvettes. Thomas Fraser, the owner, is an old race car driver and loves these machines. The company carries about 65 cars in inventory all of the time.

Fraser Dante takes trades, sells on consignment, provides appraisals and can assist in financing and shipping. In business since 1987.

STONE MOUNTAIN ANTIQUE CAR AND TREASURE MUSEUM

Stone Mountain Park (16 miles east of Atlanta on highway US 78 east of I-285 bypass)
STONE MOUNTAIN, GA 30086
Phone: 770-413-5229
www.prostman-antiques.com
Hours: Summer; March through Sept. M–Sat. 10–8, Sun. noon–8. Winter; Oct. through Feb., F–Sat. 10–5, Sun. noon–5. Admission charged.

This is a very interesting museum located inside beautiful Stone Mountain Park. On display are some 30 antique vehicles plus a number of motorcycles, motorbikes pedal cars, vintage auto parts and gasoline globes and pumps.

GEORGIA

Included in the auto collection is a Tucker and a one-of-kind 1928 Martin. And, as the name of the museum implies, there is a treasure trove of non-automotive antiques. Here, visitors will see working jukeboxes that play the golden oldies, a wide variety of antique musical instruments, electric trains and other toys, a collection of Coca-Cola memorabilia, sports items, a bottle collection, furniture, beaded purses, records and record players, clocks, fans and more. This is a real fun place. The museum is owned and operated by the Tommy Prostman family.

End of Atlanta Area

THE GENERATION GAP (Dealer)
123 Peachtree Pkwy.
BYRON, GA 31008 (12 miles south of downtown Macon on I-75)
Phone: 478-956-2678 and 888-807-8071 (toll free)
www.thegenerationgap.com
Hours: M–F 9–5

Look for the building with the big sign that says "The Generation Gap, Old Car Emporium, Antique Mall." At the entrance two vintage cars are mounted overhead on a big "T" bar. These things indicate that what you are about to see is quite unique. Inside the mall is a large auto showroom, stalls selling all kinds of antiques and a display of new car-hauling trailers which are for sale. In the auto showroom one will find a nice selection of affordable vehicles and light trucks. There will be anything from 100 point cars to fixer-uppers. The Generation Gap takes trades, sells on consignment, arranges shipping—that is if you don't buy a trailer—and helps with financing. They also have on-site and off-site auto actions during the year. The company is family-owned and has been in business since 1975.

THUNDER ROAD USA (Museum)
415 SR 53 East
DAWSONVILLE, GA 30534
(55 miles north-northeast of Atlanta on SRs. 53 and 9)
Phone: 706-216-7223
www.thunderroadusa.com
Hours: M–F 10–7, Sat. & Sun. 10–6.
Admission charged.

CLOSED

Dawsonville and Dawson County have rich histories in racing, especially NASCAR racing, and this museum celebrates that achievement. On display in the museum is a plentiful array of race cars, old and new. There is a Hall of Fame honoring notables in the sport of racing and at the entrance to the museum's attractive building is a "Winner's Circle," a place where every race car driver and owner hope one day to be. You will see a replica of an old time drive-in theater showing film footage from past races, an arcade, several motion-based racing simulators and a nice gift shop. One of the surprises in the museum is an actual (non-operative) moonshine still. So, drop in and have some fun.

CONTEMPORARY AND INVESTMENT AUTO (Dealer)
4115 Poplar Spring Rd.
GAINESVILLE, GA 30507
(North-central part of the state on I-985 and US 129)
Phone: 770-539-9111

www.ciacars.com
Hours: M–F 9–5

Here, in the beautiful lake country of northern Georgia, is an antique car dealer worthy of note. Contemporary and Investment Auto has a very nice showroom—on one of the lakes—and offers a wide variety of vintage vehicles. They sell classic cars, sports cars, muscle cars, street rods, pickup trucks and micro-cars. They also do restoration work. The company takes trades, provides appraisals and can arrange shipping and financing. This is a nice place to stop and see.

JOHNSON'S AUTO SALVAGE
1029 County Line Rd.
GRIFFIN, GA 30224
(45 miles south of Atlanta on US 10/US 41 and SR 16)
Phone: 770-227-4244
Hours: M,Tues.,Thurs.,F 8:30–5:30, W and Sat. 8:30–12:00 P.M. Small admission charged to tour the yard.

There are some 3,000 vehicles in this salvage yard ranging from the 1930s to the 1970s. This is a very clean yard with the vehicles grouped together by makes so they are easy to find. The GM stuff is over there, the Fords are over here and the Imports are down thataway. You might want to bring your lunch. It's a big yard. You'll also find a nice selection of small trucks and a few buses. In business since 1969.

AUTOMOBILEATLANTA (Dealer)
505 S. Marietta Pkwy.
MARIETTA, GA 30060 (18 miles northwest of downtown Atlanta)
Phone: 770-427-2844 and 800-792-4944 (toll free).

www.autoatlanta.com
Hours: M–F 9–5

These people know as much about Porsches as anybody—that is all they handle. The sell them, service them, overhaul them, restore them and sell parts. What more could one ask? With regard to parts, the company has the broadest line of them for Porsche 914s, 924/944s this side of Stuttgart. A parts catalog is available. In their spacious showroom, one will find up to 50 Porsches in conditions ranging from show-winners to project cars.

The company takes trades, provides appraisals, helps with shipping and financing and can provide technical advice. George Hussey IV is the man behind it all. It started as a hobby in the 1970s. And when you walk in, beware of Butzi, the watch cat!

RICHMOND HILL (13 miles southwest of Savannah on I-95)
They call this town *"The Town That Henry Ford Built"*. That's not exactly true, but it is the town that Henry Ford greatly improved and made more liveable for its citizens. In the mid-1930s Ford bought a plantation nearby and built a winter home in which he and his wife, Clara, stayed for one month each year. Ford named his Georgia home the Richmond Plantation. At that time the town of Richmond Hill was known as Ways Station and was an impoverished community whose citizens suffered a high rate of illiteracy, chronic unemployment and chronic maladies such as malaria and venereal diseases. Ford's chauffeur became a victim of malaria soon after his arrival here. Ford saw the great needs of the community and went to work to

improve the local conditions. Henry, you know, wasn't the kind of a man who could just sit around for a month. He went to work on the project and had an extensive drainage system built to drain off standing water. By 1940 these efforts had eradicated the malaria problem. He also built a medical clinic and staffed it with nurses. Ford then built chapels for whites and African-Americans, a school for African-American children, a sawmill, an industrial arts and trade school, a large community center and an agricultural research center that experimented in producing starch from locally-grown sweet potatoes and water chestnuts, in addition to making alcohol from sweet potatoes and rice for mixing with gasoline. In his schools, Ford created one of the nation's first school lunch programs. In 1941, the citizens of Ways Station renamed their community Richmond Hill in honor of Henry Ford and his nearby plantation. Henry Ford's memory is still very strong and cherished in this community.

PEBBLE HILL PLANTATION
(Historic home)
US 319 South
THOMASVILLE, GA 31799
(Southwestern part of the state near the Florida state line)
Phone: 229-226-2344
www.pebblehill.com
Hours: Tues.–Sat. 10–5, Sun. 1–5.
Last tour at 4. Admission charged.

This is an old southern plantation established in 1820. Through the years it has had a succession of wealthy owners who converted the main house into a lavish "winter cottage". The main house is open to the public as are the gardens and the other buildings on the plantation. In the garage is a collection of 8 antique cars, some of them used on the plantation.

AUTO QUEST INVESTMENT CARS
(Dealer)
710 W. 7th St.
TIFTON, GA 31793
(South-central part of the state on I-75, exit 62, and US 82)
Phone: 229-382-4750
www.auto-quest.com
Hours: M–F 8:30–5

This dealership is housed in a very nice single story building with large glass windows. That way, you can get a good look at the cars in the showroom before you even walk in the door. Here at Auto Quest you will see vintage cars, exotic cars, high performance cars, sports cars, muscle cars and classic trucks. And, bring your lady friend. Inside the showroom is a home furnishing and apparel store known as "The Cabin Shop." Here one will find accessories for the country home, classic apparel for men and women, fishing shirts and car-theme shirts, all at outlet prices. When it comes to the cars, Auto Quest takes trades, offers appraisals, has a locator service and helps with shipping and financing. And, they're old-timers in the business having been automotive specialists since 1926.

LITTLE WHITE HOUSE STATE HISTORIC SITE (Historic home)
SR 85W South (US 27 Alt.)
WARM SPRINGS, GA 31830
(30 miles northeast of Columbus)

President Roosevelt's 1938 Ford convertible equipped with hand controls so that he could drive without the use of his legs. Behind is the entrance to his Warm Springs home.

Phone: 706-655-5870
www.fdr-littlewhitehouse.org
Hours: Daily 9–4:45, tours available.
Admission charged.

This was the vacation home of President Franklin D. Roosevelt which he built for himself in 1932, and the place where he died on April 12, 1945. Roosevelt chose this location so that he could be near the local waters and spa facilities of Warm Springs which he believed helped his lower-body paralysis, which was the result of an attack of polio he suffered as a young man. On display at the historic site are many items pertaining to his life and presidency including two of his personal pre-war automobiles. One is a 1938 Ford convertible and the other a 1941 Willys convertible. Both vehicles are specially equipped with hand controls that allowed him to drive without the use of his legs. There is also a large museum focusing on Roosevelt, his family and his presidency. Other amenities include a gift shop, snack bar and picnic area.

A & B AUTO PARTS

(Salvage and display)
3411 Memorial Dr.
(South of town on US 1)
WAYCROSS, GA 32501
(Southeastern part of the state)
Phone: 912-285-1776
Hours: M–Sat. 8–5

Eighteen acres and 2,000 cars—that's A & B Auto Parts—one of the largest yards in Georgia. They have a wide variety of domestic vehicles and some imports. 1955-56-57 Chevrolets are a specialty and A & B has a number of whole cars, set aside in a separate part of the yard, that are good candidates for restoration. They include Corvettes and some early V-8 Fords. And here's a surprise...this yard has a small museum of vintage vehicles—a very rare thing in the salvage yard business. Most of the vehicles belong to the proprietor, Jim Bennett. Also in the museum are vintage toys, railroad memorabilia and a soda fountain. This is a good place to stop on your way to Florida. A & B has been around since 1962.

IDAHO

HOT ROD CAFE
1610 Schneidmiller Av.
POST FALLS, ID 83854 (8 miles west of Couer D'Alene off I-90)
Phone: 208-777-1712
www.hotrodcafe.com
Hours: Daily 11 A.M.–midnight

I'll have a *Back Fire Chili Burger* and some *Piston Rings* (onion rings). That's only a sample of the items on the menu of this very unique, 1950s and Hot Rod-oriented cafe. Other menu delights include *Wrench fries, Deuce Coupe fettuccine* and *Intake Manifold Meatloaf*. It's all the idea of Rob Elder who started the cafe in 1998. The inside of the cafe is like a museum. There are actual hot rods suspended from the ceiling and you'll see pedal cars, vintage gas signs and pumps, chrome auto parts, a Buick front end, neon signs, an occasional motorcycle, and other interesting stuff. Fifties' music is usually playing in the background. Besides food, car buffs can purchase t-shirts, jackets, coffee mugs, boxer shorts with cars on them—and more.

When you get off the Expressway, look for a square white building with a big red horse above the entrance, and a hot rod on the roof.

VINTAGE AUTOMOTIVE (Salvage)
2290 N. 18th East
MOUNTAIN HOME, ID 83647 (42 miles southeast of Boise on I-80N)
Phone: 208-587-3743
www.jimsvintageautomotive.com
Hours: M–F 9–6, Sat. 10–5

This is a 1,300-vehicle salvage yard with mixed makes and body styles from the teens through the 1970s. Vintage Automotive has an unusually large number of Nash Metropolitans in the yard and the owner has several restored Mets in his personal collection. The company also sells new parts of Mets. This is a relatively dry part of the state and, as a result, many of the cars are rust-free, or nearly so. Vintage will search for parts in other yards and customers may browse the yard supervised. Car clubs are always welcome. The owner is Jim Hines and the yard's been in business since 1972.

VINTAGE WHEEL MUSEUM
218 Cedar St.
SANDPOINT, ID 83864
(Just south of the Canadian border)
Phone: 208-263-7173
www.ohwy.com/id/v/vintwhmu.htm
Hours: M–Sat. 9:30–5:30, Sun. 11–5

CLOSED

This is a privately-owned museum with about 50 displays centered around a collection of carefully restored antique automobiles, horse-drawn vehicles, and steam engines. There is also an interesting gift shop in the museum.

L & L CLASSIC AUTO (Salvage)
2742 S. Hwy. 46
WENDELL, ID 83355
(20 miles northwest of Twin Falls)
Phone: 208-536-6606 or
208-536-6607
E-Mail llclassicauto@AOL.com
Hours: M–F 8–5. Please phone
ahead to make sure someone
is in attendance.

L & L is one of the largest salvage yards
in the west with some 9,000 vehicles on
100 acres of dry sagebrush-covered land.
Vehicles run from the late 1920s to the
1980s with the highest concentration being in the 1950s and 1960s. The lot has an
unusually large number of Lincolns and
Mercurys. Most of the other vehicles in
the yard are also American-made. There
are project cars, and L & L has a parts
locator service. Car clubs are welcome
and customers may browse the yard.
Ron Ewing is the Manager. In business
since 1965.

ILLINOIS

Galena Freeport Fox Lake Waukegan Highland Park
Rockford Evanston
Rochelle De Kalb **Chicago**
Rock Falls Aurora
Geneseo La Salle Joliet
Morris
Kankakee
Galesburg
Monmouth El Paso Watseka
Peoria
Macomb **Bloomington** Danville
Beardstown Champaign
Quincy Decatur
Jacksonville **Springfield**
Marshall
Alton Vandalia Effingham
Lawrenceville
Sandoval Salem Mt. Carmel
East St. Louis Mt. Vernon
Carmi
Marion
Carbondale

ROUTE 66

Route 66 began in Chicago, traveled for over 300 miles through Illinois and exited the state at East St. Louis. Much of the famous route has been preserved and marked by the state.

It was in Illinois that the famous Route 66 began. Specifically, it started at the intersection of Jackson Boulevard and Lake Shore Drive in downtown *Chicago*. From there it traveled some 300 miles southwest through Illinois before exiting the state at *East St. Louis*.

The State of Illinois has preserved much of the highway and marked it with signs noting **"Historic Route 66"**. Many stretches of the old road still exist as local roads or frontage roads for I-55 which parallels the route. Most of the old route is two-lane and in some rare spots the original brick surface is still is use. Many historic buildings have been preserved along the way by communities and individuals. When the route leaves the state it crosses the Mississippi River at the *Chain of Rocks Bridge*, the longest bridge on all of Route 66.

▶ LINCOLN HIGHWAY

The Lincoln Highway also ran through Illinois and sections of it are preserved like those of Route 66. This highway crossed 12 states and connected New York City with San Francisco, CA and was opened in 1915 in time for the 1915 Panama-Pacific International Exposition in San Francisco. The Lincoln Highway can be traced by following US 30 from Dyer, IN to Chicago Heights-

Joliet-Aurora, and then SR 31 to Geneva until it connects with SR 38, which then runs through DeKalb-Franklin Grove (home of the Lincoln Highway Association) and to the Mississippi River where it crosses into Iowa at Fulton, IA. Concrete markers trace the route thanks to the work of the Boy Scouts.

▶ CHICAGO AREA

CERMAK PLAZA SHOPPING CENTER
Cermak Rd. and Harlem Av.
BERWYN, IL (Eastern suburb of Chicago)

This shopping center has a number of modern sculptures on its premises including one called "The Spindle." The Spindle consists of nine automobiles, stacked one on top of the other on a tall pointed pole. Locally, it is known as "Cars on a Spike."

HARTUNG'S LICENSE PLATE AND ANTIQUE AUTO MUSEUM
3623 W. Lake St.
GLENVIEW, IL 60026-1269 (A northwestern suburb of Chicago)
Phone: 847-724-4354
www.classicar.com/museums/hartung/hartung.htm
Hours: Open daily at various hours. *Closed November through April.* Please phone for hours. Donations accepted.

This is a large museum with over 150 vehicles, including autos, motorcycles, trucks, bicycles, tractors and farm machinery. Some of the vehicles are very

"The Spindle" *at the Cermak Plaza Shopping Center in Berwyn, IL.*

rare. The oldest vehicle in the collection is a 1901 Wagner motorcycle. In addition, Hartung's visitors will see displays of hood ornaments, brass lights, old tools, spark plugs, toys, baby carriages, outboard motors, dolls, locks, and the world's most complete collection of license plates. Hartung's is owned by Lee Hartung and was established in 1971.

McDONALD'S DES PLAINES MUSEUM
400 N. Lee St.
DES PLAINES, IL 60016 (A northwestern suburb of Chicago)
Phone: 847-297-5022
http://www.media.mcdonalds.com/
Hours: Open seasonally *(Memorial Day to Labor Day)*. Please phone for hours. Free.

This was the first McDonald's restaurant opened in the Chicago area in 1955 by Ray Kroc, the founder of the McDonald's restaurant chain. The restaurant is preserved and looks as it did when it opened. There is a short movie explaining the history of the McDonald's chain of restaurants and in the parking lot are several antique autos from the 1950s.

69

ILLINOIS

Food is not served in this McDonald's, but there is a modern-day McDonald's Restaurant across the street.

MUSEUM OF SCIENCE AND INDUSTRY

In Jackson Park at S. Lake Shore Dr. and 57th St.
CHICAGO, IL 60637
www.msichicago.org
Phone: 773-684-1414
Hours: M–Sat. 9:30–4, Sun. 11–4. Closed Dec 25. Admission charged. Parking is available.

Hands-on science fun awaits all visitors, regardless of age, at this famous Chicago museum. It contains more than 800 interactive exhibits which visitors can touch, create and explore. Among the many and varied exhibits is an auto collection of some 30 vintage cars and race cars. The museum has several gift shops and restaurants.

VOLO AUTO MUSEUM AND ANTIQUE MALLS

Volo Village Rd. (one block north of Rt. 12 & SR 120)
VOLO, IL 60073 (A northwestern suburb of Chicago)
Phone: 815-385-3644
http://www.volocars.com

Hours: Daily 10–5, closed Jan 1, Easter, Thanksgiving and Dec 25. Admission charged to the museums but not to the mall buildings.

You ain't seen nothin' 'til you've seen this place! This is a 30 acre complex of several large buildings in a theme-park-like atmosphere with antique cars as the main centerpiece. There are shade trees, flowers, bubbling fountains and about 300 vintage vehicles on display in five climate-controlled showrooms. Many of the cars are for sale. Just about any type of vehicle you can imagine is here at "The Volo" including a number of celebrity cars. The museum also has its own restoration facility. Throughout the year the museum has several antique car functions such as auctions, car shows, car club events and charity events. Antique vehicle services offered include appraisals, consignment sales and trades, and aid with financing and shipping. In addition to cars, there is an armed forces exhibit, a Kids' Hollywood Showroom, several restaurants and some 350 independent dealers in the malls offering arts and crafts, gifts and antiques of all kind. And when you get tired, there are benches for resting. This place has been operating since 1960.

End of Chicago Area ◀

MAIN STREET CLASSIC CARS (Dealer)

189 S. Main St.
CRYSTAL LAKE, IL 60014
(50 miles northwest of Chicago, near the Wisconsin state line on SRs 14 and 176)
Phone: 815-459-6200

http://www.mainstreetclassiccars.com
Hours: M–F 8–6, Sat. 8–4

By stopping here, you can save a trip to Arizona. This dealer buys cars by the truckload from that area where the cars are well-known to be rust free. In their handsome showroom, you will find muscle cars, street rods, convertibles, project cars and a nice selection of vintage cars. Classic Auto takes trades, sells on consignment, offers appraisals and aids with shipping and financing. They also sell body parts for vintage cars. This is a dealer you can trust.

MY GARAGE R&D CENTER/ CORVETTE (Museum)
1 Mid America Place
(Just off US 45 North)
PO Box 1368
EFFINGHAM, IL 62401
(South-central part of the state at junction of I-57 and I-70)
Phone: 217-347-4233
Hours: M–F 8–5, Sat. 9–3
Directions: Exit I-70 onto US 45 north. The museum is straight ahead.

Here is a very unique collection of Corvettes. My Garage is a large museum attached to the main building of Mid America Designs, Inc., the world's largest supplier of Corvette parts and accessories. The 30+ Corvettes on display are mostly low mileage originals and the personal collection of Mid America's president, Mike Yager. They are often used by the company's engineers in the design and manufacture of their replacement parts and accessories. Also to be seen at My Garage is a 1910 Standard Oil of Indiana gas station, and a wide array of Corvette memorabilia including Corvette toys, model cars, pins, posters, apparel, photos and memorabilia. Car clubs and tour groups are welcome.

GATEWAY CLASSIC CARS (Dealer)
5401 Collinsville Rd.
FAIRMONT CITY, IL 62201
(6 miles east of downtown St. Louis, MO on I-55/I-70)
Phone: 800-231-3616 *nation wide (toll free), from Illinois* 618-271-3000, *from St. Louis* 314-436-2300
http://www.gatewayclassiccars.com
Hours: M–F 10–5, Sat. 9–5, Sun. noon–5

When you walk into this dealership remember where the front door is because you can get lost in their 105,000 sq. ft. showroom. Hemmings called Gateway Classic Cars the nation's eighth largest antique car dealer. The company carries some 200 vehicles on their premises including motorcycles, trucks, sports cars, race cars, muscle cars and a very large selection of vintage cars. The company takes trades, sells on consignment, provides appraisals, will search for specific vehicles, aids in obtaining insurance and financing and helps with world-wide shipping. Don't miss their gift shop—it's big. You will find lots of automobilia, Route 66 souvenirs and other items of interest here. The company welcomes car clubs, social and business events and has an annual Christmas party for its customers.

MOPAR CITY SALVAGE
6309 Brick Rd.
OREGON, IL 61061 (25 miles southwest of Rockford on the Rock River)
Phone: 815-732-7751 and 800-426-4364 (toll free)
Hours: M–F 9–5

Guess what this salvage yard specializes in? That's right, Chrysler products. They have over 800 vehicles on their 5$\frac{1}{2}$

acre lot and six buildings in which they store used, NOS and NORS parts. One of the buildings is a machine shop where they make and repair parts. In business since the 1970s.

▶ PEORIA AREA

PEORIA PUBLIC LIBRARY
107 NE Monroe St.
PEORIA, IL 61602
Phone: 309-497-2000
www/peoria.lib.il.us.
Hours: M-Thurs. 9–9, F–Sat. 9–6

Peoria was the home of the famous Duryea Brothers who many believe built the first gasoline-powered horseless carriages in America. The Peoria Public Library, in downtown Peoria, has on permanent display the oldest surviving 1899 three-wheeled Duryea trap—another word for a light horse-drawn vehicle. This trap has a motor, however.

This is the oldest surviving three-wheeled 1899 Duryea trap and is on display at the **Peoria Public Library** *in downtown Peoria.*

HUBCAP HOUSE At the corner of SW Adams St. (US 24 south) and S. Stanley St. in Peoria is a house completely covered with hubcaps.

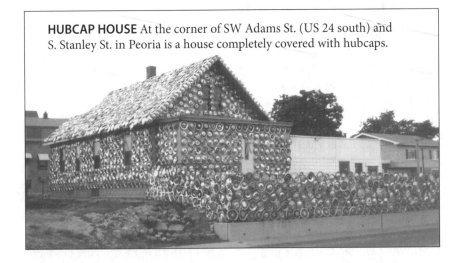

WHEELS O'TIME MUSEUM

11923 N. Knoxville Av. (SR 40)
PEORIA, IL 61525
Phone: 309-243-9020
www.wheelsotime.org
Hours: *May through Oct.* W–Sun.
noon–5. Admission charged.
Wheelchair accessible.

This is a private museum consisting of three buildings which comprise the personal collections of some 50 collectors. Some of those people collect vintage cars and about 30 of them are on display. Some of the cars were made in Peoria. Visitors will also see farm machinery, Caterpillar tractors, musical instruments, toy trains, clocks, cameras, dolls, a full-scale replica of the Red Baron's WW I tri-winged airplane, a country kitchen and many other items. The museum was founded in 1981.

End of Peoria Area ◀

HISTORIC AUTO ATTRACTIONS
(museum)

13825 Metric Dr.
ROSCOE, IL 61073
(12 miles north of downtown Rockford on SR 251 near the Wisconsin state line)
Phone: 815-389-7917
www.historicautoattractions.com
Hours: Memorial Day through Labor Day Tues.–Sat. 10–5, Sun. 11–4. Rest of year Sat. 10–5, Sun. 11–4. Admission charged.

This is a large museum—36,000 sq. ft.—with vintage autos and lots of other items. The museum is divided into several galleries and three of them are devoted to cars. They are the *"Famous Stars & Cars Gallery," "Legends of Racing Gallery"* and the *"World of Speed Gallery."* Many of the cars are associated with famous people or well-known movies and movie personalities. The other museum galleries are *"Kennedy Day in Dallas," " World Leaders," "Movieland," "Gangsterland," "Turn of the Century"* and *"TV Land/Customs."* The museum has a nice gift shop and is available for functions and parties. You'll see a lot at this museum.

AUTO GALLERY MUSEUM
(Museum and dealer)

2807 US 12
SPRING GROVE,IL 60081 (25 miles west-northwest of Waukegan close to the Wisconsin state line)
Phone: 815-675-3222
www.autogallerymuseum.com
Hours: M–F 10–7, Sat. 10–5

The Auto Gallery Museum is a classic, antique, race, and specialty interest automobile showcase situated in a landscaped 4-acre park-like setting with a beautiful 35,000 sq. ft. showroom. Visitors will find high quality vehicles here for viewing or for sale at reasonable prices. The company takes trades, sells on consignment, provides warranties and helps with financing and shipping. They also offer climate-controlled vehicle storage. The facilities are available for special events, car shows, club events and auctions.

ILLINOIS

COUNTRY CLASSIC CARS (Dealer)
2149 E. Frontage Rd.
(Historic Route 66)
STAUNTON, IL 62088
(on I-55 40 miles northeast
of East St. Louis, IL)
Phone: 618-635-7056
www.countryclassiccars.com
Hours: 9–5

When you are traveling I-55, stop for a short while to visit this dealership. It will be worth your while. They have a large selection of vintage cars and trucks in their showroom and on their lot. Also on the premises is an antique mall offering vintage car and Route 66 memorabilia along with a large selection of general antiques. The company takes trades, sells on consignment, aids in financing and shipping and does service and repair work on vintage vehicles. Look for the big white sign with the big red letters.

NORTHERN ILLINOIS CLASSIC AUTO BROKERS. LTD. (NICAB) (Dealer)
25084 W. Old Rand Rd.
WAUCONDA, IL 60084
(18 miles southwest of
Waukegan on SR 59)
Phone: 847-526-5950
www.classicmusclecars.com
Hours: M–F 9–5

These people used to be in the car auction business, so they know the antique car business very well. In their showroom, with the black and white checkerboard tile floor, you will find top quality off-body restorations, former ISCA show cars, rare muscle cars and lots of other interesting vintage vehicles. Besides the cars on display in the showroom, they have more in the warehouse. NICAB also sells new and used performance parts and accessories and offers a large selection of automobilia. The company takes trades, offers appraisals (they're very good at this having been in the auction business), helps provide financing and aids in shipping. Come on in and make a bid.

▶ WAUKEGAN AREA

CLASSIC CAR CITY (Dealer)
2727 Belvedere St. (SR 120)
WAUKEGAN, IL 60085
Phone: 847-623-1700
http://www.classiccarcity.com
Hours: M–F 9–5

There is an interesting array of antique, muscle and special interest cars and trucks in this dealer's showroom and adjacent lot. Classic Car City attempts to have classic cars available for everyone. Maybe you will find just what you are looking for. The company sells, buys and trades cars of all kinds. They sell on consignment and aid in obtaining financing and shipping.

MEMORY LANE MOTORS, INC. (Dealer)
1231 SR 176
LAKE BLUFF, IL 60044
(A southern suburb of Waukegan)
Phone: 847-362-4600
www.memorylanemotors.com
Hours: M–F 9–5, Sat. 9–3

Tour Book for Antique Car Buffs

You can buy an antique car or motorcycle here or lots of other old stuff. How about a 1955 bobsled? You'd have the only one in the neighborhood. Other than bobsleds, you will find vintage cars, special interest cars and other four-wheeled beauties in their showroom.

Memory Lane Motors takes trades, sells on consignment, provides appraisals and technical advice and helps with shipping and financing. They also offer storage for cars and other things. Chuck Requa is the owner.

End of Waukegan area ◀

INDIANA

▶ AUBURN AREA
(On I-69 in the northeastern corner of the state)

Don't whiz by this town on the interstate without stopping. It is one of the most unique places in *all* of antique cardom. There are several top-rate antique car museums here in this relatively small community.

The Auburn-Cord-Duesenberg Museum *in Auburn, IN.*

AUBURN-CORD-DUESENBERG MUSEUM
1600 S. Wayne St.
AUBURN, IN 46706
Phone: 260-925-1444
www.acdmuseum.org

Hours: Daily 9–5. Closed Jan. 1, Thanksgiving and Dec. 25. Admission charged.

When was the last time you saw an Auburn—or a Cord—or a Duesenberg?

Well here's your chance to play catch-up. There are dozens of them here. These vehicles were the high-tech and luxury machines of their day, and that point is stressed in the museum. The museum is located in the old Auburn Automobile Company factory and some of the vehicles are displayed in the factory's original 1930 art deco showroom. The remainder are shown in seven thematic exhibit galleries and the building, itself, is listed in the National Register of Historic Places. Cadillacs, Packards, Lincolns, Rolls-Royces, Mercedes-Benz and many rare Indiana-built makes are also in the exhibit. Some of the cars are associated with famous people. The museum offers ever-changing special exhibits, an appealing museum store, "The Duesy Shop", an automotive research library and full banquet and meeting facilities. The Auburn-Cord-Duesenberg Festival is held each Labor Day weekend here in Auburn and many Auburns, Cords and Duesenbergs can be seen running about on the streets of the town.

The museum was opened in 1974.

NATIONAL AUTOMOTIVE & TRUCK MUSEUM OF THE UNITED STATES (NATMUS)

1000 Gordon Buehrig Place
AUBURN, IN 46706
Phone: 260-925-9100
www.natmus.com
Hours: Daily 9–5.
Admission charged.

This fine museum is closely affiliated with the Auburn-Cord-Duesenberg Museum and occupies two of the remaining Auburn Automobile Co. buildings adjacent to the Auburn-Cord-Duesenberg Museum. NATMUS has a collection of over 100 trucks, buses, motor homes and similar vehicles. Emphasis is placed on post-World War II vehicles. There are also automotive toys, models, automotive literature, signs, automobilia and a gift shop. Groups and clubs are welcome.

End of Auburn area ◄

BEARCREEK FARMS

(Theme park with a car museum)
8339 North 400 East
(Watch for signs on SR 67 east of its Jct. with US 29)
RR 1, Box 180B
BRYANT, IN 47326 (On US 27 thirty-five miles south of Ft. Wayne)
Phone: 260-997-6822
www.bearcreekfarms.com
Hours: Thurs.–Sat. 11–4, *mid–Apr. through late Oct.*
Admission charged.

There's an antique car museum, called *"The Tin Lizzy,"* in this interesting theme park which sports a days-of-yesteryear motif.

In the park there are rides, a county fair, live theater, restaurants, an old fort, guest accommodations, retail shops and the car museum. In the latter are some 20 antique cars, many of them Model T Fords, and displays highlighting the joys and agonies of driving such vehicles during their heyday.

INDIANA

ELKHART (See South Bend/Elkhart Area)

CORVETTE CLASSICS (Museum)
6702 Pointe Inverness Way
(SW corner of I-69 and SR 14)
FORT WAYNE, IN 46804
Phone: 260-436-3444
www.corvette-classics.com
Hours: M–Sat. 10–5, Sun. 12–5.
Admission charged.

The Corvette is such a popular automobile that several museums have sprung up around the country specializing in that car. Here is one of the finest. There are about 50 Corvettes on display along with memorabilia, photos and other interesting things. Corvettes were, and still are, very popular in Indiana.

▶ GREENFIELD AREA
(20 miles east of downtown Indianapolis)

FIELD'S AUTO PARTS (Salvage yard)
5388 E. 600 N.
GREENFIELD, IN 46110
Phone: 317-326-3371 and
800-252-6291 (toll free)
Hours: M–F 8–5, Sat. 8–3

They've got so many cars in this yard that they've lost count. It's somewhere between 6,000 and 7,000, and there's a special section for the "old stuff." There you'll find a variety of domestic models and imports dating back to the late 1940s. Field's will also locate parts for you and let you browse the yard. Car clubs are welcome. Ask for Bobby. He knows where everything is.

VAIL'S CLASSIC CARS
(Restorer and dealer)
2633 W. Main St. (US 40 West)
GREENFIELD, IN 46140
Phone: 317-462-7705

www.vailsclassiccars.com
Hours: M–F 8–5

How about having your old Mustang restored? Vail's will do it for you—full restoration or partial. Up-grading Mustangs and other vehicles is a big part of their business. They also sell restored cars, again specializing in Mustangs. There are usually about 20 cars in their showroom and on their lot for sale or display. Vail's sells NOS, used and reproduction parts for Mustangs and other makes with emphasis on Fords. NASCAR and other auto memorabilia are for sale in their gift center. They do service work and appraisals, sell on consignment, will search for vehicles, and can pickup and deliver your car in their own truck. Vail's takes trades with an eye for cars that they can restore and sell. Car clubs are welcome. In business since 1985. The owner is Bill Vail.

End of Greenfield area ◀

COLLECTIBLE CLASSIC CAR MUSEUM OF HAGERSTOWN

403 E. Main St. (SR 38)
HAGERSTOWN, IN 47346
(East-central Indiana 45 miles east of Indianapolis just north of I-70)
Phone: 765-489-5598
www.collectibleclassiccarmuseum ofhagerstown.com
Hours: M–F 10–5, Sat. 10–3.
Admission charged.

CLOSED

Want to see your car displayed in a museum? Here's your chance. This museum will store and display your vehicle in a museum setting for a month or longer. A plaque identifies you and your car and a photo of your vehicle is retained for the museum's permanent collection. Because of this unique arrangement, the museum's collection is ever-changing. There are several permanent cars in the collection and some of the cars on display are for sale. Fire trucks, motorcycles and even airplanes can be seen here. There is a gift shop and car clubs are welcome. The facility is also available for social events, dances, parties, etc. Herman and Jane Rummel are the proprietors.

▶ INDIANAPOLIS AREA

CLASSIC CARS AND MORE (Dealer)

17005 Westfield Park Rd.
WESTFIELD, IN 46074 (Northern suburb of Indianapolis)
Phone: 317-867-3066
www.classiccarsandmore.com
Hours: M–F 8–5
Directions: Exit US 31 onto SR 32 west. Proceed two short blocks to Westfield Park Rd. and turn south. Proceed .4 miles and look for the Metal Powder Products Co. on the east side of the street. Classic Cars and More shares that building with its entrance on the south side.

When you walk into this dealership you will probably find its owner, Jeff Schweiger, on the phone. He sells a lot of cars that way. In his immaculate showroom will be between 35-40 beautiful and affordable machines; cars, trucks, sports car replicas and a few motorcycles. Classic Cars and More takes trades, sells on consignment, provides appraisals, does service work and some restorations. Car clubs are always welcome. Jeff's been at this game since 1998.

INDIANAPOLIS MOTOR SPEEDWAY & HALL OF FAME MUSEUM

4790 W. 16th St.
SPEEDWAY, IN 46222
(A western suburb of Indianapolis)
Phone: 317-181-8500 and 317-492-6784
www.automuseum.com
Hours: Daily 9–5, except during May (race month) 9–6. Closed Dec 25. Admission charged.

This museum is inside the track of the famous Indianapolis Motor Speedway and displays many of the race cars that have raced here in the famous "Indy 500".

Many historic race cars are on display at the **Indianapolis Motor Speedway Hall of Fame Museum.**

The Hall of Fame was created in 1956 to perpetuate the names and memories of outstanding personalities in racing and in the development of the automotive industry. The names of those so honored are inscribed on a permanent trophy and watercolor portraits of living members are on display. There is a large gift shop offering official Indy 500 souvenirs and many other items of interest. The Indy 500- mile race is held annually on Memorial Day, and a NASCAR race is held during the summer.

SPECIALTY AUTO SALES, INC.
(Dealer)
3315 Madison Av.
INDIANAPOLIS, IN 46227
Phone: 317-780-1112
www.specialtyautosales.com
Hours: M–F 9–5, Sat. 9–3

More than 75 race cars are on display and many of them are winners including the 1911 Marmon "Wasp", the winner of the very first race. There is a large collection of racing memorabilia such as trophies, helmets, photographs, etc. Video presentations of past races are shown and the museum has an extensive automotive library which is open by appointment. In addition to the race cars there is a sizeable number of antique cars, some of them made in Indianapolis.

Bus tours of the track are available and there is a Speedway-owned motel on the grounds and an 18-hole golf course, part of which is inside the track.

This dealer hates rust so he brings his cars up from the salt-free states of the south and southwest. This saves the customers from having to go to Florida or Arizona to buy rust-free cars. Specialty Sales specializes in affordable muscle cars, classic cars, Corvettes, VWs and hot rods. They also deal in motorcycles. You will find some 40 vehicles in their well-appointed showroom here on the south side of Indianapolis, and the company prides itself in giving honest assessments of the vehicles they inventory. They'll even buy it back if you are not satisfied. They take trades, sell on consignment, help with financing and shipping and they welcome car clubs.

**THE YOUTH EDUCATION
AND HISTORICAL CENTER—
INDIANA STATE POLICE**
8500 E. 21st St.
INDIANAPOLIS, IN 46219
Phone 317-899-8293
Hours: M–F 8–5. Free.

Here's a police museum with more than a dozen vintage police cars on display. They also have a motorcycle or two. As might be expected, most of the museum is devoted to a wide variety of police memorabilia and displays, but it's well worth a stop, especially if you like police cars. There's also a gift shop. The museum opened in 1994.

End of Indianapolis area ◀

THE PADDOCK (Parts dealer with a car museum)
7565 S. SR 109 (Exit 115 from I-70)
KNIGHTSTOWN, IN 46148
(35 miles east of downtown Indianapolis)
Phone: 800-428-4319 (toll free)
www.paddockparts.com
Hours: M–F 8–5, Sat. 9–4

New and reproduction parts for muscle cars are Paddock's main business, but they also have a 6,000 sq. ft. showroom filled with Mustangs, Camaros, Corvettes and other muscle cars. They are worth seeing. The Paddock is right off I-70, so stop by when you are in the area.

▶ KOKOMO AREA

AUTOMOTIVE HERITAGE MUSEUM
1500 N. Reed Rd. (US 31 North in the Johanning Civic Center)
KOKOMO, IN 46901
Phone: 765-454-9999
www.automotiveheritagemuseum.org.
Hours: Sun., W, Thurs., F. & Sat. 10–4. Admission charged.

You'll see about 100 antique vehicles in this new museum, including six Kokomo-built Haynes, Appersons and Haynes-Apperson automobiles. The centerpiece of the museum is the 1895 "Pioneer II" automobile built by Kokomo citizen Elwood Haynes. "Pioneer I," built by Haynes in 1894 and believed to be the world's first automobile, is in the Smithsonian Museum in Washington, DC.

Many displays in the museum highlight GM and Chrysler products because Kokomo has long been a GM and Chrysler town. The museum has a nice gift shop, free parking and friendly people.

ELWOOD HAYNES MUSEUM
1915 S. Webster
KOKOMO, IN 46902-2040
(40 miles north of Indianapolis)
Phone: 765-456-7500
www.kokomo-in.org
Hours: Tues.–Sat. 1–4, Sun. 1–5. Free.

This was the home of Elwood Haynes,

The **Elwood Haynes Museum,** *Kokomo, IN.*

a citizen of Kokomo, who was the inventor of America's first commercially successful automobile. It is recorded that he made the first successful road test of his first car on July 4, 1894. Haynes was involved in the formation and operation of both the Haynes-Apperson Automobile Co. and later the Haynes Automobile Co., both of Kokomo. He was also the inventor of stainless steel and other high-strength and high-heat resistant metal alloys generally known as "Stellite." The alloys were important to the successful development of modern-day jet engines and high-heat applications. In the Haynes Museum is a 1905 Haynes automobile in which the driver sat in the back seat. There are other Haynes vehicles on display as well.

End of Kokomo area ◀

La PORTE COUNTY MUSEUM

2405 Indiana Av. (US 35 South)
La PORTE, IN 46350 (Northwest corner of Indiana, 20 miles west of South Bend just south of 1-94 and the Indiana Toll Rd.)
Phone: 219-324-6767
www.dpautomuseum.com
Hours: Tues.–Sat. 10–4:30
(Closed holidays)

This is a magnificent, three-story museum operated by the La Porte County Historical Society. Their collection not only contains items of local historical interest but also distinctive automobile and gun collections. The Kesling Auto collection consists of approximately 40 vehicles and includes a number of Indiana-built cars such as the Auburn, Cord and Duesenberg. Visitors will also see a 1948 Tucker, a 1903 Winton and a 1938 Mercedes Benz Roadster.

The Jones Gun Collection contains over 1,000 pieces and is one of the finest collections in the world. In the collection are Blunderbusses, a Tommy gun and a shot gun owned by President Theodore Roosevelt.

Antique toys and vintage aircraft are also on display and there is a re-creation of a block of downtown La Porte in the 1900s. The museum has gift shop. James Rodgers is the Museum's Executive Director and Susan Richter is the Assistant Director.

RAG TOPS MUSEUM OF MICHIGAN CITY

209 W. Michigan Blvd. (Hwy. 12)
MICHIGAN CITY, IN 46360
(On the southern shore of
Lake Michigan.)
Phone: 219-878-1514
www.ragtopsmuseum.com
Hours: Sun. through Sat. 10–7.
Admission charged.

They used to make men's pants here, now they display 30,000 sq. ft. of antique cars and a lot of other neat stuff. There are about 50 antique vehicles, plus a bicycle collection, a Lionel Train collection, an old 1950s rock-and-roll diner with a juke box, a pin ball machine, a soda fountain and manikins dressed as employees and customers. Nearby is a replica of a 1950s service station complete with work bay, spare parts and all the things you would have found in such a station at that time. Manikins are in attendance here, too. Bring the kiddies because there's a big display of

The La Porte County Museum *displays both the Kesling Auto and Jones Gun Collections as well as local historical memorabilia.*

antique toys and an exhibit called Clown Alley. Bring the wife, there's a nice gift shop, too. The museum is available for social events, meetings and other get-togethers. This museum is well worth your time.

CANFIELD MOTORS (Salvage)

22–24 Main St.
NEW WAVERLY, IN 46961
(Between Logansport and Peru
on US 24)
Phone: 574-722-3230
Hours: M–F 8–4

An old, established salvage company with two yards and several buildings specializing in American-made cars from the 1940s and up. There are approximately 1,000 vehicles total and many orphans are available; Studebakers, Hudsons, Nash, and some pickup trucks. Customers may browse the yard and remove their own parts with permission. Bring your own tools and dress properly. Car clubs are welcome. In business since 1951. Robert Canfield is the owner.

VINTAGE CAMPERS (Dealer)

2574 S. Strawtown Rd.
PERU, IN 46970
Phone: 765-473-8088
www.vintagecampers.com
Hours: Wed. and Sat. 9–5

Here's something you don't see every day—an antique camper dealer. The campers are in a field behind a business called the Old House Warehouse a mile south of town. There are about 25 campers and some, but not all, are for sale. You'll see such names as Airstream, Spartan, Curtiss-Wright, Silver Streak, Boles-Aero and Yellowstone. Vintage Campers takes trades and can help with transportation. Dan Piper is the driving force behind this enterprise. Be kind to Dan, though. He has an incurable disease—*campercollectoritis!*

WAYNE COUNTY HISTORICAL MUSEUM

1150 North "A" St.
RICHMOND, IN 47374 (East-central part of the state on I-70)
Phone: 765-962-5756
www.waynecountyhistorical
museum.com
Hours: Mon.–Fri. 9–4, Sat.–Sun. 1–4. Admission charged.

Here is a fine county museum highlighting the history and progress of Wayne County, Indiana and displaying, among the many items of local interest, several of the 14 automobile marques that were manufactured in the county over the years. On display is a 1909 Richmond, a 1908 and a 1915 Wescott, a 1918 Davis a 1920 Pilot and a 1939 Crosley. The museum also has an interesting gift shop.

► SOUTH BEND/ELKHART AREA

BENDIX WOODS COUNTY PARK

32132 Timothy Rd.
(SR 2 West of South Bend near LaPorte County line.)
NEW CARLISLE, IN 46552
Phone: 574-654-3155
www.sjcparks.org

Few people know it, but the Studebaker Automobile Corporation once had its name spelled out in trees—that's right—trees. This large county park was, at one time, part of Studebaker's test ground for its automobiles. A very unique landmark still remains in the park, an arboreal sign comprising approximately 8,200 trees that spell out the word "Studebaker." The sign was planted in 1938 and is said to be the largest arboreal sign of its kind in the world. It is listed in the Guinness Book of Records and the National Historic

The arboreal sign spelling out the word "STUDEBAKER" can still be seen from above in Bendix Woods County Park.

of Miles Laboratory. The home is lavishly furnished and decorated much as it was soon after it was built in 1908. In the garage are three antique cars, a 1912 Pratt, a 1916 Milburn Electric and a 1917 Cadillac. There is also a souvenir and gift shop on the premises.

Register. The park's Club House was the home of Studebaker's last president, Sherwood Egbert, and a display on the Studebaker Company is on view in the Club House. Adjacent to the park to the east are several buildings, now in private hands, that were part of Studebaker's original test track facilities.

RUTHMERE MUSEUM

302 E. Beardsley Av. (½ mile northeast of downtown Elkhart on SR 19)
ELKHART, IN 46514
Phone: 574-264-0330
www.ruthmere.org
Hours: Museum shown by guided tour. Tours Tues.–Sat. at 10, 11, 1, 2, 3 and Sun. at 1, 2, 3. Admission charged.

This was the magnificent Beaux-Arts home of A. R. Beardsley, a co-founder

RV/MH HISTORY HALL OF FAME/ MUSEUM/LIBRARY

21565 Executive Pkwy
ELKHART, IN 46514
Phone: 574-293-2344 or
800-378-8694 (toll free)
www.rvmhheritagefoundation.org
Hours: M–F 9–5. Sat. 9–3
Admission charged.

This unique museum displays antique recreational vehicles, motor homes and related memorabilia dating back to the days before World War I. Elkhart is the center of a large RV/MH manufacturing area and the museum honors manufacturers, suppliers, dealers, park and campground owners and others involved in this very specialized industry. The growth and development of the RV and MH industry is chronicled in the museum featuring photographs,

The Studebaker National Museum *of South Bend, IN*

displays and documents. The museum is a 20,000 sq. ft. facility and contains a library of RV/MH literature, books and historic documents. Founded in 1972.

STUDEBAKER NATIONAL MUSEUM

201 S. Chapin
SOUTH BEND, IN 46601
Phone: 574-235-9714 or
888-391-5600 (toll free)
www.studebakermuseum.org
Hours: *Call for hours.*
Admission charged.

Here is one of the oldest automobile displays in the world. If you had visited the Studebaker Corporation headquarters in the 1900s, you would have seen some of the company-owned vintage vehicles you see today. That collection was eventually donated to this museum. There are 70+ vehicles displayed on a rotating basis, most of them made by the Studebaker Corporation of South Bend. Among the automobiles displayed is a 1900 Studebaker electric car, a 1927 Studebaker Commander, a 1928 Erskine, the 1956 Packard Predictor, a 1962 Studebaker truck prototype, a 1937 cab forward bus, a 1943 Weasel (a military vehicle made by Studebaker during World war II), a 1962 Studebaker GT Hawk and a 1963 Avanti. There is also a 1932 Rockne, made by Studebaker and named after the famous Notre Dame football coach, Knute Rockne. And there is a one-of-a-kind 1934 Bendix prototype airflow automobile that was never put into production. Several horse-drawn vehicles are exhibited including four presidential carriages including the carriage Abraham Lincoln took to Ford's Theater the night he was assassinated. Then too, there are exhibits on the early industrial and commercial life in South Bend. The Studebaker National Museum has extensive archives on the Studebaker company, a gift shop and a cafe. The museum is available for social and business meeting and events and car clubs are welcome any time.

TIPPECANOE PLACE RESTAURANT
(Historic home and restaurant)
620 W. Washington St.
SOUTH BEND, IN 46601
Phone: 574-234-9077
www.tippe.com

This 40-room mansion, which is now a fine restaurant, was once the home of Clement Studebaker, one of the five brothers who ran the Studebaker Corporation in its heyday. Customers of the restaurant are free to wander through the interesting building which has four floors, an elevator and 20 fireplaces. Appropriate dress is required in the dining room.

Tippecanoe Place, *the former home of Clement Studebaker, is now a fine-dining restaurant.*

End of South Bend/Elkhart area ◀

IOWA

Iowans have been in the forefront of preserving their portion of the Old Lincoln Highway, America's first coast-to-coast road. The route began at Times Square in New York City and ended in San Francisco. Through Iowa, the Lincoln Highway entered the state at Clinton on the east and exited at Council Bluffs, opposite Omaha, NE, on the west. Modern-day US 30 evolved from the Lincoln Highway and parallels sections of the old road. It is these sections that the Iowa members of the National Lincoln Highway Association endeavor to preserve. Most of the surviving sections of the old road have become local roads and some of them are unpaved. The Association has identified these sections with replicas of the original red, white and blue highway signs that consisted of a capital letter "L" on a white field. Some of the signs are mounted on concrete posts of 1928 design. Another historic touch that the Association has added are Burma-Shave signs along the route. Some of the sections of the highway have been widened to modern-day standards. Greene County, whose county seat is Jefferson,

This marker is in its original position on the grounds of the Iowa Welcome Center on US 30 near Missouri Valley.

40 miles west of Ames, has taken the lead in Iowa and preserved most of their section of the Lincoln Highway across the entire county. Citizens of Greene County are proud of the fact that their county was the first in Iowa to completely pave their section of the Lincoln Highway in 1924. The Greene County's stretch of the highway is now acknowledged as an important site and listed on the National Register of Historic Places. The community of Nevada, IA, 8 miles east of Ames, has commemorated the Lincoln Highway since 1983 with a festival each August called Lincoln Highway Days. The Iowa chapter of the Lincoln Highway Association began in 1993 to promote an annual antique car rally along the length of the Lincoln Highway in conjunction with the Nevada festival and their own annual meeting in Ames. Participants begin the rally at either end of the Lincoln Highway and end up in Nevada for the festival.

NATIONAL MOTORCYCLE MUSEUM

200 E. Main St., PO Box 405
ANAMOSA, IA 52205
(21 miles northeast of
Cedar Rapids on US 151)
Phone: 319-462-3925
www.nationalmcmuseum.com
Hours: *Summer* M–Sat. 9–5, Sun. 10–4; *winter* M–F 9–5, Sat. 10–4. Closed Sun. Admission charged.

Here is a fine motorcycle museum

with an extensive collection of vintage motorbikes. Some of the motorcycles have been associated with famous people and in movies. There is also an extensive collection of motorcycle memorabilia such as photographs, toys, postcards, and a large collection of pedal cars. The museum has a gift shop, offers a newsletter, and is available for business meetings and social events. It is also a popular destination for both motorcycle and antique car clubs.

DUFFIELD'S AUTO SALVAGE

Highway 30 West
ATKINS, IA 52206
(10 miles west of downtown Cedar Rapids)
Phone: 319-446-7141
Hours: M–F 8–5,
Sat. 8–noon.

If you like dealing with the ladies, here's your chance. This yard is owned and operated by Anne Duffield, who really knows her stuff when it comes to old cars. It is her intention to continually expand her old car inventory and to specialize more in that area. The 15-acre salvage yard has many AMCs, Fords, Studebakers, Edsels, Chevys & more dating back to the 1940s. There are about 3,800 cars total. If Duffield's doesn't have it, they'll try to find it. There are a number of whole cars here, too, ready to be restored or converted into custom cars or hot rods. Customers may browse the yard. In business since 1967.

The bill of sale of the 1949 Chrysler that Mamie and Dwight Eisenhower gave to Mamie's uncle as a surprise Christmas gift in 1948.

MAMIE DOUD EISENHOWER BIRTHPLACE

709 Carroll St. (PO Box 55)
BOONE, IA 50036 (40 miles northwest of Des Moines)
Phone: 515-432-1896
www.booneiowa.com
Hours: *June–Oct.* daily 10–5,
Apr.–May Tues.–Sun. 1–5,
rest of year by appointment.
Admission charged.

This modest home is the birthplace

Duffy's Collectible Car Connection *of Cedar Rapids, IA.*

of Mamie Doud Eisenhower, wife of General, and later President, Dwight D. Eisenhower. The main floor of the home is furnished and decorated much as it was when Mamie was born in 1896. In the lower level is a museum and library tracing the life of Mamie and her family history. In the garage are two antique cars. One is a 1949 Chrysler Windsor 4-door sedan that Mamie and Ike gave to Mamie's uncle, Joel Carlson, as a surprise Christmas gift on Dec. 24, 1948. The other car is Mamie's 1962 Plymouth Valiant donated to the museum in 1996 by Charles "Bebe" Roboza of Florida, a friend of Richard M. Nixon. Car clubs are welcome. There is a gift shop and Larry Adams is the museum's curator.

DUFFY'S COLLECTIBLE CAR
CONNECTION (Dealer and museum)

250 Classic Car Court S.W.
CEDAR RAPIDS, IA 52404
(East-central part of state off I-380)
Phone: 319-364-7000
www.duffys.com
Hours: M–F 8:30–5, Sat. 8:30–4:30.

Admission charged to tour.
Directions: Exit I-380 at the 33rd Av. S.W. Exit and go east on 33rd Av. S.W. one block to J St. S.W. Turn south on J St. S.W. one block to Classic Car Ct. Turn west of Classic Car Ct. Duffy's is at the end of the street. Watch for their rooftop display which can be seen from I-380.)

Duffy's is a large and well-known dealer of antique vehicles. They normally carry some 100 vehicles for sale and on display in their large, museum-like showroom. Many of the cars have been fully restored. Walk down memory lane and view their fascinating collection of cars from the 40s, 50s and 60s. Gas pumps, barber poles, wall murals and other memorabilia are on display, too. Many of the cars are convertibles, hardtops and muscle machines. Financing can be arranged as well as transportation including exports. Duffy's can provide appraisals, takes trades and has a fine gift shop.

▶ QUAD CITIES AREA

KLEMME KLASSIC KARS
(Dealer and Museum)
3422 Brady St.
DAVENPORT, IA 52806
Phone: 563-386-2902
www.klemmeklassickars.com
Hours: M–F 8–6, Sat. 8–1.
Free admission to museum.

At Klemme's you can buy 'em or just look at 'em. There are some 60 vehicles on display and for sale here in their museum-like showroom. There are T-birds, Packards, Model T's, Mercedes-Benz and lots of other makes. Klemme's takes trades, sells on consignment, provides appraisals, and can assist with financing and shipping. You'll like what you see here at Klemme's.

VEIT'S VETTES & COLLECTOR CARS
(Dealer with two locations)
221 E. 2nd St.
DAVENPORT, IA 52801

and 1838 State St.
BETTENDORF, IA 52722
(Bettendorf and Davenport are two of the four Quad Cities.)
Phone: *Bettendorf location:*
563-359-1074, cell 563-343-5727
Davenport location: 563-323-3107,
cell 563-343-5727
www.vettesndreamcars.com
Hours: M–F 9–5

Corvettes are big here, but they also offer classics, convertibles, muscle cars, imports and exotics. There's a goodly number of such cars in Veit's two locations. If you are in the market for a Shelby or a Javelin don't pass this place by. Veit's has the ability to transport your vehicle and they have a locator service, provide appraisals, take trades and can help with financing. There's a nice gift shop, too. These people pride themselves in the number of repeat customers they serve.

End of Quad Cities area

JIM AUSTIN'S CLASSIC CONNECTION
(Dealer)
702 N. 1st. St.
GREENE, IA 50636 (45 miles northwest of Waterloo at junction of SR 14 and CR 13.)
Phone: 866-220-9391 (toll free), 641-823-4129 (business) and 641-823-5674 (Jim Austin's home)
www. classicconnection.net
Hours: Mon. 7 a.m.–7:30 p.m., Tues.–Fri. 7–6, Sat. 9–4

When you reach Greene, IA you are in the middle of the American heartland and there, just north of downtown, is this very interesting vintage car dealer. Austin's carries a large selection of affordable vintage vehicles which include coupes, sedans, convertibles, light trucks and more. They take trades, and can provide vehicle delivery. Jim Austin says he likes to deal and it's OK to call anytime.

Van Horn's Truck Collection *of Mason City, IA.*

NATIONAL SPRINT CAR HALL OF FAME & MUSEUM

PO Box 542
Knoxville Raceway/County
Fairgrounds (1.7 miles north of
Jct. SRs 14 and 92)
KNOXVILLE, IA 50138 (38 miles
southeast of Des Moines)
Phone: 641-842-6176 and
800-874-4488 (toll free)
www.sprintcarhof.com
Hours: M–F 10–6, Sat. 10–5,
Sun. noon–5. Admission charged.

Legends of sprint car racing live on at the National Sprint Car Hall of Fame & Museum. This fine three-story facility is on the second turn of the famous Knoxville Raceway. Most of the space is devoted to the Hall of Fame and Museum, but there are also 20 luxurious skybox suites overlooking the track. In the Hall of Fame one will find the names of outstanding drivers, owners, mechanics, officials, and members of the media who have contributed to the sport of sprint racing. In the museum more than 25 restored race cars are on exhibit along with big cars, midgets, engines, trophies, tools, helmets, uniforms, etc. There is a Theater and Library/Archives Research Center which houses archives and other historic documents related to sprint racing. Many such items are on display in the museum. There is a large museum gift shop offering die-cast toys, clothing, jewelry, artwork, books, videos and other collectibles.

VAN HORN TRUCK COLLECTION
(Museum)

15272 North St.
(Highway 65 North)
MASON CITY, IA 50401
Phone: 515-423-0550;
off season, 515-423-9066
www.globegazette.com
Hours: *May 25 through Sept. 22*
M–Sat. 9–4, Sun. 11–4.
Admission charged.

CLOSED

You will see more than 60 of the country's oldest and rarest antique trucks on exhibit with many of them displayed in settings of the era in which they were built. Some of the trucks date back to the teens. There are also trailers on display and a Circus Room with a 1920 GMC circus truck as its centerpiece. Other displays include an early gas engine collection, old farm implements, tractors, crawlers, gas pumps, gas globe signs and equipment and old country store items. The museum has a gift shop and an old time coffee lounge. Free brochure upon request. Lloyd and Margaret Van Horn are the museum's owners.

OLSON LINN MUSEUM

Village Square
VILLISCA, IA 50864 (Southwest
corner of the state on US 71)
Phone: 712-826-2756
www.villiscaiowa.com
Hours: *June 1 through Oct. 1,*
Sat. noon–5 and Sun. 1–5.
Admission charged.

This three-level museum has a fine
collection of antique cars, trucks, buggies
and farm equipment. Among the 25 or
so vehicles is a 1917 Allen, a 1917 Cole
Cloverleaf Roadster, a 1918 Ford delivery
van, a 1929 Ford Model AA truck, a 1910
Maxwell, a 1918 Sampson truck and a
1924 Star touring car. Actually, this is
much more than a car museum. There
are exquisite wall murals depicting the
town of Villisca at the turn of the 20th
Century and a myriad of other items
on display. Darwin Linn, the museum's
owner, is a man of many interests. The
museum also owns and preserves the
"Ax-Murder House" a short distance from
the museum. This is the scene of one of
Iowa's most famous unsolved mysteries.

In 1912 eight people were axed to death
in this house. Six were members of the
family and two were neighbor children
staying overnight. While at the museum,
you might inquire about the house and
those interested in seeing it are sometimes driven there in one of the museum's
antique cars. Car clubs are welcome at
both locations and the car museum has
been in operation for some 30 years.

OLD CARS ON THE HILL (Dealer)

1956 Charles Av.
WEST BRANCH, IA 52358
(14 miles east of Iowa City on I-80)
Phone: 319-643-2280
www.oldcarsonthehill.com
Hours: M–F 9–5

Look for the car up on the post. That's
Old Cars On The Hill. Inside their showroom visitors will find a broad selection
of classics cars and trucks, most of which
are in the affordable range. Vintage and
hard-to-find vehicles are their specialty.
The company buys and sells vehicles,
takes trades and helps with shipping and
financing. Ask for Dave.

KANSAS

When **US Highway 66** was the main route from Chicago to Los Angeles, a short stretch of it crossed the extreme southeastern tip of Kansas between the towns of *Galena* and *Baxter Springs*. In recent years these two communities have joined together to preserve this 10 mile stretch of the old highway for its historical value. Both towns have museums devoted to Route 66.

EISENHOWER CENTER (Historic home and presidential museum)
200 S.E. 4th St.
ABILENE, KS 67410
(22 miles east of Salina on I-70)
Phone: 785-263-4751 and
877-746-4453 (toll free)
www.eisenhower.archives.gov
Hours: Daily 9–4:45; closed
Jan. 1, Thanksgiving and Dec. 25.
Admission charged.

This is the site of the boyhood home of Dwight D. Eisenhower. The center consists of five main entities; the family home, the Eisenhower Museum, the Eisenhower Presidential Library, the Visitors Center and the Place of Meditation which is his final resting place and that of his wife, Mamie. Within these building is recorded the life and career of Eisenhower and members of his family. In the Eisenhower Museum are several military vehicles and two antique automobiles. One automobile is a 1914 Rauch and Land Electric which was owned by Mamie Eisenhower's parents, Mr. & Mrs. John S. Doud. Eisenhower, as a young man, drove the car frequently when he came to see Mamie. The other car is a 1942 Cadillac 4-door sedan used by Eisenhower in Europe as a staff car when he was commander of Allied forces there during World War II. Eisenhower used the car in the U.S. upon his return after the war and then it followed him back to Europe when he became Supreme Allied Commander in the early post-war years. When Eisenhower returned again to the U.S. the car remained in Europe and served his successor, Gen. Gruenther. In 1956, the car was declared surplus by the Army and by then it had its third engine and 200,000 miles on the odometer. A group of Eisenhower's friends bought the car, restored it and gave it to Ike. He, in turn, gave it to the museum.

SCOTTY'S CLASSIC CARS
(Museum and dealer)
302 N. 9th St. (US 69 Bypass)
ARMA, KS 66712 (Southeastern corner of the state 5 miles from the Missouri border)

Phone: 620-347-8387
www.scottysclassiccars.com
Hours: Tues.–Sat. noon–4.
Museum free.

If this is your first time in Arma, Kansas you'll want to stop here and see these nice cars and maybe take one home. Scotty's is both a museum and an antique car dealership. They carry about 20 affordable and driveable classic autos, and maybe a small truck or two in their showroom which is tastefully decorated with automobilia, displays of local history, a doll collection and other accoutrements. There is also a library and a gift shop. Car clubs are always welcome. If you are interested in buying or selling a car Scotty's will oblige. Scotty's takes trades, sells on consignment, will search for specific vehicles, helps with shipping and financing and does appraisals. Scotty's Classic Cars is owned and operated by Scotty Bitner and his lovely wife, Phyllis, and they've been in this location since 1999.

KANSAS AUTO RACING MUSEUM
1205 Manor Dr., PO Box 549
CHAPMAN, KS 67431
(On I-70, 75 miles west of Topeka)
Phone: 785-922-6642
www.raceindustry.com
Hours: M–F 8–5, Sat. 9–5, Sun. 1–5

Did you ever sit in a NASCAR racing machine? You can do it here. This is a hands-on museum where visitors can get up close to the cars and, with permission, sit in them and have their picture taken. In addition to the race cars, there is a lot of racing memorabilia including videos and trophies. The museum emphasizes racing in Kansas and honors many Kansas race drivers in the museum. There are also several interactive NASCAR-style games where a person can sit behind the controls and actually program racing events. The museum hosts an actual racing team and its activities can be viewed by visitors when they are in the process of preparing for a race. You will have fun here. Look for the signs on I-70.

PRIDE AUTOPLAZA (Dealer)
228 N. Baltimore (SR 15)
DERBY, KS 67037 (10 miles southeast of downtown Wichita)
Phone: 316-788-2898
www.prideautoplaza.com
Hours: M–F 9–5, Sat. 9–3

When you are in the Wichita area stop by this dealership and take a look. Pride Autoplaza has a nice assortment of muscle cars, classics and special interest cars in their spacious showroom. The company takes trades, sells on consignment, and assists with financing and shipping. The people at Pride pride themselves in giving honest and accurate descriptions of their vehicles—and they back it up with a money-back guarantee. Check the window sticker; most of the information is there. The company is owned and operated by two long-time car enthusiasts, Bill Roberts and Charles Carver. They've been having fun at this game since 1988.

WALTER P. CHRYSLER BOYHOOD HOME & MUSEUM
102 W. 10th St.
ELLIS, KS 67637 (West-central part of the state at Exit 145 on I-70)

The **Walter P. Chrysler Boyhood Home** *in Ellis, KS.*

Phone: 785-726-3636
www.ellis.ks.us/Chrysler/chrysler.
html
Hours: *After Labor Day weekend
and until Memorial Day Weekend*
Tues.–Sat. 11–3, Sun. 12:30–4:30.
Rest of year Tues.–Sat. 9:30–4:30,
Sun. 12:30–4:30. Admission
charged.

Walter P. Chrysler, founder of the
Chrysler Corporation, spent most of his
youth in Ellis and his boyhood home is
preserved and open to the public. It is
furnished much as it was when he lived
here with his family. His father worked
for the railroad. The house is listed on
the National Register of Historic Places
and there is a museum on the grounds
behind the home displaying additional
items of interest related to Chrysler,
his life in Ellis and the Corporation he
founded. There are family photos and
memorabilia as well as the desk Chrysler
used during the later years of his business career. A 1924 Chrysler automobile,
the first year of production for that
marque, is on display in the museum. It

was here in the Ellis railroad shops that
Chrysler, as a young man, learned the
metal-working trade before going east
to work in the automobile industry. His
wife, Della Forker Chrysler, was from
Ellis and they were married here. The
museum has a gift shop offering many
Chrysler-related items and souvenirs.

"EASY JACK" & SONS (Salvage)
2725 S. Milford Lake Rd.
(6 miles west of Junction City
on I-70 at Exit 290)
JUNCTION CITY, KS 66441
(60 miles west of Topeka on I-70)
Phone: 785-238-7541 and
785-238-7161
Hours: M–F 8–5:30, Sat. 8–2.

Here's an old-timer in the salvage
business. "Easy Jack" has been in the
Business since 1963. There are between
2,500 and 3,000 vehicles here ranging
from the 1920s and up, and there is a
large selection of whole cars ready for the
loving hand of a restorer or a hot rod enthusiast. Many parts have been removed
and are in storage for easy inspection and

quick shipping. These people also search for parts they can't supply. "Easy Jack" advertises that they are the "Largest Antique Auto Parts Store in the Midwest."

 # KANSAS CITY AREA

KC CLASSIC AUTO (Dealer)
10101 Lackman Rd.
LENEXA, KS 66219 (A southern suburb of Kansas City, KS)
Phone: 913-888-1234 and
800-551-0903 (toll free)
www.kcclassicauto.com
Hours: M–F 10–5, Sat. 10–4. Very low admission charge for browsers.

This is a vintage car dealer decked out to look like a museum. There are not only vintage cars in their showroom, but a whole host of auto memorabilia. KC Classic Auto carries a broad line of antique vehicles from the four-pedals-on-the-floor types to the two-pedals-on-the-floor types. They take trades, sell on consignment and provide appraisals. You will be glad you stopped here.

WAGNER CLASSIC CARS (Dealer)
741 E. Front St. (20 minutes from the Kansas City Airport)
BONNER SPRINGS, KS 66012
(Western suburb of Kansas City)
Phone: 913-422-1955
www.wagnersclassiccars.com
Hours: M–F 8:30–7, Sat. 9:30–5:30

Willie Wagner owns this dealership that sells a wide variety of vintage vehicles including muscle cars and street rods. They specialize in investment-quality class and collector cars and trucks. Between 20 and 35 vehicles can be seen in their spacious showroom which is located in a former Ford dealership building decorated in a 1960s motif. On an adjacent lot, Wagner sells current model used cars. Wagner's takes trades, sells on consignment, will search for specific vehicles, and provides shipping and financing. Car clubs are welcome. In business since 1968.

End of Kansas City area

H Z SMITH MOTORS (Dealer)
1701 N. 1399 Rd. (At mile marker 6 on East K-10 Hwy.)
LAWRENCE, KS 66046
Phone: 785-842-3200
www.hzsmithmotors.com

There're a lot of antique cars at this dealership—some 160. Many of them are convertibles and classics, and there are some trucks. In their inventory of cars one will find fully restored vehicles ready for that parade as well as fixer-uppers for the more adventurous souls. The company takes trades and sells on consignment.

KENTUCKY

NATIONAL CORVETTE MUSEUM

350 Corvette Dr. (Exit 28 off
I-65 just south of the GM
Corvette Assembly Plant)
BOWLING GREEN, KY 42101
Phone: 270-781-7973 or
800-538-3883 (toll free)
www.corvettemuseum.com
Hours: Daily 8–5. Admission
charged. Free parking with ample
turn-around space for RVs and
trucks.

This is a large exquisite museum,
opened in late 1994, to preserve and
honor the history of the Corvette automobile from its inception to the present
day. It is next door to General Motors'
Corvette Assembly Plant in Bowling
Green. Many models of Corvettes are
on display at the museum from the
first models introduced in 1953
to, and including, the 1 mil-
lionth Corvette produced here
in Bowling Green. The cars are
displayed in authentic settings
representing the stages of the
Corvette's development. There
are also exhibits on racing, design, building and marketing the
Corvette and its impact on the
American auto industry. A Hall
of Fame honors those individuals who have been instrumental
in the automobile's development
and marketing and there is a
library and archives collection.

Guided tours are available and the museum is available for parties, weddings,
corporate functions, etc. There is a large
gift shop offering Corvette clothing,
jewelry, books, and rare models. Free
tours of the Corvette Assembly Plant
are also available.

SWOPE'S CARS OF YESTERYEAR MUSEUM

1100 N. Dixie Av.
ELIZABETHTOWN, KY 42701
Phone: 270-765-2181 and
270-763-6156
www.swopemuseum.com
Hours: M–Sat. 10–5. Free and
handicapped accessible.

There's a guy here in Kentucky named
Bill Swope who loves to collect old cars
and loves to show them to people. That's

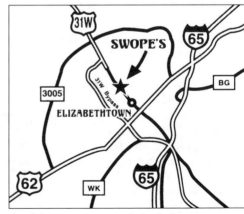

Here's how to get to Swope's Cars of Yesteryear
Museum.

General George S. Patton was fatally injured in the back seat of this 1938 Cadillac limousine when it was involved in an automobile accident in Germany soon after the end of World War II.

why this attractive museum exists. On display are over 30 antique vehicles, all in good condition and all running. Swope collects both domestic vehicles and imports. Bill has a string of new-car dealerships, but this is his pride and joy. Car clubs and bus groups are always welcome, so come on in. Museum founded in 1999.

PATTON MUSEUM OF CAVALRY & ARMOR

4554 Fayette Av., PO Box 25
FORT KNOX, KY 40121 (20 miles south of Louisville on US 31W)
Phone: 502-624-3812 and
888-212-6767 (toll free)
www.generalpatton.org
Hours: M–F 9–4:30, weekends
& holidays 10–6. *May 1 through Sept. 30* M–F 9–4:30, weekends

and holidays 10–4:30. Closed Dec. 24, 25 and 31 and Jan. 1. Free.

This fine museum is devoted to the memory of World War II General George S. Patton, Jr. and to those who served in the U.S. Cavalry and armored units of all American wars. Among the many military vehicles on display is a caravan truck used by General Patton during World War II and the Cadillac sedan in which he was fatally injured in December 1945. The museum is administered by the U.S. Army Armor Center, Fort Knox, and is one of the largest in the U.S. Army Museum System. Every July 4 a World War II battle re-enactment takes place near the museum using many of the museum's vehicles. You will be happy to have stopped at the Patton Museum.

LOUISIANA

SELECT MOTOR CO. (Dealer)
6205 Monroe Hwy. (US 165)
BALL, LA 71405
(10 miles north of Alexandria)
Phone: 318-640-4584 and
800-716-9635 (toll free)
www.selectmotors.net
Hours: M–F 8–6

American muscle cars are the big thing here, but they also carry classics and other vintage vehicles. They have between 25 and 30 cars in stock at all times, and will search for the vehicle of your choice if they don't have it. They also do restorations and service work. The company takes trades, sells on consignment, offers appraisals, and can assist with shipping and financing. Car clubs are always welcome. Every year, on the Saturday before Halloween, there's a car show here held in conjunction with the city fathers of Ball. Select Motors has been in business since 1991.

ARK-LA-TEX ANTIQUE AND CLASSIC VEHICLE & SHREVEPORT FIRE FIGHTER'S MUSEUM
601 Spring St.
SHREVEPORT, LA 71101
Phone: 318-222-0227
www.carmuseum.org
Hours: Tues.–Sat. 9–5, Sun. 1–5.
Admission charged.

This attractive museum is in a handsome old three-story, 24,000 sq. st. building that once was a Graham Bros. dealership and a Dodge dealership. The showrooms—that's right, plural—are on the first floor. The museum is also home to the Shreveport Fire Fighter's Museum. Altogether there are about 50 vintage cars plus fire trucks and more than a dozen motorcycles. Many of the cars are on loan from local collectors so the exhibits rotate. Some of the cars are for sale. There is also a research library. The museum participates in several annual antique car events, is available for parties etc. and has an impressive gift shop. Car clubs are welcome.

MAINE

▶ BANGOR AREA

COLE LAND TRANSPORTATION MUSEUM

405 Perry Rd.
BANGOR, ME 04401 (South-central part of the state on I-95)
Phone: 207-990-3600
www.colemuseum.org
Hours: *May 1 through Nov. 11*
daily 9–5. Admission charged.

The mission of this privately-owned museum is to collect, preserve and display an historic cross-section of Maine's land transportation equipment. On display are some 200 pieces of such equipment. Not only are there antique automobiles, but there are tractors, trucks, railroad equipment, snowmobiles, bicycles, wagons and sleighs. The museum possesses one of the most extensive collections of early commercial vehicles in the country and claims to have the largest collection of snow-removal equipment in America. There are various auto-related artifacts on display, as well as displays of military equipment. On the museum's grounds is a World War II memorial with a WW II Jeep as its center piece. The museum has a gift shop with many interesting items for sale.

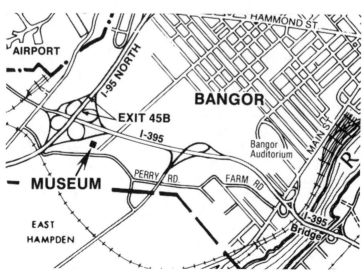

The Cole Land Transportation Museum *is just off the intersection of I-95 and I-395.*

MAINE

CONCEPT AUTOWORKS, INC.
(Dealer)
891 Main St.
BRADLEY, ME 04411 (12 miles
northeast of Bangor on SR 178)
Phone: 207-866-0082
http/www.dealsonwheels.com/
dealers/conceptautoworks/
Hours: M–F 10–6

You will find an interesting selection
and general line of antique vehicles at
this dealer. Some 20 vehicles are on
display in their modern showroom. The
company will search for specific vehicles
for customers, take trade-ins, sell on
consignment and help with shipping. Ted
Pomeroy, the owner, says car clubs are
always welcome. In business since 1993.

End of Bangor area

BOOTHBAY RAILWAY VILLAGE
(Multi-attraction village museum)
586 Wiscasset Rd.
(3¹/₂ miles north on SR 27)
BOOTHBAY, ME 04537
(On the coast 35 miles
northeast of Portland)
Phone: 207-633-4727
www.railwayvillage.org
Hours: *May 31–Oct. 12* daily
9:30–5. Admission charged.

This is a museum village of approximately 30 buildings representing life in
Maine as it was at the beginning of the
20th Century. Among the several buildings is a blacksmith shop, a restored
school house, a general store, a doll
museum and a well-stocked gift shop. A
steam train operates from the old station
and 15-minute rides are offered through
the nearby woods. There is also an
antique car museum with approximately
50 vehicles including horse-drawn carriages, shays, pre-World War I vehicles,
trucks and, of course, autos. Also in this
museum are displays of old gasoline
engines, license plates, gas pumps and
other automobile memorabilia. Museum
founded in 1963.

CLASSIC FORD SALES (Salvage)
PO Box 60 (Office)
EAST DIXFIELD, ME 04227
(Western part of state on US 2)
Phone: 207-562-4443 and
800-894-4300 (toll free)
www.classicford.com
Hours: M–F 9–5

They call it "Ford Heaven" because
this is where Fords go in their afterlife,
and it is high up on a mountain top and
not easy to get to. Visitors who wish to
visit the yard are advised to phone first
for directions. The yard is "located up
the road a bit" at South Carthage. Upon
arrival, though, visitors will see one of
the largest Ford salvage yards in the
world. There are more than 1,000 Fords
here from 1949 through 1972 and later.
Classic Ford Sales has many T-birds,
Fairlanes, Falcons, and can supply NOS
parts as well as used. But, guess what,
no Mustangs! On the other hand, Classic Ford Sales has a sizeable inventory
of large Ford trucks beginning with
the F100 series through tandem rigs.
Project cars are available for those who
do their own restoration. Visitors can
browse the yard and Phil McIntyre, the

owner, welcomes car clubs and groups. He says that if the numbers justify it, he'll prepare a cookout. Phil started the yard in 1992.

AYER EUROPEAN AUTO
(Restorer and dealer)
Brunswick Rd. (SR 201)
GARDINER, ME 04345
(7 miles south of downtown
Augusta on SR 24)
Phone: 207-582-7372 (sales),
207-582-3618 (shop)
www.ayereuropeanauto.com
Hours: M–F 7:30–5:50 (sales),
M–F 7:30–4:30 (service)
Directions: *Heading north on I-295*
take exit 27 (SR 201). Turn right
and proceed 2.5 miles. Dealership
is on the right. *Heading south on the
Maine Turnpike (I-95)* take exit 14B
onto I-295. Take exit 27 (SR 201),
turn left and proceed 2.5 miles.
Dealership is on the right.

This interesting company restores and sells high-end vintage vehicles such as Porsches, Mercedes-Benz, Packards, Ferraris, etc. They take great pride in their restoration work and back it up by providing references and testimonials. They also do service and repair work. In their showroom one will find 6 to 8 examples of their work. More vehicles are displayed on an adjoining lot. Ayer European Auto takes

trades, searches for specific vehicles and assists in financing and shipping. The company was founded in 1958 by Everett Ayer and is now run by his son, Ray.

THE STANLEY MUSEUM
40 School St., PO Box 77
KINGFIELD, ME 04947 (47 miles
north-northwest of Augusta)
Phone: 207-265-2729
www.stanleymuseum.org
Hours: *May through Oct.*
Tues.–Sun. 1–4; *Dec. through Mar.*
M–F 10–4. Admission charged.

Here's a very interesting museum. It is housed in a 1903 school building and honors the Stanley family of Stanley Steamer fame. There are several Stanley Steamer automobiles in the museum, including models from 1905, 1910 and 1916. Photos and memorabilia relate the history of this famous Maine family, especially Francis E. and Frelan O. Stanley, the inventive twin brothers who were the driving forces behind the Stanley Motor Carriage Company, which was located in Watertown, MA. Photography was

The **Stanley Museum** *of Kingfield, ME*

103

An interior view of the Owls Head Transportation Museum, *Owls Head, ME.*

also important to the Stanley family and that fact is highlighted in the museum in that they were the owners of the Stanley Dry Plate Co., which produced an early form of film making equipment. This company was the source of the family's wealth. Information on the company and its products are on display along with vintage cameras and photographs of local life in Maine at the turn of the century taken by sister Chansonetta, who was an accomplished photographer.

The museum publishes a newsletter 4 times a year containing historical and technical information on steam engines and newsbriefs of steam-related events. Museum was founded in 1981.

OWLS HEAD TRANSPORTATION MUSEUM

2 Miles South of Rockland on SR 73 at Knox County Airport
OWLS HEAD, ME 04854
(On Penobscot Bay 40 miles southeast of Augusta)

Phone: 207-594-4418
www.olwshead.org
Hours: *Apr.–Oct.* daily 10–5. *Rest of year* M–F 10–5. Admission charged.

This is a large museum displaying one of the finest collection of antique cars, motorcycles, bicycles, buggies, engines and airplanes on the eastern seaboard. Emphasis is on pre-1920 transportation. Some 75 vintage cars, including some very rare and unusual models, are on display. Some of the vehicles are on loan to the museum by their owners, so the displays change from time-to-time. On weekends during the summer, various pieces of equipment are taken out of the museum and operated on the museum grounds. The Owls Head Museum is host to many social and business events throughout the year.

SEAL COVE AUTO MUSEUM

Pretty Marsh Rd. (SR 102)
SEAL COVE, ME 04674

One of the many rare and unique vintage autos at the Seal Cove Auto Museum, *Seal Cove, ME.*

(On the Ocean just southwest of Acadia Natl. Park)
Phone: 207-244-9242
www.sealcoveautomuseum.org
Hours: June 1 through Sept. 15, daily 10–5. Admission charged.

This is a privately-owned museum with approximately 100 antique cars and some 30 antique motorcycles. Some of the cars are extremely rare and many of them are of pre-World War I vintage. A significant number of the cars have been restored to world-class condition. You will see vehicles here that you won't see anywhere else. The museum also has a gift shop with many interesting auto-related items. This is a popular destination for car clubs.

WELLS AUTO MUSEUM
Highway US 1
(Exit 2 off Maine Turnpike)

WELLS, ME 04090
(30 miles southwest of Portland)
Phone: 207-646-9064
http://seacoastnh.com/dct/
wellsautomuseum.html
Hours: *Labor Day to Columbus Day 10–5. Closed rest of year.*
Admission charged.

This fine museum has a display of some 80 vehicles including New England's largest display of "Brass Era" cars. The museum is the outgrowth of collections made by the prominent Gould Family of Wells. Included in the collection are Stanley Steamers, early electric cars, a 1918 Stutz Bearcat, a 1934 Chrysler Airflow, a 1935 Lagonda, a 1935 Bantam and a 1941 Chrysler Town & Country. There are displays of New England license plates, old toys, tools, hubcaps, nameplates and photos. Visitors will also see exhibits of motor-

1912 Pathfinder from the collection of Brass Era autos at the Wells Auto Museum *of Wells, ME.*

cycles, bicycles, nickelodeons, arcade picture machines, orchestrions, Regina Hexaphones and many more items. The museum has a well-stocked gift shop offering toys, jewelry, models, books and other auto-related items.

MARYLAND

US ARMY ORDNANCE MUSEUM
Building 2601
Aberdeen Proving Ground
ABERDEEN PROVING GROUND,
MD 21005 (25 miles northeast
of downtown Baltimore)
Phone: 410-278-3602 and
410-278-7473
www.ordmusfound.org
Hours: Daily 10-4:45. Free
admission and parking.

This is a large Army museum displaying many pieces of equipment and items
of war associated with the US Army's
Ordnance Department and the Aberdeen Proving Ground. A large selection
of military vehicles can be seen here.
Included in that collection are several
antique cars including Gen. John Per-
shing's 1917 Locomobile and German
Kubelwagens and Schwimmwagens
from World War II. Schwimmwagens
are amphibious Volkswagens. The
museum also has a gift shop.

FLEMING'S ULTIMATE GARAGE
(Dealer)
318 6th St.
ANNAPOLIS, MD 21403
Phone: 410-280-3700
www.flemingsultimategarage.com
Hours: M-F 9-5

When you buy a car from this dealer,
they ship it free and enclosed to anywhere in the U.S. And when you visit

their waterfront showroom, you will
have a nice selection of vintage cars
from which to chose. They offer classic
cars, sports cars, exotics, special interest vehicles and motorcycles. Each of
their vehicles has been serviced with
an eye for safety, reliability and good
looks making them turn-key cars and
motorcycles ready to drive off the floor.
Fleming's takes trades, offers warranties,
will locate specific vehicles, and helps
with financing and insurance. Tony
Fleming is the owner and has been in
business since the mid-1980s.

VOGT'S AUTO RECYCLERS (Salvage)
2239 Old Westminster Pike
PO Box 400
FINKSBURG, MD 21048
(20 miles northwest of downtown
Baltimore on US 140)
Phone: 410-848-1300 or
800-492-1300 (toll free)
www.vogtsbaweb.com
Hours: M-F 8-5, Sat., 8-noon
Directions: From Baltimore Beltway
695, take Exit 19 (Rt. 795). Go
to Exit 9B (Rt. 140 West). Go 5
miles to traffic light. Turn left onto
Greenmill Rd. Bear right to stop
sign onto Old Westminster Pike.
They're on the left at 2239 Old
Westminster Pike.

This is an old established salvage yard
with some 3,000 vehicles on 17 acres
of land. They carry a generous mix of

MARYLAND

American-made and imported vehicles, including light trucks from 1935 to the 1990s. The inventory is computerized and there is a parts showroom. If they don't have it, Vogt's will search other yards for specific parts. The company is run by the Vogt family. In business since 1956.

MASSACHUSETTS

▶ BOSTON AREA

LARZ ANDERSON AUTO MUSEUM: THE MUSEUM OF TRANSPORTATION
15 Newton St. in Larz Anderson Park
BROOKLINE, MA 02146
(A western suburb of Boston)
Phone: 617-522-6547
www.mot.org
Hours: Tues.–Sun. 10–5. Admission charged.

There are about 25 vintage cars on display in the 1888 carriage house of the former home of the famous diplomat, Larz Anderson. Most of the cars were collected by Larz Anderson and his wife, Isabael, and is the oldest private collection of antique cars in the country. Changing exhibits in the museum reflect the influence of the automobile on various periods of American history and with various themes. Many of the permanent cars are from the turn of the Century. The Museum hosts an annual car auction, Concours d'Elegance and many car club events. Other displays in the museum highlight the lives of the famous Anderson family and there are exhibits telling of the early life in the Brookline area. The museum also has a nice collection of vintage carriages and an interesting and pleasant gift shop. The museum was founded in 1949.

HATCH & SONS AUTOMOTIVE, INC.
(Dealer)
533 Boston Post Rd.
WAYLAND, MA 01778
(Western suburb of Boston on US 20 and SR 126)
Phone: 508-358-3500
www.hatchandsons.com
Hours: M–F 9–5, Sat 9–3.

In this company's spacious showroom you will see 25,000 sq. ft. of beautiful iron such as Mercedes-Benz, Ferraris, Porsches and other top-of-the line vintage vehicles. They do all of their own restoration work in house except for plating. With regards to restoration, they are perfectionists and have an award-wining history to prove it. The company also does service work. Hatch & Sons Automotive has sold cars world-wide and are well-known in the high quality vintage vehicle field. They take trades, search for specific vehicles, offer appraisals and aid in shipping and financing. Ask for either of the Jims, Jim Horgos or Jim Hatch.

End of Boston area ◀

MASSACHUSETTS

TANGO CLASSIC AUTOS, INC.
(Restorer and dealer)
38 William Way
BELLINGHAM, MA 02019
(South central part of state, just
north of Woonsocket, RI)
Phone; 508-966-4260
www.shelbymustang.com
Hours: M–F 8–5

If you like Shelby Mustangs, this is
the place for you. Tango Classics restores
them, sells them, sells parts for them, and
offers a wide selection of Shelby apparel
and other collector items in their gift shop.
There about 20 Shelbys and other vehicles
in their showroom for sale at all times.
And, if you own a Shelby and want it restored, they will do it. The Shelby Mustang
muscle cars were produced jointly by Mr.
Carroll Shelby and Ford Motor Co. from
1965 through 1970. The company does a
lot of sales over the internet.

STEVENS AUTO WRECKING
(Salvage and dealer)
160 Freeman Rd.
CHARLTON, MA 01507 (10 miles
southwest of Worcester on I-90)
Phone: 508-248-5539 or
508-832-6380
Hours: M–F 8–5, Sat. 8–2:30.

Stevens Auto Wrecking is a large
salvage yard of approximately 3,000
vehicles with cars and trucks from the
1930s to the 1980s. The heaviest concentration is from the late 1940s to the early
1970s. Vehicles are of mixed makes and
models and mostly American-made.
Stevens also offers used and recondi-
tioned cars for sale and will search other
yards for parts. Customer may browse
the yard. Car clubs welcome. In business
since 1958. Joe Stevens is the owner.

HERITAGE MUSEUMS & GARDENS
Grove and Pine Sts. off SR 130
SANDWICH, MA 02563
(West end of Cape Cod)
Phone: 508-888-3300
www.heritagemuseumsandgardens.
org
Hours: *May 1–Oct. 31*, daily 9–6
and 9–8 on Wed. Please phone for
winter hours. Admission charged.

Here is a fine museum founded by J.
K. Lilly III to display some of his family's
collection of Americana. Housed in a
Shaker round stone barn are some two
dozen vintage autos including President
William Howard Taft's 1909 White
Steamer, a 1922 American-made Rolls-
Royce, a 1912 Mercer Raceabout, a 1915
Stutz Bearcat and a 1930 Duesenberg
once owned by Gary Cooper. Tours of the
estate are available in a jitney and there
are three gift shops on the grounds. This
is also the site of the Cape Cod Baseball
Hall of Fame. In the other buildings are
displays of American handicrafts, art,
firearms, flags, a carousel with free rides
for everyone and many other items.
The grounds are lavishly decorated
with trees, shrubs and some 100,000
rhododendrons. Also on the grounds
are a labyrinth, a maze and a 200 year old
windmill that is still operational.

INDIAN MOTORCYCLE MUSEUM
33 Hendee St. (Exit I-291
at Saint James St)
SPRINGFIELD, MA 01104
Phone: 413-737-2624
http:/www.sidecar.com
Hours: Daily 10–4.
Admission charged.

This is a museum devoted to Indian
Motorcycles, the first gasoline-powered

motorcycles to be manufactured in the United States. It is located in the last building owned by the company. The Indian Motorcycle Company began manufacturing here in Springfield in 1901 and continued until the company went out of business in 1953. Many examples of Indian motorcycles are on display, including some of the earliest models; some were used by American paratroopers in World War II. There is also a large display of toy motorcycles and motorcycle memorabilia. The Indian Motorcycle Company, at various times, also manufactured outboard motors, airplane engines and automobiles. A 1927 Indian automobile is on display. The museum has a gift shop offering many interesting items.

LONGFELLOW'S WAYSIDE INN

72 Wayside Inn Rd. (US 20 west)
SUDBURY, MA 01776 (22 miles west of downtown Boston)
Phone: 978-443-1776
www.wayside.org

This is an old restored inn made famous by Henry Wadsworth Longfellow who composed his poem "Tales of a Wayside Inn" while sitting by the Inn's fireplace. The Inn offers lodging and meals and there are a number of interesting and historic outbuildings on the grounds including the Martha-Mary Chapel, a gristmill and Mary Lamb Schoolhouse. In the 1920s the Inn was abandoned and in decay when Henry Ford came to its rescue and restored it once more into a working inn. Ford restored the gristmill and moved a schoolhouse onto the property from Sterling, MA which he believed to be the original schoolhouse immortalized in the McGuffey Reader classic "Mary Had a Little Lamb". Henry Ford and his wife,

Clara, loved the Wayside Inn and visited it often and attended many of its square dance parties. In 1939, Henry Ford build the Martha-Mary Chapel and named it after his mother and his wife's mother. After restoring the Wayside Inn, Ford went on to create his famous Ford Museum and Greenfield Village complex in Dearborn, MI now known as The Henry Ford.

DEARBORN AUTO (Dealer)

16 Maple St.
TOPSFIELD, MA 01983
(on US 1, 10 miles north of Lynn)
Phone: 978-887-6644
www.dearbornauto.com
Hours: M–F 9–5, Sat 9–3

This dealer specializes in vintage Mercedes-Benz automobiles up to 1971. That alone tells you a lot. Occasionally, they have other European sports cars and all of their cars are backed by a buy-back warranty. There's always a nice selection of M-Bs in their wood-paneled showroom, but if you don't see the car you want, Dearborn Auto will try to find it. Dearborn Auto can provide service records and restoration histories for many of their cars. They also have a detailer and work closely with two local restorers so they can provide a turn-key vehicle for you to drive off the floor. The company sells cars on consignment, takes trade-ins, does pre-purchase inspections, provides appraisals, and aids in shipping and financing. The owner, Alex Dearborn, is a very interesting individual. He has been a race car designer, a race car driver, a concourse judge and, in his earlier years, designed the popular "Deserter," a series of cars uniquely blending sports car and dune buggy with VW underpinnings. In business since 1972.

MICHIGAN

If you want to see all the antique car sites in Michigan, you had better count on a month or more to do so. The state is loaded with them. This is where a large percentage of the old cars that people collect today came from, and the state is proud of that fact and has made a concerted effort to perpetuate its automotive heritage.

All over the state you will find plaques, monuments, buildings, parks, street names, interstate highways, and other entities named after famous automotive personalities and their products. And everywhere you will find Henry Ford. Henry Ford stands heads and shoulders above all other automotive personalities because he produced so many cars. For example, in 1919, half of the cars in the world were Ford Model Ts.

During the summer months antique car activities proliferate; swap meets, auctions, car shows, club functions, automotive-oriented bus tours and more. So join in. This is a fun state for antique car buffs.

WALTER P. CHRYSLER MUSEUM
One Chrysler Dr. (Corner of Featherstone and Squirrel Rds.)
AUBURN HILLS, MI 48326
(4 miles east of Pontiac, MI on I-75)
Phone: 888-456-1924 (toll free)
www.chryslerheritage.com
Hours: Tues.–Sat. 10–6, Sun. noon–6. Admission charged.

This is a large and excellent museum devoted to preserving the history of the Chrysler Corporation and its founder, Walter P. Chrysler. There are three stories displaying some 75 beautifully restored Chrysler production cars, concept cars, trucks, race cars, muscle cars, their famous "Hemi" engines, and other Chrysler firsts and important

The Walter P. Chrysler Museum *in Auburn Hills, MI.*

engineering advancements. There are also interactive displays and vignettes related to the company, and a small theater which shows various films on the company's history. Included in the many displays are replicas of Walter P. Chrysler's original workshop and office complete with cast manikins representing Chrysler and some of his closest associates. The museum, which opened in October 1999, also has a gift and souvenir shop, restoration shop, archive and research section and a courtyard.

TOWNE & COUNTRY MOTORS
(Dealer)
    78927 North SR 51
    DECATUR, MI 49045

(25 miles west of Kalamazoo)
Phone: 269-423-3131
Hours: M–F 9–7, Sat. 9–5.

Muscle cars and street rods are what Towne & Country Motors is all about. But, you will also see a few classics and antique vehicles in their showroom. This fast-growing company carries about 50 cars in inventory and sells cars worldwide. They can provide an inventory list, take trades, sell on consignment, do repairs, do appraisals, have a gift shop, arrange financing and insurance, and will search for specific vehicles for customers. Greg Gorzelanny, the owner, says car clubs are welcome any time. Your contact man at Towne & Country is Dave Peters. In business since 1973.

▶ DETROIT AREA ("MOTOR CITY"—"MOTOWN")

During the first half of the 20th Century Detroit emerged as America's automobile capital, a title which it retains to this day. Many cities contended for the honor, but it was here that the big names and survivors in the very competitive early automotive industry assembled and thrived. By doing so, they propelled Detroit into one of America's great industrial centers. As a result, the city and its suburbs abound with historic automotive sites. Here are the international headquarters and major factories of the automotive giants, the homes of many of the famous personalities of the industry, their monuments, their museums, their philanthropic works and their gravesites. One need travel just a few blocks in the city in any direction to run into a street, a park, a school or a building bearing an historic automotive name. Visitors will dart about the city on the *Edsel Ford Freeway*, the *Chrysler Freeway* and the *Fisher Freeway*. They will encounter *General Motors Tech.*, the *General Motors Building*, the *Fisher Building*, *Walter P. Reuther Library*, *UAW World Headquarters*, *Dodge Brothers State Parks*, the *Henry Ford Hospital*, *Henry Ford Centennial Library*, *Henry Ford Auditorium*, *Henry Ford Academy*, *Henry Ford Community College*, *Henry Ford High School*, *Henry Ford Junior High School*, *Henry Ford Elementary School*, *Ford Road*, *Ford Avenue*, several of Henry Ford's small hydroelectric power plants, and buildings or historic markers noting some of the 15 homes Henry and Clara Ford lived in from 1888 to 1947. From many parts of the city one can see the high-rise buildings of the *Renaissance Center*, which was the inspiration of Henry Ford II and is now *General Motors' World Headquarters*.

AUTOMOTIVE HALL OF FAME

21400 Oakwood Blvd. (Adjacent to The Henry Ford museum complex) **DEARBORN**, MI 48124 (Southwestern suburb of Detroit) Phone: 313-240-4000 www.automotivehalloffame.org Hours: Daily 9–5; *Closed Mondays, Nov. through April.* Admission charged.

The Automotive Hall of Fame is designed to be a place of honor and an educational resource. It celebrates accomplished people of the worldwide motor vehicle industry for the purpose of inspiring others, especially young people, to higher levels of achievement in their own work and lives. It is a unique "people place" of innovation and inspiration where interactive experiences and one-on-one demonstrations are entertaining and enlightening.

Some of the several hundred names that will be found in the Hall of Fame are Gordon M. Buehrig, designer of the Auburn, Cord and Duesenberg cars; Elmer Wavering, inventor of the car radio

The Automotive Hall of Fame *in Dearborn, MI is a place of innovation and inspiration.*

and the alternator; John W. Koons, Sr. of Falls Church, VA, the world's largest Ford dealer; Ralph Teetor, a blind engineer and inventor of cruise control; and Soichiro Honda, founder of the Honda automotive empire. The museum has a gift shop and facilities for large corporate meetings and events. School groups are always welcome. The museum was founded in 1975 and is wheelchair accessible.

CLASSIC AUTO SHOWPLACE (Dealer)
  31435 Stephenson Hwy.
  MADISON HEIGHTS, MI 48071
  (northern suburb of Detroit off I-75)
  Phone: 248-589-2700
  www.classicautoshowplace.com
  Hours: M–Thurs. 10–6, F–Sat. 10–4, Sun. noon–4.

This dealership has been selling antique vehicles since 1984, and they're in the heart of "The Motor Capital of the World." In their spacious showroom you will find classics, hot rods, muscle cars, sports cars and special interest cars. They do a lot of business on the Internet and have multiple Internet sites. The company takes trades, sells on consignment, locates specific cars, provides appraisals and can arrange financing and shipping. This is a busy place. They say that up to 1,000 people visit them each week. The company also has a sister dealership in Grand Rapids.

DETROIT PUBLIC LIBRARY,
NATIONAL AUTOMOTIVE HISTORY
COLLECTION
  Skillman Branch Library
  121 Gratiot Av.
  DETROIT, MI 48226
  Phone: 313-628-2851 or 313-628-2750

http://.detroit.lib.mi.us/nahc/
Hours: M–F 10–6, Free.

The National Automotive Historical Collection (NAHC) contained within this library has the largest public automotive archive collection on the North American Continent. They have hundreds of thousands of books, magazines, photographs, manuals and documents covering such subjects as company histories, products, people, progress, events, racing, restoring, advertising, servicing, court cases, novels, parts manuals, chronologies, cartoons, calendars, posters, business records and music. The collection is open to the general public interested in automotive history. A reference service is offered and the collection publishes "Wheels, Journal of the National Automotive History Collection". The library can also recommend private researchers for in-depth inquiries. The NAHC is supported, in part, by Chrysler, Ford, General Motors and donations from other sources. Tours are available by appointment. The collection was established in 1953.

THE FISHER MANSION
(Historic home)
  383 Lenox Av.
  DETROIT, MI 48215
  Phone: 313-331-6740
  www.fishermansion.com
  Hours: Mansion offers tours F–Sun. at 12:30 through 6.
  Admission charged.

This was the magnificent riverfront home and estate of Lawrence Fisher, founder of the Fisher Body Co. and President of Cadillac Motors. Completed in 1927, this two bedroom—that's right, two

The Fisher Mansion, *former home and estate of Lawrence Fisher, founder of Fisher Body Co. and President of Cadillac Motors.*

bedroom,—Mansion is remarkable for its ornate stone and marble work, wood crafted doors and archways, stained glass windows, Art Deco tile work, exquisite chandeliers and black walnut parquet floors. Over 200 ounces of gold and silver leaf decorate the ceilings and moldings. Fisher was a friend of William Randolph Hearst and certain aspects of this mansion were patterned after Hearst's famous San Simeon Estate in California. On the water front is an enclosed dock so that visitors can arrive by boat. It also served as a slip for Fisher's 104 Ft. yacht. Fisher was a flamboyant character and remained single until he was 63.

The Mansion is the home of the Bhaktivedanta Cultural Center which is inspired by the spiritual teachings of His Divine Grace A. C. Bhaktivedanta Swami Prahudapa of the Hare Krishna Movement. The Center was established by Alfred Brush Ford, great-grandson of Henry Ford and Elisabeth Reuther Dickmeyer, daughter of United Auto Workers Union President, Walter Reuther who jointly purchased the estate in 1975. Inside the mansion is "Govinda's," a fine dining vegetarian restaurant.

EDSEL & ELEANOR FORD HOUSE
(Historic home)
  1100 Lake Shore Rd.
  GROSSE POINTE SHORES, MI 48236 (A northern suburb of Detroit)
  Phone: 313-884-4222
  www.fordhouse.org
  Hours: *April through Dec.,* tours are given on the half hour Tues.–Sat. 10–4, Sun. noon–4. *Rest of year,* Tues. through Sun. noon–4. Admission charged.

  This was the 60-room lake-front mansion and 87-acre estate of Henry

The **Edsel & Eleanor Ford House,** *Grosse Pointe Shores, MI.*

Ford's only son, Edsel, his wife Eleanor and their four children, Henry II, Benson, Josephine and William Clay. The house was begun in 1926 and completed in 1929. It was modeled after the home in England, "Cotswold," which the Fords had visited many times. Edsel Ford lived here until his death in 1943 and his wife lived on in the house until 1976. The house was opened to the public in 1978 and is decorated much as it was when the Fords lived in it. There are numerous examples of fine furniture, oriental rugs, oil painting, crystal chandeliers and English walnut paneling. The grounds are well landscaped and can be toured. Several vintage cars belonging to the family are on display and there is a Tea Room which is open from 11:30 to 2:30. The Edsel & Eleanor House hosts several antique car events each year.

HENRY FORD HOME "FAIR LANE"
(Historic home)
   4901 Evergreen Rd. on the
   University of Michigan–Dearborn
   Campus off US 12
   DEARBORN, MI 48128-1491
   (An eastern suburb of Detroit)
   Phone: 313-593-5590
   www.henryfordestate.com
   Hours: Thirty minute tours
   are offered *April–Dec.* M–Sat.
   at 10, 11, 1, 2, and 3, Sun. 1–4:30,
   and *rest of year* M–F at 1, Sun.
   1–4:30. Admission charged.

This was the 31,000 sq. st. residence and 1300-acre estate of Henry Ford, founder and owner of the Ford Motor Co. and his wife, Clara. Henry Ford was born in Dearborn and as he made his fortune he brought his home town

117

"Fair Lane", Henry and Clara Ford's home in Dearborn, MI.

along in the shadow of his success by building within the city limits the huge Rouge River factory complex and other Ford manufacturing facilities, the World Headquarters of the Ford Motor Co., The Henry Ford museum complex, and ultimately, his own home and estate, "Fair Lane". The estate was named after an area in Ireland where Ford's ancestors had lived. The house and grounds are open to the public and appear much as they did when the Ford family live here. Most of the original furniture, however, was sold at auction in the 1950s. The Fords entertained many important people of their day in their home including such world-renowned people as President Herbert Hoover, Charles Lindbergh, the Duke of Windsor, Harvey Firestone and John Burroughs. The estate had a suite of rooms reserved for Ford's good friend,

Thomas Edison. Fair Lane reflects the mechanical genius of Ford in that the estate has its own phone system and power house, a private laboratory, a 4,000-book library, a summer home, a man-made lake, a root cellar, a vegetable garden, a 10,000-plant rose garden, a "Santa's Workshop" and a scaled-down working farm for the grandchildren, a water piano and a vacuum tube-operated hair dryer. There are also some 500 bird houses. The Fords were very active ornithologists. The estate has dining facilities open to the public that offer food prepared according to some of Clara Ford's favorite recipes.

THE HENRY FORD (Formerly the HENRY FORD MUSEUM & GREENFIELD VILLAGE)
  20900 Oakwood Blvd.
  (Village Road & Oakwood Blvd.)

The Henry Ford, *Dearborn, MI.*

DEARBORN, MI 48124
Phone: 313-982-6001 or
800-835-5237 (toll free)
www.hfmgv.org
Hours: *Museum;* Daily 10–5
year around. *Greenfield Village;*
Mid–June–late Aug. daily 10–9, late
Aug.–Dec.31 and April 1–mid–June
daily 10–5. Admission charged,
group discounts available.

The Henry Ford is the world's largest indoor-outdoor museum spanning
over 90 acres. Holdings include more
than one million objects and 25 million
historical papers. Henry Ford founded
the museum and village in 1929 to
show how far and fast America had
come in technological achievements.

The Museum's statement is that, in a
brief moment of history, America was
transformed from a farming society to a
gigantic manufacturing society. Visitors
are invited to take a look back at 300
years worth of American resourcefulness
and innovation. The museum complex
has an Imax Theater, the Benson Ford
Research Center and offers tours to the
nearby River Rouge Plant which has
been redeveloped into a modern-day
industrial complex. One of the most
popular exhibits at the museum, as
might be expected, focuses on the automobile and showcases its development
and transformation through the years.
This exhibit features some 100 cars and
trucks, part of the museum's much larger
collection. Among the significant ve-

119

hicles on permanent display are the only existing 1886 Duryea Motor Wagon, the first production car in America; presidential limousines, including the one in which President John F. Kennedy was assassinated in 1963; and an astonishing array of many makes and models significant to auto history, including one-of-a-kind concept cars. The exhibit also includes car memorabilia and cultural milestones of America's automotive past, including a classic 1946 diner, a tourist cabin, an original Holiday Inn room and a McDonald's sign flashing "15-cent Hamburgers." And, speaking of food, there are a number of cafes and restaurants in the complex and plenty of shops to peruse. Among the exhibits personally related to Henry Ford is his 1886 Quadricycle, his first "horseless carriage," a huge Highland Park engine which was one of the nine that powered the Ford Highland Park plant from 1912 to 1930, Ford's watch repair tools, and a spinning wheel that was a gift from Mohandas Gandhi.

Greenfield Village is adjacent to the museum and is a collection of historic buildings celebrating the resourcefulness of, and telling the stories of, famous and not-so-famous Americans. In Greenfield Village you will find the actual buildings and homes in which America's greatest inventions, the auto, the airplane and the light bulb were developed. Part of its charm is in the incongruous conjuncture of famous inventors; only in Greenfield Village do the Wright Brothers live around the corner from Thomas Edison's laboratory.

FORD PIQUETTE AVENUE PLANT
(Historic site)

411 Piquette Av.
DETROIT, MI 48202
Phone: 313-867-8960
www.tplex.org
Hours: *May–Oct.* 3rd Sat. of each month 1–5. Admission charged.

Here is one of the most historic automobile plants in the world. It was here, at the turn of the century, that Henry Ford entered the automobile business producing his first automobiles, the Models B, C, F, K, N, R and S. Then lightning struck. In 1908, Henry Ford designed his Model T automobile in a secret room in this building, initiated the idea of the moving assembly line, and built the first 12,000 Model Ts at such a high production rate that he set a world record for automobile production. The price of the Model T was so low that millions of people could afford them and the car was very dependable. Here, too, in this building, was Henry Ford's office from which he directed his soon-to-mushroom enterprise. Sales of the Model T were so great that

The Piquette Avenue Plant *is the birthplace of the Ford Model T, the most significant automobile of the 20th Century.*

Meadow Brook Hall, *the Dodge-Wilson mansion in Rochester, MI.*

the plant outgrew its capacity within a year and Model T production moved to the newly-built, and much larger, Highland Park Model T Plant. The Model T automobile, which is now recognized as the most significant car of the 20th Century, remained in production until 1927 and captured nearly one-half of the world's automobile market.

MEADOW BROOK HALL
(Historic home)
Walton Blvd. & Adams Rd. (3 miles west of Oakland University)
ROCHESTER, MI 48309-4401
(A northern suburb of Detroit)
Phone: 248-370-3140
www.meadowbrookhall.org
Hours: *Guided tours are given every 45 minutes from Memorial Day to Labor Day* daily 10:30–3, *rest of year* M–F at 1:30, Sat.–Sun. 12:30, 1:30 and 2:30. Garden tours and group tours are available. The mansion is wheelchair accessible and a sign-language interpreter can be provided upon request. Admission charged.

Directions: From I-75, take University Drive (Exit 79) east to Oakland University main entrance. Turn left at Squirrel Rd. Turn right at Walton Blvd. then right at Adams Rd. Turn right at the east campus entrance to Oakland and follow the signs to Meadow Brook Hall.

This 110-room Tudor-revival style mansion is now a part of Oakland University. It was built in 1929 at the cost of $4 million by Matilda Raush Dodge Wilson, the widow of John Dodge, the automotive pioneer. The home is lavishly decorated with needlepoint draperies, hand-carved paneling, priceless art treasures and a sculptured ceiling in the dining room. There are 24 fireplaces, a great hall, a ballroom and the grounds are beautifully landscaped. There is a gift shop and a coffee shop on the grounds and the Mansion is available for corporate meetings, weddings and other events. An automotive concours d'elegance is held here each year on the first Sunday in August.

MICHIGAN

The Motorsports Hall of Fame *honors many famous racing personalities and has race cars on display.*

MEMORY LANE MOTOR CARS
(Dealer)

> 36024 Michigan Av.
> *WAYNE*, MI 48184 (Western suburb of Detroit on US 12)
> Phone: 734-721-2355
> www.memorylanemotorcars.com
> Hours: Tues.– Sat. 10–6

If you like muscle cars you'll like this place. It's their specialty and they always have a nice selection of such vehicles in their indoor showroom. Their inventory is listed on the web. If you can't find what you are looking for, Memory Lane Motor Cars will search for it. The company takes trades, sells on consignment, buys cars outright, and will help in financing and shipping. They call themselves *"Your Muscle Car Connection."*

MOTORSPORTS HALL OF FAME MUSEUM

> 43700 Expo Center Dr.
> (Southwest corner of I-96 and Novi Rd. (exit 162) at the base of the water tower)
> *NOVI*, MI 48375 (A northwestern suburb of Detroit)
> Phone: 248-349-7223
> www.mshf.com
> Hours: *Memorial Day through Labor Day* daily 10–5, *rest of year* Thurs.–Sun. 10–5.
> Admission charged.

This Hall of Fame museum, located in Novi's spacious Expo Center, honors outstanding personalities in auto, motorcycle, airplane and boat racing. Some of those honored in the museum include "Cannonball" Baker, Gen. Jimmy Doolittle, A. J. Foyt, "Big Daddy" Don Garlits, Phil Hill, Bill Muncey, Barney Oldfield and Richard Petty. The museum has on display some 40 racing and high-performance vehicles such as race cars, motorcycles and boats. Some of them are vintage vehicles and some are modern-day. Its annual induction ceremony takes place in June prior to the NASCAR Winston Cup race here in Michigan. The museum has a gift and souvenir shop which offers many items of interest to racing fans.

SHOWDOWN MUSCLE CARS (Dealer)
34165 Gratiot Av.
CLINTON TWP., MI 48035
Phone: 586-791-0777 and
586-791-9243
www.showdownmusclecars.com
Hours: M and Thurs., 10–8; Tues.,
W, and F, 10–6; Sat. 10–4

Muscle cars from the 1950s, 1960s
and 1970s are what you will find in this
progressive dealer's showroom. There
will also be some classic cars, street rods
and even a few motorcycles—some 50
vehicles in all. Showdown Muscle Cars
accepts trades, offers appraisals, will
search for vehicles of your choice and
helps with financing and shipping. The
company began operations in 1989 and
its owner, Sonny Gandee, has been in
the business for 35 years.

End of Detroit area ◀

The Alfred P. Sloan, Jr. Museum, *Flint, MI.*

THE ALFRED P. SLOAN, JR. MUSEUM
1221 E. Kearsley St. (In the Flint
Cultural Center Mall)
FLINT, MI 48503
(40 miles northwest of Detroit)
Phone: 810-237-3450
www.sloanmuseum.org
Hours: M–F 10–5, Sat.–Sun.
noon–5. Tours available.
Admission charged.

This large museum honors the man
who was the president of General Motors from 1923 to 1946, during which
time General Motors became No. 1 in
the automotive industry. The museum
has about 100 automobiles, including
a large collection of GM's experimental
cars. Only about half of the collection
is on display at any one time. Other
Flint-made automobiles are also on
display, some of them very unique
and rare. There is an exhibit honoring
William Crapo Durant, the founder

of General Motors Corp., a native of Flint. The museum hosts a "Summer Auto Fair" each June and is the site of many other auto-related activities. There are also displays on chemistry, physics, local history and a *"Temporary Gallery"* which accommodates traveling exhibits. A small 1950s-style cafe, the *"Halfway Cafe"*, is in the museum, and the museum is available for parties, meetings and other gatherings. The museum has a nice gift and souvenir shop with many interesting items.

CLASSICAUTO SHOWPLACE (Dealer)

002 84th St.
Bryon Center
GRAND RAPIDS, MI 49315
Phone: 616-301-9090
www.classicautoshowplace.com
Hours: M–F 10–6, Sat. 10–4

This dealer has a wide selection of vehicles including antique, muscle, sports, special interest cars and hot rods displayed in an attractive showroom. The company takes trades, sells on consignment, will locate specific cars, provides appraisals, and can arrange financing and shipping worldwide. You will like what you see here at ClassicAuto Showroom. The company also has a sister dealership in Madison Heights in the Detroit area.

GILMORE CAR MUSEUM

6865 Hickory Rd.
HICKORY CORNERS,

MI 49060 (15 miles northeast of Kalamazoo)
Phone: 269-671-5089
www.gilmorecarmuseum.org
Hours: *May through Oct.* M–F 9-5, Sat.–Sun. 9-6. Admission charged.

It used to be a farm, now it's a big car museum. Within its big red barns, several of which were moved here from other sites, are some 200 antique, classic and special interest vehicles. Many of the vehicles are very rare. Also on the grounds is a 1930s service station, a small town railroad station and some three miles of paved roads. When visiting the Gilmore Museum it's not uncommon to see one or more of the vehicles being driven around on the roads or an old car event in progress. The museum is host to many events in the summer. Other exhibits include a

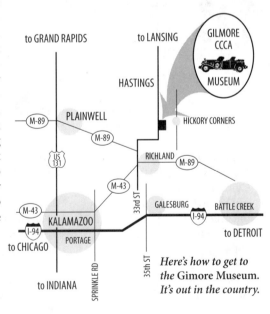

Here's how to get to the Gimore Museum. It's out in the country.

Several of the antique REO automobiles on display at the R. E. Olds Transportation Museum *in Lansing, MI.*

display of some 75 pedal cars and one of America's largest collection of automotive hood ornaments and name badges. The museum opened in 1966 and is the brainchild of Donald S. Gilmore and his wife, Genevieve. Don't miss this one; it's well worth your time.

R. E. OLDS TRANSPORTATION MUSEUM

240 Museum Dr. (down in town)
LANSING, MI 48933
(South-central part of the state)
Phone: 517-372-0529
www.reoldsmuseum.org
Hours: Tues.–Sat. 10–5, Sun. noon–5. Closed Sundays Nov.–March. Admission charged.

This is a large city-owned museum preserving the history of Lansing, and honoring automotive pioneer, Ranson E. Olds, a local resident who developed both the Oldsmobile and REO lines of automobiles. The museum has been voted one of the ten best automobile museums in the U.S. Some 30 vehicles are on display, most of which were made by Olds' companies. The oldest vehicle is an 1897 Olds Motor Wagon and there are also Star, Durant and Viking vehicles. Other exhibits include engines, a large collection of automobile wheels, machinery, vintage automobile advertising, a Lansing-built bicycle carriage, aviation materials and photos and memorabilia of the Olds family and home. The museum has a gift and souvenir shop. After you see this museum you'll be humming *"In My Merry Oldsmobile."*

MICHIGAN

WILLS SAINTE CLAIRE AUTOMOBILE MUSEUM

2408 Wills St.
MARYSVILLE, MI 48040
(55 miles northeast of downtown Detroit near Port Huron.
Phone: 810-987-2854 or 810-364-3612
Hours: *Jun.–Aug. 2nd and 4th Sun. of the month,* 1–5, *rest of year* 2nd Sun. of the month 1–5. *Group tours by appointment.* Admission charged.

Here's how to find the Wills St. Claire Automobile Museum.

Here's a good one, if you can make it during their limited hours. There are between 6 to 8 Wills St. Claire automobiles on display; some restored, some original. That's about as many Wills St. Claires that you see anywhere in the world considering that only about 80 Wills St. Claires still exist. Also on display is automobilia related to the Wills St. Claire vehicles and a replica of Henry Ford's first motorized vehicle, his "Quadricycle." The museum is available for meetings and car club events and offers automobile storage. It is located in a WW II munitions factory and is run by the local Wills St. Claire Auto Club.

C. Harold Wills was a fascinating individual. He was Henry Ford's first employee, rose to be chief designer on the Model T, and created the Ford logo still in use today. Wills left Ford in 1919 on friendly terms with a $1.5 million severance pay to start his own automobile company. There was no competition for Ford, however. Wills St. Claire automobiles sold for around $3,500 while Ford's Model Ts sold for $450.

AUTOMOTIVE HERITAGE COLLECTION AND CORVAIR MUSEUM

112 E. Cross St.
(In historic *Depot Town*)
YPSILANTI, MI 48198
Phone: 734-482-5200
www.ypsiautoheritage.org
Hours: M–F 1:30–5:30, Sat. 9:30–5, Sun noon–5. Admission charged.

This museum consists of three adjacent buildings of a 1920s-era and tends

A 1946 Hudson convertible on display at the Ypsilanti Automotive Heritage Collection. *The convertible top mechanism was manufactured in Ypsilanti.*

to favor Hudson automobiles, other orphan cars, and cars with a Ypsilanti connection. The westernmost building was used by Miller Motors, the last Hudson dealer to have operated. This is also the home of the Corvair Museum, that automobile having been made in Ypsilanti at the Willow Run Plant. There are other displays in the museum highlighting Ypsilanti's automotive history, which is considerable for a town of its size. For example, Ypsilanti is the home of the famous Willow Run Plant, built by Henry Ford during World War II to mass produce B-24 bombers on an assembly-line basis. After the war, Kai-ser-Fraser automobiles were made at the Willow Run Plant. After Kaiser-Fraser passed into history the huge Willow Run plant continued to manufacture a number of well-known General Motors vehicles including the Corvair.

The museum also has information on Preston Tucker, a Ypsilanti native, and producer of the Tucker automobile. In the museum's collection is a fiberglass Tucker used in the movie *"Tucker, The Man and His Car"*. There are other automotive displays and a gift shop. Every year the museum is host to a unique car show called "The Orphan Car Show."

▶ UPPER PENINSULA OF MICHIGAN

FORD INDUSTRIAL COMPLEX During the 1920s Henry Ford invested heavily in the western sector of the Upper Peninsula of Michigan and created a small industrial empire to provide his huge network of factories in the Detroit area with wood products, iron ore, coal, limestone and silica. Many of the wooden parts for Ford's station wagons came from this area. Much of that industry has declined today, but some of the old buildings and industrial sites can still be seen. Some are still operating businesses while others are abandoned or have been donated to worthy enterprises. Visitors interested in seeing a particular site should inquire locally as to its location and accessibility.

The cities and operations involved in the Ford industrial complex are:

ALBERTA: A sawmill. The town of Alberta was named after Alberta Johnson, the wife of one of Henry Ford's brothers-in-law.

BIG BAY: A sawmill. Ford built a hotel named "Big Bay Lodge" in the 1920s which was later sold and re-named. Parts of the movie "Anatomy of a Murder" were filmed in the hotel. An exclusive residential area existed outside Big Bay known as "The Huron Mountain Club" where many Ford executives lived.

IRON MOUNTAIN: A factory producing finished wood parts for Ford vehicles.

ISHPEMING: The "Blueberry" Iron Mine.

KINGSFORD: A sawmill, a hydro-electric plant, an automobile assembly plant and a chemical plant making charcoal briquettes out of sawdust. The "Kingsford" brand of charcoal is still popular to this day.

L'ANSE: A large lumber operation including a sawmill and a factory producing finished wood parts for Ford vehicles. This was also the site of Ford's main dock facilities.

MICHIGAMME: The "Imperial" Iron Mine.

MUNISING: A sawmill.

PEQUAMING: At one time Ford owned this entire town. Located here was a sawmill and Ford's private summer home, known as "The Bungalow". He visited the area frequently. In recent years, The Bungalow has been a bed and breakfast inn.

SIDNAW: The site of Ford's first lumbering operation in the Upper Peninsula.

RANDY HALLMAN SPECIALTY CARS
(Restorer and dealer)
N 3792 US Hwy. 2
IRON MOUNTAIN, MI 49801
(Western end of the Upper Peninsula on the Wisconsin state line)

Phone: 906-774-5897
www.randyhallmanspecialtycars.com
Hours: M–F 8–5, Sat. 9–noon.

Randy Hallman has chosen to do his old car thing in one of the most beautiful parts of the country. Randy and his crew do partial or ground-up restorations on antique vehicles, hot rods and custom cars. They specialize in Ford V-8s from 1932 to 1953. In the showroom are approximately 25 vehicles for sale, some of them restored here. The company takes trades, offers appraisals, will search for specific vehicles, arranges financing and shipping, and delivers in their own truck. In business since 1976 and car clubs are always welcome. When you come up this way, don't forget your fishing pole.

MILLIONAIRES' CARS AND DISNEY STARS MUSEUM

1498 W. US 2
ST. IGNACE, MI 49781
(At the northern end of the famous Mackinac Bridge)

Phone: 906-643-6643
Hours: Open 7 days a week during the tourist season.

According to its owners, Jim and Margaret Plouffe, this museum isn't really a museum. Instead, it's a place where visitors can touch, sit in, and even take a ride in a beautiful old car. Several of Plouffe's cars are set aside for this purpose. In this non-museum you will see classics, sports cars, hot rods along with a lot of Disney memorabilia, a second love of the Plouffe's. Mickey Mouse and Donald Duck live here part of the year. There's also a few old-timey Coke machines around that provide modern-day ice cold Coca-Colas. You can't help but have fun here at this place with the rhyming name.

MINNESOTA

FRENCH LAKE AUTO PARTS
(Salvage yard)
    3531 County Rd. 3 NW
    ANNANDALE, MN 55302
    (60 miles west-northwest of
    Twin Cities on SR 55)
    Phone: 320-274-8497 or
    320-286-2560
    www.frenchlakeautoparts.com
    Hours: Tues.–F 8–5, Sat. 8–3

There aren't many places in the country where you can see 13,000 vehicles in one place, but you can see them here. French Lake has, on their 100-acre lot, a generous assortment of makes and models from way back to the present, and they have a large selection of whole cars, some ready to drive and some ready to restore or customize. They ship parts worldwide and have personnel that speak Spanish. The company also has a nickname—"Junktown USA." The company began in 1956 which is a pretty good indicator that they'll be around for years to come.

AL'S AUTO PARTS (Salvage)
    SR 10 East (4 miles east of town)
    GLYNDON, MN 56547 (Five miles
    east of Fargo, ND off I-94)
    Phone: 218-498-2797
    Hours: M–F 10–5, Sat. noon–5,
    best to phone first.

Need a part for your Hupmobile, Crosley, Nash, Studebaker, Kaiser, Fraser or Hudson? If so, call Al's. He's got 'em on his 40-acre lot. Al's also has many vintage Fords, Chryslers and GM vehicles. There are some light trucks too, especially from the 1950s and 1960s. There are some whole cars ready for the customizer or the restorer. Al's Auto Parts was started in 1955 by Al Gardner and is now run by his son, Randy. Randy says car clubs are welcome to come and visit.

MINNESOTA'S MACHINERY MUSEUM
    County Rd. 18, one block west of
    SR 23.
    HANLEY FALLS, MN 56245
    (Southwestern part of the state
    on SR 23)
    Phone: 507-768-3522 or
    507-768-3580
    www.mnmachinerymuseum.com
    Hours: *May through Sept.*
    M–Sat. 10–4, Sun. 1–4:30. Free but
    donations requested. Handicapped
    accessible.

This is a six-acre complex comprising 5 large buildings, a camp ground and parking area. The museum buildings are full of vintage machinery and pioneer household items. There is an old time blacksmith shop, general store, farm kitchen, toys and many other items. Included in the displays are about a dozen antique cars, mostly American-made. Most of the cars are on loan from local collectors, so the displays change from time-to-time. During the second weekend in August each year when the town celebrates the "Threshing Show and Old Timers Reunion" some 50 to 70 vintage cars are on display in and around the museum. The museum is available for meetings, reunions, and other events. There is also a gift shop selling products made in Minnesota.

GREYHOUND BUS ORIGIN MUSEUM
1201 Greyhound Blvd.
HIBBING, MN 55746 (Northeastern part of the state on US 169)
Phone: 218-263-5814
http://greyhoundbusmuseum.org/
Hours: *Mid–May through* late Sept. M–Sat. 9–5, Sun. 1–5. *Rest of year* open by appointment. Admission charged.

Most people don't know it, but the Greyhound Bus Lines Company started here in Hibbing. The story of Greyhound's founding and early days is explained in this museum by pictorial displays, audio-visual presentations and a VCR show entitled "The Greyhound Story." The museum has on display 11 vintage buses beginning with a 1927 White and there are hundreds of artifact and memorabilia on display related to the bus industry. There's also one lone antique car here, a 1914 Hupmobile, with an interesting story behind it. Another display consists of a diorama illustrating how Greyhound contributed to the World War II effort. Meetings and social events are sometimes held in the museum and there is a nice gift shop.

MENAHGA AUTO SALES (Dealer)
225 Aspen Av. NW, PO Box 273
MENAHGA, MN 56464 (West-central part of the state on US 71)
Phone: 218-564-5866
E-mail: acar4u@wcta.net
Hours: M–F 9–5:30, Sat. 9–1.

When you're zipping along US 10, you might want to check out this dealership. He's just up the road a piece on US 71. The company offers a general line of antique, classic and collectible vehicles and has about 20 to 25 in stock most of the time in their nice showroom. They will also search for cars for customers, take trades, provide appraisals and help with financing and shipping. Menahga Auto Sales sells cars on consignment and has a gift shop. Tom Halverson is the owner.

▶ MINNEAPOLIS/SAINT PAUL AREA

ELLINGSON CAR MUSEUM
(Museum and dealer)
20950 Rogers Dr. (Northwest of downtown Minneapolis off I-94 at the Rogers exit)
ROGERS, MN 55374 (Northwestern suburb of Minneapolis)
Phone: 763-428-7337
www.ellingsoncarmuseum.com
Hours: Museum, Daily 10–5. Admission charged to the museum.

This is an educational museum covering the whole spectrum of the American automobile from its inception to the present. The museum's collection is arranged in chronological order beginning with the early teens and unique settings have been devised to display the cars. All told, there are about 100 cars, trucks and motorcycles on display. Some of the vehicles are for sale. Other displays include an automobilia display and a large doll collection.

Yesterday's Auto of Minneapolis offers a selection of about 35 antique vehicles for sale from this multi-story location.

The museum has a nice gift shop with hundreds of automotive-related books and a 1950s-era malt shop called *"Clarabelle's Ice Cream Parlor."* Clarabelle's is open Sat. and Sun., Memorial Day through Labor Day. Make mine a strawberry malt with whipped cream and a cherry on top!

YESTERDAY'S AUTO (Dealer)
2800 Lyndale Av. South
MINNEAPOLIS, MN 55408
Phone: 612-872-9733
www.yesterdaysauto.com
Hours: M–F 10–5, Sat. 10–2.

This dealer of antique vehicles carries a regular inventory of about 35 vehicles of mixed makes and models. The dealership is located in a building built in 1911 to house the Eklund Brothers Bus Company, the first supplier of buses to Greyhound. They usually have a good selection of classic American and British cars and light trucks and they ship worldwide. The showroom is decorated with antique automobile dealer signs and gas station signs. Yesterday's Auto, which is owned and operated by Al Hagen, can arrange transportation and financing and provide appraisals.

End of Minneapolis/Saint Paul Area ◀

WINDY HILL AUTO PARTS (Salvage)
9200 240th Av. NE
NEW LONDON, MN 56273 (40 miles southwest of Saint Cloud on SR 23)
Phone: 320-354-2201
http://www.windyhillautoparts.com/
Hours: Daily 8–5

They pack some 7,000 vehicles onto this large salvage yard which covers 160 acres. Most are American-made cars and trucks from 1915 to the mid-1980s. There is also a good selection of military trucks. Customers may browse the yard and remove their own parts. In business since 1966. Finding the yard is not easy. You may want to phone for directions.

HOOKED ON CLASSICS
(Dealer and restorer)
701 Jefferson Av. SW (SR 25)
WATERTOWN, MN 55388
(25 miles west of downtown Minneapolis midway between US 12 and SR 7)
Phone: 952-955-2706
www.hookedonclassics.com
Hours: M–F 9–5, Sat. 10–4, Sun. noon–4.
Directions: Take 494 to Hwy. 7, then take 7 west for 25 miles to Hwy. 25. Take Hwy. 25 north for 3 miles and *Hooked on Classics* will be on your left as you enter Watertown.

Classics, muscle cars, street rods, sports cars, restorables—all these can be found at Hooked on Classics. And, if you pick a restorable, the company can give you a partial or complete restoration job in their in-house restoration shop. At times, some 250 vehicles are available to choose from and the company can provide an inventory list. Hooked on Classics takes trades, helps arrange financing and shipping, provides appraisals, will search for the vehicle of your heart's desire and is well known for handling estate sales both in cars and parts. Car clubs and other interested groups are always welcome.

SCHWANKE'S MUSEUM
3310 Business Hwy. 71 South
(Across from Wal-Mart)
WILLMAR, MN 56201
(Southwestern part of state on US 71 and US 12)
Phone: 320-231-0564
E-Mail: ddikken@willmar.com

Hours: *May–Oct.* M–Sat. 1–4, rest of year by appointment. Admission charged.

You'll see a lot more than vintage cars here. There's trucks, fire trucks, tractors (lots of them) and other highway and farm equipment. Over 80 of the vehicles are automobiles. It took more than 45 years to create this collection and you can enjoy it in a little more than an hour. Also on display are gas engines, gas pumps, antique signs and other automobilia. Don't forget to check out the gift shop. It's a fun place for the whole family.

VALLEY MOTORS (Dealer)
1773 Mobile Dr. (Hwy. 61 South)
WINONA, MN 55987 (120 miles southeast of Minneapolis/Saint Paul on the Mississippi River)
Phone: 507-452-0859 or 888-452-0859 (toll free)
www.valleymotorsofwinona.com
Hours: M–F 8–6, Sat. 9–4

It is very pretty country in this part of Minnesota — on the Mississippi River. Here you will find Valley Motors, a dealer in affordable vintage vehicles. They usually have about 40 cars in stock in their indoor showroom and on an adjacent lot. The company also deals in boats, motorcycles, trailers and parts. Valley Motors provides many services; they do repairs, help arrange financing, offer appraisals, sell on consignment, take trades, provide an inventory list and will search for the vehicle you are looking for. Also on display and mostly for sale at Valley's, is a nice assortment of automobilia such as signs, books, models, etc. Free soda pop, coffee and cookies are available for car clubs and groups.

MISSISSIPPI

SANDIFER'S AUTO & TRUCK SALVAGE

6062 Osyka-Progress Rd.
MAGNOLIA, MS 39652 (Southern part of the state off I-55 just north of the Louisiana border)
Phone: 601-542-5429 and
601-542-3684
Hours: M–F 8–5, Sat. 8–noon

When you drive down to New Orleans, here's an interesting salvage yard to visit on the way. Sandifer's is easy to find and is just off I-55 in the Magnolia, MS area. It's a big place with some 1,000 vehicles scattered out so that each car is easily accessible. Customers can remove their own parts with their own tools and there are some whole cars suitable for restoring or customizing. This is a family-run business run by Norman, Dale and Darryl Sandifer. They'll be glad to see you.

BENCH MARK WORKS MOTORCYCLE MUSEUM & CAMPGROUND

3400 Earles Fork Rd.
STURGIS, MS 39769
(About midway between Tupelo and Jackson on SR 12)
Phone: 662-465-6444
www.brenchmarkworks.com
Hours: Campground open daily, museum open M–F 8–3.

Here's a very unique place. You can camp overnight and see an interesting motorcycle museum as you do. Elaine and Craig "Vech" Vechorik run the operations and are both motorcycle lovers. They specialize in pre-1970 BMW cycles, which Vech works on and restores and displays in the museum. There are a few other makes of motorcycles in the museum along with a couple antique cars. Bench Mark also stocks and sells parts for BMW motorcycles. Car clubs and, of course, motorcycle clubs are always welcome. In business since 1996.

Special note: Sturgis, MS has created a nation-wide motorcycle rally, called the *"Little Sturgis Rally,"* patterned after the big motorcycle rally held each year in Sturgis, SD. The Mississippi rally has grown by leaps and bounds in recent years and is held each August. If you like motorcycles, this is the place to be.

TUPELO AUTOMOBILE MUSEUM

1 Otis Blvd.
TUPELO, MS 38804
(Northeast corner of the state)
Phone: 662-842-4242
www.tupeloautomuseum.com
Hours: Tues.–Sun. 10–6.
Admission charged.
Directions: Exit west off Bypass US 45 onto Main St. You'll see the museum to your right.

Here's a museum that is well worth your time. It's big—120,000 sq. ft.—and

134

beautiful and designated an official Mississippi State museum. It contains about 150 vintage vehicles from all over North America and Europe. Some of the cars are very rare and others are associated with well-known people including Elvis Presley. Presley was born here in Tupelo in a two-room shack which is now something of a shrine. The museum also has an old-time service station named *"Goob's* (as in goober) *Garage"* which is complete with antique gas pumps, tools, oils cans and a weathered garage. Hanging around the museum are vintage gasoline station signs and other automobilia. There is a nice gift shop, a dining area and the museum is available for business and social events.

MISSOURI

Some 70 vintage cars are on view at Auto World Museum *along with trucks, tractors, fire trucks and many other items of interest.*

AUTO WORLD CAR MUSEUM & KINGDOM EXPO CENTER

200 Peacock Dr.
FULTON, MO 65251 (22 miles east-southeast of Columbia, MO)
Phone: 573-642-2080
www.autoworldmuseum.com
Hours: April–Nov. M.–Sat. 10–4, Sun. 12:30–4.
Admission charged.

Here is one of the finest antique car collections in the Midwest. More than 70 vintage and special-interest cars are on display in this former K-mart store with 37,000 sq. ft. of space. The oldest vehicle is an 1895 Haynes, only one of two surviving models, and that's just one of nine pre-World War I vehicles.

Also on display are vintage fire trucks, tractors, model trains, Hit and Miss engines, old tools, a miniature carnival and lots of auto-related memorabilia. Convention space and meeting rooms are available with ample free parking. There is a small theater and the museum has a fascinating gift shop with many items of interest to old car buffs. The museum started in 1996.

HARRY S TRUMAN HISTORICAL SITES of INDEPENDENCE, MO
(An eastern suburb of Kansas City)

Independence, MO was the home of President Harry S Truman and several sites significant to his life and presidency are located within the city and are

This 1941 Chrysler Royal 2-door coupe was purchased by Harry S Truman while he was still a Senator and used by him in Washington, DC throughout most of World War II.

known collectively as the ***Harry S Truman Historic Sites***. At two of these sites are automobiles that either belonged to him or were used by him as president.

At the ***Harry S Truman Library and Museum*** on the northeast edge of town at US 24 and Delaware St. are two cars: a 1941 Chrysler Royal 2-door purchased by Truman in Nov. 1940 and used by him in Washington, DC throughout most of the war when he was Senator and Vice President; a 1941 Chrysler Windsor 4-door sedan also purchased in Nov. 1940 and driven by his wife, Bess, throughout the war.

At the ***Truman Home*** on the corner of Truman Rd. and Delaware St. is a 1972 Chrysler Newport 4-door sedan. As one may guess, Truman was a "Chrysler man". This was the last car Truman purchased and his wife drove it until her death in 1982. It is still parked in their garage as it was on the day Bess died, and has 18,000 miles on the odometer. The car is kept clean, waxed and in running order.

LOST 'N THE 50s CLASSIC CARS
(Museum and dealer)
   12941 Memory Ln.
   NEOSHO, MO 64850
   (15 miles south of Joplin at junction of US 71 and SR 86)
   Phone: 417-451-8888 or
   417-850-5999
   www.lostnthe50sclassiccars.com
   Hours: M–Tues., Thurs.–F 10–6.
   Wed. 12–6. Sat. 9–1

At *Lost N the 50s* you can look at 'em or buy 'em—or both. This company carries a nice inventory of vintage cars, muscle cars, classic trucks, street rods and concentrates on Mopar products. Most of the cars are on display in their showroom.

On the selling side of the business, the company take trades, sells on consignment, locates specific vehicles for customers and can help with financing and shipping. The cars in their inventory are listed online. Dale Stanley is the General Manager.

MISSOURI

AMERICAN CLASSIC AUTOS, INC.
(Dealer)
1 Impala Ct.
PARK HILLS, MO 63601
(1 hour south of St. Louis at
junction of US 67 and SR 32)
Phone: 314-882-7000
www.americanclassicautos.com

There's mostly American-made cars at this dealership and they are beauties. American Classic Autos specializes in nice original and restored cars and light trucks. They also carry hot rods and custom vehicles, and have been known to have a few car hauler trailers. They take trades, offer appraisals, help with financing and ship worldwide. There is also a good inventory of antique car parts. Count them in when you are looking to buy your next car.

▶ SPRINGFIELD AREA

CLASSIC MUSCLE CARS (Dealer)
779 N. 20th St.
OZARK, MO 65721 (13 miles south
of Springfield on US 65)
Phone: 417-485-7569
www.classicmuscle.net/
Hours: M–F 9–5

When you're on your way to Branson, here's an interesting place to stop. As the company name implies, muscle cars are the specialty here. Walk into their nice indoor showroom, and there on the black and white checkerboard tile floor you will see beautiful examples of this segment of the antique car field. Cars you will see might include Chevelle SSs, Plymouth GTXs, Ford Mustangs, and even a few pickup trucks. The company takes trades, provides appraisals, lists their inventory on the web, and can help with shipping and financing. Then too, you might stop a second time on your way back from Branson.

PREMIER SPORTSCARS CO. (Dealer)
1950 E. Chestnut Expressway
SPRINGFIELD, MO 65802
Phone: 417-831-6065
www.premiercars.com
Hours: M–F 9–5

As you approach this dealership you will certainly notice that they have a magnificent showroom building. Inside, you will likewise find a generous collection of magnificent vintage cars. This company believes in selling vehicles with a pedigree history, high attention to details and service after the sale. All of their vehicles are stored inside under climate-controlled conditions. There is a three-bay detail area that provides concourse-quality detailing, and every newly-acquired car goes through this area and is inspected thoroughly. Premier Sportscars Co. takes trades, provides appraisals, leases cars, gives written guarantees and warranties, offers financing and shipping options. They also sell and install radar detection systems.

End of Springfield area ◀

MEMORYVILLE, U.S.A.
(Museum, restorer, dealer)
3220 N. Bishop Av. (at junction of
I-44 and US 63 north of Rolla)
ROLLA, MO 65401
Phone: 573-364-1810
www.memoryvilleusa.com
Hours: M–F 8–6, Sat. 9–6, Sun.
9–5:30. Group tours available.
Admission charged to museum.

This is a large antique car museum,
restoration facility and antique store. In
the car museum there are some 40 to
60 cars on display. Some of the cars are
for sale. Other displays in the museum
include works of art, antique engines, a
variety of storefronts representing early
20th century Rolla, and a large gift shop.
Memoryville's restoration shop is one of
the largest in the country and does partial
to complete frame-off restorations on
their own vehicles and those of others.
Visitors to the museum can watch work
in progress in the restoration shop. All
this is the brain child of George Carney,
owner. In business since the 1970s.

FAST LANE CLASSIC CARS (Dealer)
427 Little Hills Industrial Blvd.
(Just north of the intersection of
SR 370 and SR 94 north of down-
town St. Charles.)
ST. CHARLES, MO 63301
(25 miles N.W. of downtown
St. Louis off I-70)
Phone: 636-940-9969
www.fastlanecars.com

Tour Book for Antique Car Buffs

Hours: M 9:30–9, Tues.–Thurs.
9:30–6, F 9:30–7, Sat. 9:30–5.

They'll pick you up at the airport if
you wish. It's only 10 minutes away, and
your trip will be well worth it. Fast Lane
Classic Cars offers up to 140 vintage
cars, muscle cars, convertibles, light
trucks, street rods, exotics and post-1980
special interest vehicles. Motorcycles are
also to be seen here. The company takes
trades, does repairs and detailing, helps
with financing and shipping and has
a nice gift shop. David Williams and
his beautiful wife, Laura, are the proud
owners of Fast Lane Classic Cars. They
invite you to stop by.

PATEE HOUSE MUSEUM
12th & Penn Sts.
SAINT JOSEPH, MO 64503
(45 miles north of Kansas City on
the Missouri River)
Phone: 816-232-8206
www.stjoseph.net/ponyexpress/
museums.shtml
Hours: Apr.–Oct. M–F 10–5, Sun.
1–5. Feb.–Mar. and in Nov. Sat.
10–5, Sun. 1–5. Admission charged.

This is a fine local museum located
in an elegant old hotel built in 1858
which is registered as a National Historic Landmark. The museum has many
displays on the early history of the area
including exhibits on the Hannibal-St.
Joseph railroad, Pony Express artifacts
and memorabilia on the famous outlaw,
Jesse James. There is also a display of
about a half dozen antique autos including an electric car built in St. Joseph and
several old buggies. Patee House served

as Headquarters for the Pony Express in 1860 and next door is the Jesse James Home Museum where the outlaw was killed Apr. 3, 1882. Jesse's wife, mother and children stayed at the Patee House after Jesse was gunned down. Featured also are artifacts found in his grave when it was exhumed for DNA tests in 1995 to prove that the body in the grave was actually that of Jesse James.

▶ ST. LOUIS AREA

HYMAN LTD. CLASSIC CARS (Dealer)
2310 Chaffee Dr. (Near the St. Louis International Airport)
ST. LOUIS, MO 63146
Phone: 314-524-6000
www.hymanltd.com
Hours: M–F 9–5, Sat. 9:30–3:30.
Directions: Exit I-270 onto Page Ave. west. Proceed three blocks to Schultz Rd. and turn left (north). Go two blocks to Wesline Industrial Dr. and turn left (west). Proceed two blocks and turn right onto Chaffee Dr. Hyman's is straight ahead.

This company started in a 4,000 sq. ft. rented garage in 1989, but look at them now! They have a beautiful 35,000 sq. ft. facility with a wonderful showroom and restoration facilities. The company specializes in selling (and buying) pre-war classic cars, post-war American collectibles and both pre-war and post-war American and European sports cars. They are always on the lookout for the unusual. The company takes trades, accepts select consignments, offers appraisals, does repairs and restorations, arranges shipping, does estate planning with regard to vintage automobiles, offers consultation for museums and can help in financing and insurance. Mark Hyman, with assistance from buyers like you, put all of this together.

NATIONAL MUSEUM OF TRANSPORT
3015 Barrett Station Rd.
ST. LOUIS, MO 63122
Phone: Museum, 314-965-7998; information and reservations, 314-965-8008; gift shop 314-965-5709
www.museumoftransport.org
Hours: Tues.–Sun. 9–5.
Closed Mondays.
Tours available.
Admission charged.
Handicapped accessible.
Directions: Exit I-270 onto Dougherty Ferry Rd. (exit 8). Go west on Dougherty Ferry Rd. about 1 mile to Barrett Station Rd. and turn left (south). You'll see the museum on your right.

This is a large county-owned and operated museum, established in 1944, displaying a wide spectrum of transportation equipment. There are displays of locomotives and rail cars, aircraft, streetcars, buses, trucks, horse-drawn vehicles, boats and some 35 automobiles including a 1901 St. Louis automobile (built in St. Louis). The cars are located in their own building. Many smaller exhibits are also in the museum all dealing with transportation.

The larger items, such as railroad

Singer Bobby Darin's 1960 custom-built Dream Car is on display at the National Museum of Transport. *(See previous page.)*

equipment and aircraft are outside and everything is well-marked.

End of St. Louis Area ◀

DRIVIN' DREAMS (Dealer)
328 Memory Lane
SEYMOUR, MO 65746 (30 miles east of Springfield on US 60)
Phone: 417-935-4999
www.fidnet.com/-dreamin/index.htm
Hours: M–F 9–5, Sat. 9–3

If you like cars from the 1950s and 1960s, you will be in your element here. There will be plenty of examples of these vehicles in the company's showroom just waiting to find a home. Included in their inventory might be a few light trucks and hot rods. Drivin' Dream takes trades, sells on consignment,

provides appraisals, and will provide accurate information on all of their cars. They also will help with shipping and financing. You'll like being in Seymour. It's beautiful hill country.

HAPPY DAYS DREAM CARS (Dealer)
812 E. Young
WARRENBURG, MO 64093
(On US 60 fifty miles east south-east of Kansas City.
Phone: 660-422-7177
www.happycarz.com
Hours: Tues.–F 10–5:30, Sat. 10–3
Directions: Exit US 50 onto SR 13 south. Proceed to the second stop light which is Young St. Turn left (east) onto Young St. and you'll find the dealership about 6 blocks ahead

on your right.

Come by and meet John and Helen Meyer. They own and operate this interesting antique car dealership in the delightful community of Warrenburg. You'll see some 50 original classics, street rods, muscle cars, light trucks and other vehicles in their 16,000 sq. ft showroom. They do a lot of business online, so you can contact them that way too. Happy Days Dream Cars take trades, will search for vehicles and helps with shipping. By the way, John and Helen are very much in love with each other and with '57 Chevys.

WILSON MOTOR COMPANY (Dealer)
679 International Av.
WASHINGTON, MO 63090 (45 miles west of downtown St. Louis on the south shore of the Missouri River and SRs 100 and 19)
Phone: 636-239-6781
www.wilsonmotorco.com
Hours: M–F 9–5, Sat. 9–3

You can visit this dealer in your boat because Washington is on the Missouri River. Here at Wilson Motor Company you will find a grand selection of British, German, Italian and American classic cars, sports cars and special interest cars.

Some of the vehicles are rare and quite unique. The cars in their inventory are listed on their website. The company takes trades, sells on consignment, offers appraisals and can help arrange shipping and financing. The company is owned by Dennis Wilson, whose father started in the car business in 1934 and trained Dennis long and well.

DREAM CAR STORE (Dealer)
US 60/63 Junction
(Southeast of town)
PO Box 506
WILLOW SPRINGS, MO 65793
(South-central part of the state on US 60/63)
Phone: 417-469-2886
www.dreamcarstore.com
Hours: M–Sat. 9–3

You'll find this place at latitude 36:59:32 N, longitude 091:58:11 west and 1,257 ft. above sea level. You'll also find here in their showroom between 20–30 affordable-priced vintage cars, most of them muscle cars. The Dream Car Store takes trades, sells on consignment, offers appraisals and will help with shipping, finance and insurance. Chris Purvis, the owner, says car clubs are always welcome. He's been in the

MONTANA

MISSOULA AUTO SALVAGE
9905 Inspiration Dr.
MISSOULA, MT 59808
Phone: 496-542-0600
Hours: M-Sat. 8:30-5:30
Directions: Leave I-90 at Exit 96 in
Missoula. Drive south and veer left on
I-90 Business to Inspiration Dr. Turn
right and the yard is on your left.

This is Big Sky Country and also big
salvage lot country. This yard has some
6,000 vehicles spread out across the flat
Montana grass lands. Cars range in age
from the 1940s to the present—this is
a company that doesn't like to send old
cars to the crusher. There's a nice selection of 1950s-era Chevy pickup trucks
and 1960s T-Birds. Some of the cars are
whole and restorable and some of the
really good stuff is kept inside. Donavan
Russell, ex-hot rodder, is the owner.

MIRACLE OF AMERICA MUSEUM
58176 US 93 South
POLSON, MT 59860
(Northwestern Montana at the
south end of Flathead Lake)
Phone: 406-883-6804
www.cyberport.net/museum
Hours: *Memorial Day through
Labor Day* daily 8–8, *rest of
year* M–Sat. 1:30–5. Reasonable
admission charged.

The Miracle of American Museum *has something for everyone, plus antique autos.*

143

This is just a fraction of the 30,000 cars to which Freman's Auto Salvage *has access.*

Here is a very unique museum with a wide selection of displays that includes something for everyone. In all, there are 28 buildings offering displays of military vehicles and weapons, logging equipment, snow-removal equipment, pioneer and Indian artifacts, toys, dolls, musical instruments, old signs, posters, cowboy items, boats, farm equipment, horse-drawn vehicles, some 20 antique cars, about 40 antique motorcycles and a nice display of automobilia. The Miracle of America Museum has been called *"Montana's Smithsonian"* because of its wide variety of displays. Stop by and take a look; you'll like this place.

DANIELS COUNTY MUSEUM AND PIONEER TOWN

7 West County Rd.
SCOBEY, MT 59263 (Northeastern corner of the state on SR 13)
Phone: 406-487-5965 and 406-487-5559
www.scobey.org
Hours: *Memorial Day through Labor Day* daily 12:30–4:30, *rest of year* Tues. only 10–2. Admission charged.

Here is a restored pioneer town portraying early 20th-century homestead life in this part of Montana. There are many period antiques, furnishings, pieces of farming equipment, clothing and the like from that era. Also on display are some 50 antique cars and trucks. Some of the vehicles are permanent but most are on loan from local collectors so the display is ever-changing. Each June, during Scobey's Pioneer Days Festival, a Threshing Bee is held at the museum as well as a variety show, complete with dancing girls. The theatrical production is called *"The Dirty Shame Show."* It's held in the *"Dirty Shame Saloon"* on the museum grounds. The museum has a nice gift shop with lots of interesting stuff.

FREMAN'S AUTO SALVAGE

138 Kountz Rd.
WHITEHALL, MT 59759
(20 miles east of Butte on I-90)
Phone: 406-287-5436
www.fremansauto.com
Hours: M–F 8–5

Did you ever try to count to 30,000? That's how many vehicles this huge salvage company has access to on their own lots and in other locations. They can provide parts for cars from the 1940s through the 1980s and also have lots of project cars available. There's an extensive collection of Mopar parts as well as parts for muscle cars and light trucks. Freman's does some restoration work and operates its own 18-wheeler coast to coast for shipping cars. They also ship world-wide. Neil Freman and his son, Mike, are the owner-operators of the company and they've been in business since the 1980s.

NEBRASKA

CARHENGE (Curiosity)
Along US 385 north
(2.5 miles north of town)
ALLIANCE, NE 69301
(Northwest corner of the state)
Phone: 308-762-1520
(Alliance Chamber of Commerce)
www.carhenge.com

This is a very unique automotive sculpture inspired by the famous Stonehenge monument in England. Old car bodies, mostly from the 1960s, have been up-ended and partially-buried in a large circular pattern similar to the large stones at Stonehenge. The rear ends of the cars have been buried so that the headlights all point skyward. Other car bodies have been placed horizontally across pairs of partially-buried cars. Carhenge can be seen from the highway and visitors are free to park and wander around the site. There are picnic tables, educational displays and other sculptures at the site, including "Ford Seasons" which was inspired by Vivandi's "Four Seasons." This sculpture consists entirely of Fords and depicts

Nebraska's landscape seasonal changes as wheat is planted, grows, is harvested, and then the fields lie dormant during the winter months. The main sculpture was created in 1987 by local artist Jim Rienders as a memorial to his father who lived on the farm where Carhenge is located. The monument is maintained by a local group known as the Friends of Carhenge.

PLAINSMAN MUSEUM
210 16th St.
AURORA, NE 68818
(70 miles west of Lincoln on I-80)
Phone: 402-694-6531
Hours: *April 1 to Oct. 31* M–Sat.
9–5, Sun. 1–5; *rest of year* daily 1–5.
Closed Jan. 1, Easter, Thanksgiving and Dec. 25. Admission charged.

This museum, consisting of two large buildings, is devoted to preserving the local and regional heritage of the plains. There are exhibits on the plains Indians, early explorers, the first settlers and local individuals of note. In the museum are period homes including an original log

This is Carhenge, Nebraska's version of the famous Stonehenge monument in England.

cabin, a Sod house, a Victorian house and a prairie chapel. The homes are equipped with period furnishings. There are also about 20 antique autos and light trucks on display.

CHEVYLAND U.S.A. (Museum)

7245 Buffalo Creek Rd.
ELM CREEK, NE 68836 (south central part of the state off I-80)
Phone: 308-856-4208
www.classicar.com
Hours: *Memorial Day through Labor Day* daily 8–5. *Rest of year* by appointment.
Directions: Leave I-80 at Exit 257 and proceed a few yards north on US 183, then travel 1 mile east on a gravel frontage road to the museum.

This is the only exclusively Chevy Museum in the USA. When you stop here, you will see over 110 cars on display, mostly in original condition and all running. The oldest is from 1914. There are also displays of automobilia and a large hub cap collection. Somehow—no one seems to know how—a few Fords, Cadillacs and a 1928 Whippet got into the collection.

EASTERN NEBRASKA AUTO RECYCLERS (Salvage)

Mile Marker 351 on US 34,
PO Box 266
ELMWOOD, NE 68349
(22 miles east of Lincoln)
Phone: 402-994-4555 and 402-475-1135
Hours: M-F 9–6

There are approximately 1,500 cars and trucks of mixed makes in this lot in-

cluding many 1940s models. Other cars range in age up to the 1980s. Some cars are restorable. Towing and mechanical repair services offered and customer may browse the yard and car clubs are welcome. In business since 1980.

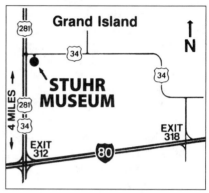

Directions to the Stuhr Museum.

STUHR MUSEUM OF THE PRAIRIE PIONEER

3133 W. US 34
GRAND ISLAND, NE 68801 (90 miles west of Lincoln on I-80)
Phone: 308-385-5316
www.stuhrmuseum.org
Hours: The Main Building and Fonner Rotunda are open daily all year long 9–5. Other exhibits open May 1 through Oct. 15. Admission charged.

This is a very large museum with some 50 buildings spread out over 200 acres of the Nebraska prairie. Each building is of historic significance and was brought here from various locations all over Nebraska. In the *Main Building*, which is a two-story museum, are many displays on the culture and times of the early settlers, an art gallery, a gift shop and a short orientation film narrated by the late Henry Fonda, a native of Grand Island. Within the complex is *Railroad Town*, a completely reconstructed town depicting a typical Nebraska small town in the late 1800s and early 1900s. In the town is the house where Henry Fonda was born. Of interest to car buffs is the Antique Farm Machinery and Auto Exhibit building which houses some 200 vehicles of all types—15 of them autos, some of them over 100 years old.

HASTINGS MUSEUM

1330 N. Burlington (US 281)
HASTINGS, NE 68901
(15 miles south of I-80 Interchange)
Phone: 402-461-4629 and
800-508-4629 (toll free)
www.hastingsmuseum.com
Hours: M 9–5, Tues.-Sat. 9–8, Sun.
10–6. Admission charged.

This museum has extensive displays on natural history, pioneer history, local Indian tribes, a 50-seat planetarium and a 200-seat large-screen-format theater. Among the many and varied exhibits are some dozen antique autos, most of them pre-World War I. Included in the collection is a 1903 Cadillac, a 1909 Sears Motor Buggy, a 1910 Brush and a 1912 Rauch and Lang Electric. There are also sizeable displays of clocks and guns. Spanish translations are provided for many of the displays. Car clubs are welcome and the museum has an interesting gift shop. The museum was founded in 1927. Teresa Hodson is the Curator.

NEBRASKA PRAIRIE MUSEUM

2701 Burlington St. (US 183 North)
HOLDREGE, NE 68949 (South-central part of the state 65 miles

southwest of Grand Island)
Phone: 308-995-5015
www.nebraskaprairie.org
Hours: M–F 9–5, Sat. 10–5,
Sun.1–5. Donations requested.

This fine museum traces the history of Phelps County and the surrounding area from pioneer days to the present. Included in the displays are about a dozen antique vehicles including a restored 1916 Ford Model T, a rare 1914 Republic truck, a 1920 Federal truck, a restored 1852 Buick and an old Dodge truck that was converted into a well-driller. There are also horse-drawn vehicles on display as well as Cushman motor scooters. The museum has what they call the *"Old Car Corner"* with a large display of automobilia. One of the premier exhibits in the museum relates to the World War II prisoner-of-war camp, Camp Atlanta, that was just southwest of town. Car clubs are welcome at the museum and if they know you are coming they just might provide a catered lunch. Angela Cooper is the Executive Director.

HEARTLAND MUSEUM OF MILITARY VEHICLES

606 Heartland Rd. (US 283)
LEXINGTON, NE 68850 (South-central part of the state on I-80)
Phone: 308-324-6329
www.heartlandmuseum.com
Hours: M–Sat. 10–5, Sun. 1–5.
Admission charged.

Have you ever seen a Downed Airman Retriever? There's one here. This vehicle was designed and built to retrieve downed airmen in snowbound areas during World War II. It's a very rare machine. Other vehicles on display are restored Jeeps, military trucks, military ambulances and half-tracks. Some of the vehicles were used by local farmers after World War II when tractors were scarce, but there was a surplus of military vehicles. In all, there are about 60 vehicles. The museum has a project to restore most of the vehicles and make them operative. There is also an extensive library on military vehicles.

HAROLD WARP PIONEER VILLAGE (Museum)

Junction US 6/34 and SR 10
(12 miles south of I-80 exit 279)
MINDEN, NE 69859
(South-central part of state 43 miles southwest of Grand Island)
Phone: 308-832-1811 and
800-445-4447 (toll free)
www.pioneervillage.org
Hours: Daily 8–sundown.
Admission charged.

This is a very large museum and village complex with the main theme being *"See How America Grew."* Thousands of items are displayed in chronological order so that the visitor can see the progress and developments through the years. There are displays of farm equipment, airplanes, toys, bicycles, motorcycles, electric lighting, musical instruments and an unusual exhibit of seven generations of rooms including kitchens, living rooms and bedrooms. Of primary interest to antique car buffs is the museum's collection of some 350 antique cars, most of which are pre-1930. They are housed in three separate buildings in the Pioneer Village, which is adjacent to the main museum building. The Village consists of more than 25 historic building, each with its own unique display. In addition to cars, the antique car buff will be interested in the Fire House which displays several antique fire trucks; the Antique Tractor and Truck Building which has vintage tractors, trucks, engines, etc.; the Antique Farm Machinery Building which has antique farm equipment; and the Livery Stable which has many horse-drawn vehicles. The museum complex also has a motel, restaurant, snack bar and a campground. In the museum is a gift shop with many interesting items.

CLASSIC AUTO SALES (Dealer)

10848 Blondo St.
OMAHA, NE 68164
Phone: 402-496-0123
www.classicautosales.com
Hours: M–F 9–6, Sat. 9–3
Directions: Exit I-680 at SR 64.
Proceed west on SR 64 for 1 block to 108th St, go south on 108th to Blondo St., turn right (west) and Classic Auto Sales will be in sight.

You'll find top-of-the-line antique vehicles for sale at this fine dealership; exotics, sports cars,

Watch for the unique signs that lead to the Harold Warp Pioneer Village.

149

NEBRASKA

luxury vehicles and some motorcycles. The company prides itself in being able to find the vehicle of your dreams. They have numerous contacts in this regard. They take trades, buy outright, offer leases, aid with shipping and financing and can provide extended warranties. In business since the 1970s.

NEVADA

CAR MUSEUM AT ST. JUDE'S RANCH FOR CHILDREN

US Highway 93
BOULDER CITY, NV 89005
(20 miles southeast of Las Vegas
on US 95 and US 93)
Phone: 800-492-3562 (toll free)
www.stjudesranch.org
Museum Hours: daily 9-6,
donations requested.

Here's a way to have fun and help kids at the same time. St. Jude's Ranch for Children cares for abandoned, abused and neglected children and has, on its campus, a car museum with some 20 world-class antique vehicles on display. Some of the vehicles are on loan from local owners so the exhibit changes from time-to-time. The museum also has automobilia and a sizeable collection of automotive art. There is a gift shop which, like the museum itself, is run by volunteers. You'll feel good when you walk out of this museum.

PONDEROSA RANCH
(Attraction)
100 Ponderosa
Ranch Rd.
(SR 28)
**INCLINE
VILLAGE**, NV
89451

(North end of Lake Tahoe)
Phone: 775-831-0691
www.ponderosaranch.com
Hours: Mid-Apr.-Oct. 31 daily
8-9:30. Admission charged.

This is a large western theme park built around the original television set of the ranch house used on the long-running television show "Bonanza". The Bonanza ranch house is open to the public and provides information and memorabilia related to the production of the show. Other buildings and structures in the park consist of an old time saloon, general store, frontier chapel, mystery mine, petting zoo, playground, kiddyland, prop lots and other attractions. There are several museums on the grounds and displayed in them and on the grounds are some 50

The Car Museum *at* St. Jude's Ranch for Children *in* Boulder City, NV.

151

These two restored antique GMC trucks are part of the sizeable collection of antique vehicles at the **Ponderosa Ranch.**

antique cars and trucks. At the northern end of the park is a significant collection of military vehicles in an open lot. There is also a large collection of wagons and other horse-drawn vehicles. The park has several restaurants and gift and souvenir shops. It's a fun place for the whole family.

CLASSIC AUTO EXHIBITION HALL
(Museum)
Laughlin's Riverside Resort
Hotel & Casino
1650 Casino Way
LAUGHLIN, NV 89029
(Southernmost tip of Nevada
on the Colorado River)

Phone: 702-298-2535 and
800-227-3849 (toll free)
www.riversideresort.com
Hours: Auto Exhibition Hall:
Sun.–Thurs. 9 a.m.–10 p.m.,
F–Sat. 9 a.m.–11 p.m. Free.

This fine collection of antique vehicles will be found at Laughlin's Resort Hotel & Casino in Laughlin. There are some 70 cars in the collection along with a collection of vintage motorcycles. Some of these vehicles are associated with well-known people. A few are for sale and others are on loan from local collectors. Mark Osborn is the museum's curator.

▶ LAS VEGAS AREA

THE AUTO COLLECTIONS (Museum-
Dealer)
Imperial Palace Casino complex
(5th floor of the parking structure)
3535 Las Vegas Blvd. South
LAS VEGAS, NV 89109

Phone: 702-794-3174
www.autocollections.com
Hours: Daily 9:30 a.m.–9:30 p.m.
Admission charged.

"Our goal is to provide for the collector

a place to visit in a relaxed atmosphere, to buy, sell, or trade some of the most desired vehicles in the world." This is what the owners and operators of The Auto Collections say of their operation—and it says it well. Gathered here in one of largest antique auto museums in the world, some 125,000 sq. ft., are over 250 of the most exotic, most rare and most desirable vehicles on the planet. And most of them are for sale. But you are also invited to just go in and look around. You will also see motorcycles and boats on display. This is one of the top tourist attractions in Las Vegas. The very knowledgeable staff can discuss every vehicle in detail, giving you its history and background. Many of the cars are associated with famous people. Since the cars come and go, the collection is ever-changing so multiple visits are worthwhile. There is also a well-stocked gift shop. If you like, The Auto Collections can arrange complete packages for your stay in Las Vegas including lodgings, dining and admissions to other attractions. Car clubs and groups are most welcome and can be provided for in the same manner.

CLASSIC & COLLECTIBLE CARS
(Dealer)
> 3542 Siris Av.
> *LAS VEGAS*, NV 89102
> Phone: 702-873-2222
> www.classiccarslasvegas.com
> Hours: M-F 10-5, Sat. 10-2.

After you make that big killing at the roulette table, drop by this antique car dealer and buy yourself a nice antique car. They offer a wide variety of collectible cars from their indoor 10,000 sq. ft. showroom. Most cars are in the affordable range and there is an average of some 40 vehicles on display at all times. An inventory list is available. The company will buy cars, sell on consignment, take trades, arrange transportation and do appraisals. The dealership has been owned and operated by the Nicholl family since 1982.

The Harley-Davidson Cafe *in Las Vegas, NV. (See next page.)*

NEVADA

HARLEY-DAVIDSON CAFE

3725 Las Vegas Blvd. South
(In the heart of the Strip)
LAS VEGAS, NV 89109
Phone: 702-740-4555
www.harleydavidsoncafe.com

If you would like to eat good food and look at beautiful motorcycles at the same time, this is the place to go. As its name implies, this is a restaurant with the Harley-Davidson motorcycle theme. A very unique moving assembly line, hanging from the ceiling, slowly travels around the restaurant carrying real motorcycles. The walls are covered with photos, documents and other displays. And the menu is a thing of joy. You can start off with a cocktail from the bar—a *"Wheelie"* or perhaps a *"Malibu Low Rider."* Then, for the main course, you can select a *"The Harley Hog"* or *"Harley Hero"* sandwich, or *"Harley Texas Style Beef Chili,"* or one of several *"Side Cars."* And

you can top it all off with a *"Tank full of Sundae."* Bon Appetit and *Vroooom!*

THE LIBERACE MUSEUM

1775 E. Tropicana Av.
LAS VEGAS, NV 89109
Phone: 702-798-5595 and
800-626-2625 (toll free)
www.liberace.com
Hours: M-Sat. 10-5, Sun.
Admission charged.

This museum, consisting of two buildings, is devoted to the memory of the late entertainer, Liberace. Among the many items on display that belonged to this popular showman are about half a dozen of his personal cars, including a customized Duesenberg covered with rhinestones. Most of the cars were used in his performances. There is also a collection of rare pianos and Liberace's elaborate costumes. The museum has

This is one of the cars in the Liberace Museum, his Bicentennial Rolls-Royce.

The Shelby assembly plant and museum *in Las Vegas, NV.*

a cafe and an elegant gift shop selling many Liberace-related items including copies of some of his glitzy jewelry.

CARROLL SHELBY MUSEUM AND ASSEMBLY PLANT

6755 Speedway Blvd. (At the entrance to the Las Vegas Motor Speedway on the north side of town.)
LAS VEGAS, NV 89115
Phone: 702-643-3000
Hours: M-F 8-5. Tours offered at 10:30 a.m. and 3:30 p.m. Free.

Here's where they assemble the fa-mous Shelby sports cars. Housed in the same facility is the Shelby Museum, which displays some of the vehicles assembled here and earlier models of the famous Shelby marques such as the Cobras and Shelby Mustangs. Nearly all of the cars are from Carroll Shelby's personal collection. Visitors can tour the factory floor and watch the current-day Shelbys being assembled. Personnel are on hand to conduct the tours, explain the features of the various models, and answer questions. There is also a pleasant gift shop offering Shelby-related items.

End of Las Vegas area ◀

WHISKY PETE'S HOTEL-CASINO

Off I-15 at the Nevada/California state line
PO Box 19119
PRIMM, NV 89019-9119
Phone: 702-382-1212 and 800-386-7867 (toll free)

www.bonnielovesclyde.com
Hours: Open 24 hours a day, 7 days a week.

In the lobby of this Hotel-Casino is the famous "Bonnie and Clyde" death car, a 1934 Ford V-8 four-door in

155

The Bonnie & Clyde death car is on display at **Whiskey Pete's Hotel-Casino** *24 hours a day, 7 days a week.*

which the two notorious outlaws were ambushed and killed. The car is original and unrestored and has 167 bullet holes in it.

▶ RENO AREA

NATIONAL AUTOMOBILE MUSEUM (The Harrah Collection)

10 Lake St. South (Near downtown Reno)
RENO, NV 89501
Phone: 775-333-9300
www.automuseum.org
Hours: M-Sat. 9:30-5:30, Sun. 10-4.
Admission charged.

This is one of the most famous automobile collections in the world. It was begun by the late Reno businessman William F. "Bill" Harrah and still bears his name. Harrah collected and restored antique, classic and special-interest autos for over 40 years in his own restoration shop in nearby Sparks,

The **National Automobile Museum,** *Reno, NV.*

NV. After Harrah's death in 1987, a generous selection of the most rare and unique vehicles were donated to the National Automobile Museum (The Harrah Collection). Today there are over 220 cars in the museum, which are displayed in galleries and period street scenes depicting each quarter of the 20th Century. Some of the vehicles are associated with famous people. There are lots of automobilia items on display and the museum has a research library, a multimedia theater, a very nice gift shop and a cafe.

SPORTHAUS MOTOR CARS (Dealer)
9732 S. Virginia St.
RENO, NV 89511
Phone: 775-329-1447
www.sporthausinc.com
Hours: M-F 9-5.

Directions: Exit US 395 at S. Meadows Pkwy. Proceed west on S. Meadows Pkwy. three blocks to S. Virginia St. Turn left (south) onto S. Virginia St. and Sporthaus Motor Cars is about 200 yards ahead on the east side of the street.

When you walk into this dealer's elegant showroom, you will see on the outside of the building such names as Porsche, Mercedes-Benz, Audi and the like—and—that's what you'll see inside. Here are some of the finest examples of high-quality vintage sports and luxury cars to be seen anywhere. The company does service work, sells parts, takes trades, helps with shipping and will search for specific vehicles. Happy browsing!

End of Reno area ◀

NEW HAMPSHIRE

CLASSIC CARS OF NEW ENGLAND
(Dealer)
714 Daniel Webster Hwy.
MERRIMACK, NH 03054
(Southern part of the state midway between Nashua and Manchester.)
Phone: 603-262-2002
www.classiccarsofne.com
Hours: M–F 9–5, Sat. 9–3

American muscle cars, Corvettes, collectibles, special-interest cars... that's what you find here in this New Hampshire dealership. They are not only sellers of such vehicles, but are active buyers who offer top dollar for the really good stuff. The company takes trades, sells on consignment, provides appraisals, does service and repair work, arranges financing, insurance and shipping. Bring your fishing pole; they're right near the Merrimack River.

NEW JERSEY

SPACE FARMS ZOO AND MUSEUM

218 County Rd. 519
(in Beemerville)
BEEMERVILLE, NJ 07461
(Northwestern corner of
the state west of Sussex)
Phone: 973-875-5800
www.spacefarms.com
Hours: *May 1 through Oct. 31*
daily 9–5. Admission charged.

This 100-acre, 11-building complex
houses a zoo with over 500 animals,
including a petting zoo and an animal
nursery which are big hits with the kids.
There is an agricultural museum with
antique farm equipment, sleighs, wagons and Indian artifacts, and an antique
car museum. In the car museum are
some 50 vintage cars, mostly pre-1940,
and a collection of antique motorcycles
and bicycles. Other buildings house a
collection of antique weapons, a doll
collection, a blacksmith shop and a
children's toy collection. Food is available and there is a picnic area. The
museum also has a well-stocked and
interesting gift shop.

THE STABLE, LTD. (Dealer)

217 Main St.
GLADSTONE, NJ 07934
(25 miles east of downtown
Newark)
Phone: Sales 908-234-2055;
Service 908-234-1755
www.stableltd.com

Hours: M–F 9–6, Sat. (sales only)
9–5

Prime examples of fine European and
American cars are the big thing at The
Stable. You'll find some 50 top-quality
vintage machines offered for sale in their
two showrooms. An inventory list is
available upon request. The company
does its own service work in addition to
work for customers. The Stable will take
trades, sell on consignment, provide
appraisals, assist in arranging financing
and shipping, provide storage, search
for specific vehicles and arrange leases.
Car clubs are most welcome and Italian
is spoken here. Tom Rossiter is the
president and founded the company in
1973 in a stable.

KUSER FARM MANSION

(Historic home)
2090 Greenwood Av.
HAMILTON, NJ 08650 (Eastern
suburb of Trenton)
Phone: 609-890-3630
www.fieldtrip.com
Hours: *May through Nov.*
Thurs.–Sun. 11–3; *Feb. through
Apr.* Sat.–Sun. 11–3 only. Last
tour starts at 2:30 pm. Free.

This 17-room 1892 mansion was the
"Country Home" and estate of the late
Fred Kuser, a prominent New Jersey
businessman. The Kuser family was
instrumental in forming the Fox Film

159

Corporation which, after a merger, became 20th-Century-Fox. The Kuser family, along with the Roebling family, manufactured the Mercer automobile. Scattered throughout the museum are photos and memorabilia of the Mercer Motor Car Company. Most of the mansion's rooms are open to the public, including Kuser's private projection room. The formal gardens and the many out-buildings can be visited by taking the self-guided walking tour.

UNIQUE AUTO & TRUCK (Salvage)
470 Chandler Rd.
JACKSON, NJ 08527
(20 miles east of Trenton at junction of SRs 528 and 571)
Phone: 732-363-0677 and
973-332-5130
Hours: M–F noon–6, Sat. 9–6

There is no vehicle in this yard newer than 1975, and there's some 2,000 of them. Unique Auto & Truck specialize in American-made vehicles including many orphans. There is a good selection of light trucks and vans and some whole cars available for restoration. The company prides itself in giving fair and honest descriptions of parts and vehicles. Car clubs are welcome. In business since 1998.

FUTURE CLASSICS (Dealer)
1165 SR 88 West
LAKEWOOD, NJ 08701 (18 miles southwest of Long Branch)
Phone: 732-370-8800
www.futureclassicsnj.com
Hours: M–Sat. 9–9

This is one of the larger antique car dealers on the east coast offering up to 100 muscle cars, classic, exotic, street rods and motorcycles for sale in their new and modern showroom. Celebrity cars are sometimes available. Future Classics actively buys cars, sells on consignment, arranges financing and transportation and has a substantial business in leasing antique cars. The company has a facility for light restoration work and an interesting gift shop.

In business since 1988.

C & C AUTO SALES, INC. (Dealer)
613 St. Mihiel Dr.
RIVERSIDE, NJ 08075
(Opposite Philadelphia on US 130)
Phone: 856-764-9300
www.ccautosales.com
Hours: M–F 9–5.

C & C Auto Sales is a family owned and operated establishment specializing in antique and classic cars, muscle cars and hot rods. They also offer project cars for the more ambitious customers. The company motto is "The Original Home of the Oldies" and the cars are housed in a warehouse-like indoor display. The company takes trades, sells on consignment, buys cars and will help with transportation. Come in and take a look.

BLACKTIECLASSICS.COM (Dealer)
6 South Rt. 30 E. White Horse Pike
STRATFORD, NJ 08084 (20 minutes east of Philadelphia)
Phone: 856-309-8808
www.blacktieclassics.com
Hours: M–Sat. 9–6

There's about 35 cars in this dealer's showroom most of the time and another 50 in the warehouse. Behind the warehouse is a boneyard of restorable cars. That makes for a nice selection of classic cars, hot rods, imports, convertibles, trucks and other collectibles here at Blacktieclassics.com. Pontiac GTOs are a specialty and the company normally carries about 30 in stock. Their growing inventory of Chevy muscle cars is a close second. The company takes trade-ins, offers leases, sells on consignment, provides service and restoration, and can help with transportation and financing. They will also search the marketplace for specific cars. If you like to keep your car nice and shiney, they offer a specially-made cleaner and polish called Black Gold.

RITT JONES USED AUTO PARTS (Salvage)
780 Oak Grove Rd.
SWEDESBORO, NJ 08085
(South of Philadelphia on the New Jersey Turnpike)
Phone: 609-467-4644
Hours: M–F 9–5:30, Sat. 9–2
Directions: From the junction of US 322 and US 130 head north on US 130 ¼ mile then turn right onto Barker Rd. which dead ends into Rt 44. Turn left onto Rt. 44 then proceed to Rt. 671 (Oak Grove Rd.) The yard is ¼ mile ahead just before the I-295 underpass.

As the sign says, this is Ritt Jones' place. Ritt has a well-organized salvage yard with some 2,000 vehicles ranging from the 1940s to the 1970s. The different makes of cars are grouped together. The Chevys are over there, the Mustangs are down that way and the T-birds are back yonder. Ritt doesn't like to see good parts destroyed by the crusher, so he hangs on to the old stuff. This is a pull-it-yourself yard, but Ritt will do it if you wish.

MUSCLECAR GARAGE (Dealer)
1107 SR 23 South (Also US 202)
WAYNE, NJ 07470 (6 miles west of downtown Paterson)
Phone: 973-694-9400
www.musclegarage.com
Hours: M–F 9–5, Sat. 9–3

You can see them through the big glass windows as you approach this dealer's showroom - muscle cars - some 20 of them. They range from the 1930s to the 1970s and all are turn key ready to drive away. There are nice original cars and cars that have been meticulously restored. The people at Musclecar Garage want the experience of purchasing a car from them to be nothing but pure fun. The company will locate vehicles, sell on consignment, take trades, lease cars and aid in financing and shipping. They can also provide references. If you like, you can put your name on their mailing list and they will keep you informed as their inventory changes.

161

NEW MEXICO

 New Mexico is one of the states that has made an active effort to preserve parts of historic highway US 66. I-40 parallels US 66 in many places and the old stretches of US 66 are currently being used as frontage roads, especially in eastern New Mexico near the Texas state line. In *Gallup* the city fathers have made efforts to preserve many of the old buildings along the section of US 66 that ran thru their town. This is being done both for historical preservation and because the buildings and road are often used by the movie and TV industries as filming locations.

NORTH 54 SALVAGE, INC.

7066 US 54 North
PO Box 387
ALAMAGORDO, NM 88310
(South-central part of the state 80 miles north of El Paso, TX)
Phone: 800-624-4941 and
505-437-4188
www.north54salvage.com
Hours: M–F 8–5, Sat. 8–noon

It is hot and dry in this part of the country and car parts, along with many other things, last a long time. You will find that true with parts from North 54 Salvage. They have about 2000 vehicles on their 25-acre lot from the late 1930s to the present. They have a goodly number of convertibles, hardtops, wagons and pickups. Furthermore, there's an inventory of large trucks and military vehicles from the 1950s and 1960s. They also have whole cars suitable for restoration. Customers may roam the yard and remove their own parts with permission. Car clubs are welcome. Important! Wear proper attire for tall grass and desert conditions. George Smith and his pretty daughter, Amy, run the show here, partner. In business since 1947.

▶ ALBUQUERQUE AREA

DISCOUNT AUTO PARTS (Salvage)

4703 Broadway SE
ALBUQUERQUE, NM 87105
Phone: 505-877-6782 and
800-748-1537
www.car-parts.com/dealersaz.shtml
Hours: M–F 8–5:30, Sat 8–1.

This is a large salvage yard with approximately 1400 vehicles specializing in

Volkswagens from day one to the present. New Volkswagen parts also offered and Discount Auto will search for parts. Car clubs are welcome and Spanish is spoken here. In business since 1967.

J & R VINTAGE AUTO MUSEUM
(Museum and dealer)
3650 SR 528 (½ mile south of Hwy 44 on Hwy 528)
RIO RANCHO, NM 87124
(A northern suburb of Albuquerque)
Phone: 505-867-2881
www.jrvintageautos.com
Hours: *Summer* M–Sat. 10–6, Sun. 1–5, *winter* M–Sat. 10–5. *Closed Sun. November through April.*
Admission charged to the museum.

Here is a very interesting place for old car buffs. In the front of the building is a large automobilia store selling die cast models, books and many other auto-related items. In the back is a 60-car museum, and out further in the back yard are vehicles awaiting restoration by J & R's own restoration shop. Many of the cars in the museum are for sale. There are also displays of Cushman motor scooters and construction equipment in the museum. As the vehicles come and go, the display is ever changing. Car clubs are always welcome here.

UNSER RACING MUSEUM
1776 Montano NW
ALBUQUERQUE, NM 87105
Phone: 505-341-1776
www.unserracingmuseum.com
Hours: Daily 10–4, admission charged.

Everyone who follows racing knows of the Unsers; Al, Bobby, Little Al, Jerry, Al III and Jason Tanner. Here's where they keep their trophies, old race cars and other memorabilia. Exhibits in this 13,000 sq. ft. museum trace the Unser's racing careers from the Pike's Peak Hill Climb to the Indy 500 which, together, they won 9 times. Unser family member, team members, mechanics and others are also identified and honored in the museum. Displays go back to the time when family patriarch Jerry Unser opened his garage on US 66—in 1936—and a Design and Engineering gallery traces the progress of race car design. After visiting this museum, you will feel that you know the Unsers personally. They are really down-to-earth folks.

End of Albuquerque Area

DEMING LUNA MIMBRES MUSEUM
301 S. Silver St.
DEMING, NM 88030 (Southwest corner of the state on I-10)
Phone: 505-546-2382
Hours: M–Sat. 9–4, Sun. 1:30–4. Closed Thanksgiving and Dec. 25. Donations requested.

This museum contains exhibits pertaining to the history of the southwest, the Mimbres Indians, cowboy memorabilia, pioneer artefacts such as clothing, household items, quilts, dolls, mounted animals, room furnishings and a re-creation of a 19th-century funeral home. Artefacts from the Mimbres Indians

This is the War Eagle Museum's *immaculately restored 1936 Packard Super 8 Roadster.*

include pottery, clothing, baskets, tools and weapons. The museum also has an annex devoted to historic transportation which includes a small collection of antique vehicles, military vehicles and fire trucks displayed in period street scenes.

WAR EAGLE AIR MUSEUM

2012 Airport Rd. on the grounds of the Santa Terese Airport. (Exit 11 from I-10, go west) *SANTA TERESA*, NM 88008 (A western suburb of El Paso, TX) Phone: 505-589-2000 www.war-eagle-air-museum.com

Hours: Tues.–Sun. 10–4.
Admission charged.

This is a fine and spacious air museum dedicated to preserving, restoring and flying military aircraft from the World War II and Korean War eras. Mixed in with the many aircraft and other displays are a number of military vehicles and more than a dozen civilian antique autos. All of the cars are in running condition. The War Eagle Museum also conducts educational programs and has special exhibits from time-to-time. There is a large gift shop offering auto-related, air-related and military-related items.

NEW YORK

▶ BUFFALO AREA

BUFFALO HARLEY-DAVIDSON
(Distributor and museum)
    4220 Bailey Av. (SR 62)
    AMHERST, NY 14226
    (Northeastern suburb of Buffalo)
    Phone: 716-832-7159
    www.buffaloharley.com
    Hours: M–Sat. 9–6. Free.

Here's a place where you can buy a used or a brand new shiny motorcycle and just look at the old ones, or both. This is a Harley-Davidson dealership with its own museum. The museum is adjacent to the business part of the enterprise and is open to the public. There are about 35 vintage motorcycles on display and others that come and go, so the display is ever-changing. Some of the bikes are classics and very rare. The walls of the museum are decorated with photos, artifacts and other Harley memorabilia. Both motorcycle clubs and car clubs are welcome. The business, here and at other locations, has been operating since 1922.

**THE BUFFALO TRANSPORTATION
PIERCE-ARROW MUSEUM**
    263 Michigan Av. at 201 Seneca St.
    BUFFALO, NY 14203
    Phone: 716-853-0084
    www.pierce-arrow.com

Hours: F & Sat. noon–5. Open some Sundays. Admission charged.

How many Pierce-Arrows have you seen in your lifetime? Here's your chance to catch up. How about Thomas Flyers—seen any of those lately? Both were manufactured in Buffalo. When you visit this new museum, which is in the heart of the old transportation center in downtown Buffalo, you will see lots of Pierce-Arrows and a smaller collection of Thomas Flyers. Many of the vehicles are in restored condition. You will also see lots of artifacts and memorabilia related to the two companies along with memorabilia from other Buffalo-area automotive manufacturers. Not only did they make automobiles in Buffalo, but they made trucks, automobile bodies, motorcycles, bicycles, radiators, windshield wipers and more. Associated with this large non-profit museum is a very interesting filling station designed by the famous architect, Frank Lloyd Wright in the late 1920s, but never built—until now. The station has a "living room" for customers waiting for their cars to be serviced, gasoline storage tanks on the roof, totem poles and signs identifying it as a Tydol Oil Company station. They like to say at the museum that *"The Buffalo Transportation Pierce-Arrow Museum has the WRIGHT stuff."* The museum and the service station are the results of the efforts of James T. Sandoro, a local business man and a long-time Pierce-Arrow collector.

TERRY YOUNG'S CLASSIC CAR CENTER (Dealer)

5110 Camp Rd.
BUFFALO, NY 14075
Phone: 716-649-6400 or
877-302-5291 (toll free)
www.tycc.net
Hours: M–Sat. 9–6:30

You can have a lot of fun here at Terry Young's place. There are lots of beautiful antique and classic cars and trucks in the showroom and on the lot. Most of the cars are American-made and range from the 1920s and up. The company takes trades, sells on consignment, provides appraisals, offers a video of their cars that they send by mail, and assists with financing and shipping. The company also participates in an annual car auction each September.

End of Buffalo area ◄

CORVETTE AMERICANA HALL OF FAME (Museum)

SR 38 South (3 miles south of Cooperstown)
COOPERSTOWN, NY 13326 (50 miles west of Schenectady at the southern end of Lake Otsego)
Phone: 607-547-4135
http://www.vettenet.org
Hours: *March 1 through Oct. 31*

daily 9–6, *longer hours in the summer* time, closed *rest of year.* Admission charged.

This 30,000 sq. st. museum traces the history of the Corvette automobile from its beginning to the present. The museum has 35 Corvettes displayed in chronological order and each car is integrated into a color co-ordinated Hollywood-type set

The Indy Festival car is one of the displays at the **Corvette Americana Hall of Fame** *in Cooperstown, NY.*

of a famous American landmark such as Mt. Rushmore, the Alamo, Gateway Arch and Niagara Falls. At each display there is a multi-media show with music, TV, movies, sports, news events, commercials and personalities corresponding with the year of the car. Visitors walk through a time tunnel and into time capsules representing a particular year. The museum has a large display room featuring every Corvette sales brochure, postcard, plastic model, magazine, ad, promo model and owner's manual ever made. There are also memorabilia displays of pop culture celebrities such as the Beatles, James Dean, Marilyn Monroe and others. Yet another room is an old-time theater displaying cars featured in the Corvette-oriented movies *"Corvette Summer"* and *"Death Race 2000"*. Behind the theater is a re-creation of the famous Indy 500 racetrack with Corvette pace cars of 1978, 1986 and the Indy Festival car of 1990.

STONEBRIDGE MOTOR COMPANY
(Dealer and restorer)
 363 E. Market St. extension
 CORNING, NY 14830
 (On US 15 and SR 17 east of
 Elmira and just north of the
 Pennsylvania state line)
 Phone: 607-738-9605
 www.stonebridgecars.com
 Hours: M–F 9–5, Sat. 9–3

European sports cars, American classics, vintage competition cars and Superformance MK III Roadsters are the specialty at this dealer and restorer. Examples of their restored vehicles are on display and for sale in their showroom. Occasionally, they will have vintage motorcycles to offer. Stonebridge Motor Company has a world-wide buying

service for the enthusiast and collector of fine automobiles; they sell parts, lease storage space and sell original photography and art work by noted motorsports artists Bob Gillespie and Robert Tariach. While you are in the area, you might want to visit the famous Watkins Glen Grand Prix Race Track which is nearby.

PLATINUM CLASSIC MOTORCARS
(Restorer and dealer)
 108 Lincoln Pkwy.
 E. ROCHESTER, NY 14445
 Phone: 716-248-0580
 www.platinumclassics.com
 Hours: M–F 9–5, Sat. 9–3

This company is dedicated to the restoration of a wide range of antique vehicles, brass era automobiles, classic cars, muscle cars and high-performance cars. Most of the work is done in-house. The company offers top quality workmanship and reasonable prices. Some of the cars they restore are for sale in their showroom. They take cars on consignment, sell parts, and help with transportation.

AUTOSPORT DESIGN, INC. (Dealer)
 203 West Hills Rd.
 HUNTINGTON STATION, NY
 11746 (On Long Island 10 miles
 east of Queens on SR 25A)
 Phone: 631-425-1555
 www.autosportdesigns.com
 Hours: M–F 9–5, Sat. 9–3

This is a big dealership specializing in quality imports and vintage vehicles. In their spacious showroom one will find a nice selection of cars which might include Aston Martins, Ferraris, Porsches and other top-of-the-line cars. Behind the showroom is a 6,500 sq. ft. workshop and service center with a machine shop, a body shop, a maintenance center and a tuning center which tests and confirms that your car will get the highest level of performance. The company takes trades, offers appraisals, sells parts, has an interesting photo gallery, aids in shipping and financing and offers storage.

THE FRANKLIN D. ROOSEVELT LIBRARY, MUSEUM & HOME

Albany Post Rd. (US 9)
HYDE PARK, NY 12538
(Halfway between New York City & Albany on the Hudson River)
Phone: 845-229-9115 or
845-229-2502 (Sat. & Sun.)
www.fdrlibrary.marist.edu
Hours: Daily 9–5. Closed Jan. 1, Thanksgiving, Dec. 25.
Admission charged.

This is the home and 200-acre estate of President Franklin D. Roosevelt. It is now a National Historic Site with a presidential library and a museum. Among the many belongings of the President on display is a 1938 Ford 4-door convertible with special hand controls that he used to get around this estate and the local area. Roosevelt's legs were crippled by polio when he was a young man and he could not use them to drive.

BRITISH AUTO (Salvage)

703 Penfield Rd.
MACEDON, NY 14502 (15 miles east-southeast of Rochester)
Phone: 315-986-3097 and
800-458-4575 (toll free)
www.britishauto.com
Hours: M–F 8–5.

This interesting salvage yard specializes in British-made cars only from 1950 to the present. In the yard one will find Austins, Austin-Healys, Jaguars, Jensens, Lotuses, MGs, Triumphs, TVRs, English Fords, Sunbeams and others. There are some 800 cars total and the company has parts from another 400 dismantled vehicles. Some whole cars are available for restoration or for parts cars. British Auto has new and NOS parts, imported parts, a parts locator service and a complete repair service. They also sell car manuals and have an extensive reference library. Car clubs are welcome and visitors may browse the yard. In business since 1975.

▶ NEW YORK CITY AREA

When in **NEW YORK CITY**, many people visit *Times Square*. This was the official eastern terminus of the famous **Lincoln Highway** that crossed America in the early days of automobile travel. The Highway, officially sanctioned in 1921, crossed 12 states, covered 3,389 miles and terminated in San Francisco, CA. Ironically, the length of the Lincoln Highway in New York state was only about one mile long. It traveled west along 42nd St. to the Hudson River, then automobiles were carried by ferry to *Weehawken, NJ*. From there, the highway continued westward.

CHRYSLER BUILDING
405 Lexington Av.
(in downtown New York City
between 42nd and 43rd Sts.)
NEW YORK, NY 10174-0002

Walter P. Chrysler was a man who thought big and this building is a perfect example of that thinking. In the late 1920s, two new "skyscrapers" were under construction in New York City, the Bank of Manhattan and the Chrysler Building. It was announced that the Bank of Manhattan building would be the taller of the two. But Walter P. Chrysler had was not a man who liked second place. As the buildings rose, a tower was secretly constructed for his building that would win the race into the sky. One week after the Bank of Manhattan Building had reached its announced height, Chrysler installed his tower. The 77-story Chrysler Building became the tallest building in the world. It also had the distinction of being the first building to be higher than the Eiffel Tower in Paris. The year was 1930. Chrylser's triumph was short-lived, however, because in the next year the Empire State Building was completed and was taller than the Chrysler Building. The Chrysler building is a perfect example of the Art Deco style of architecture of the times. A considerable amount of stainless steel, then a new high-tech material, was used in the construction of the building, and reference to Chrysler's automobile empire can be seen in the gargoyles which depict Chrysler car ornaments, and the tower which is modeled after a radiator grille. Also, abstract automobiles can be seen in the building's masonry walls. On a clear day, Chrysler could see his building from his home on Long Island. The Chrysler Corporation eventu-

ally lost control of the building and it is now in the hands of others—but the name remains.

WALTER P. CHRYSLER HOME— US MERCHANT MARINE ACADEMY
Steamboat Rd.
KINGS POINT, NY 11024
(West end of Long Island on the north shore)
Phone: 516-773-5387
www.usmma.edu
Hours: Daily and weekends 9–4:30. Closed federal holidays and during summer and winter leave periods. Free.

The US Merchant Marine Academy was built on the former estate of Walter P. Chrysler in 1942 during World War II. The mansion was left intact and remains on the grounds of the Academy and is in daily use. It can be seen by visitors during the general tour of the Academy offered to the public.

COOPER CLASSIC COLLECTION
(Dealer)
137 Perry St. (between Washington and Greenwich)
GREENWICH VILLAGE, NY 10014
Phone: 212-929-3909 and 800-719-3909 (toll free)
www.cooperclassiccars.com
Hours: M–F 9–5:30, Sat. 10–5

Everyone knows there are some very nice art galleries in Greenwich Village. Here's one that sells both fine art and fine quality vintage cars—*"rolling sculptures"*—they call them. The cars are displayed in a refined gallery setting with collector quality paintings and photographs on the walls. Both American and European high quality vehicles will be found here. This unique company has had many magazine articles written about it and was designated by both the "New York Magazine" and the "Time Out Magazine" as the best vintage car facility in New York. The company takes trades, offers appraisals, has a locator service and helps with financing and shipping. Elliot Cuker is the man behind this very interesting dealership.

PAR PORSCHE SPECIALISTS (Dealer)
310 Main St.
NEW ROCHELLE, NY 10801
(Northeastern suburb of New York City on Long Island Sound)
Phone: 914-637-8800
www.parcars.com
Hours: M–F 9–5

Guess what these people specialize in? You guessed it—Porsches. Examples of this fine automobile will be found aplenty in their showroom and online. They usually have some 200 cars from which to choose. You are invited to browse through the collection. Most of the cars have been road tested and inspected by the company's factory trained technicians. The company takes trades, sells on consignment, provides new and used parts, sells accessories

including Recaro Seats, and helps with financing and shipping.

VINTAGE CAR STORE OF NYACK (Dealer)
40 Lydecker St. (Foot of High Av.)
NYACK, NY 10960 (Northern suburb of New York City on the west bank of Hudson River at the Tappan Zee Bridge)
Phone: 845-358-0500
www.vintagecarstore.com
Hours: M–F 9–5, Sat. 9:30–5, Sun. noon–5.

The town of Nyack is a huge antique center for metropolitan New York City, so it is an ideal location for an antique car dealership like Vintage Car Store of Nyack. Here, in a big warehouse, can be found between 40 and 60 vintage cars of various makes and models. Many of the vehicles are quality cars such as Cadillacs, Ferraris, Jaguars, etc. An inventory list is available upon request. Vintage Car Store of Nyack can arrange financing and transportation, takes trades, sells on consignment, provides appraisals, leases cars, offers limited storage and will search for that special car you have always wanted. Gary Blankfont is the owner and extends a standing invitation to car clubs to come and visit.

End of New York City ◀

NORTHEAST CLASSIC CAR MUSEUM
24 Rexford St. (SR 23)
NORWICH, NY 13815
(38 miles northeast of Binghamton on scenic SR 12)
Phone: 607-334-AUTO (2886)
www.classiccarmuseum.org
Hours: Daily 9–5.
Closed Thanksgiving, Christmas, and New Year's Day.
Admission charged.

At the Old Rhinebeck Aerodrome *antique planes and cars perform together in a weekly air show.*

Take the scenic drive along SR 12 and the Chenango River and you will come to the beautiful town of Norwich. There you will find this three-building museum with a first class display of some 125 classic automobiles. Most of the cars are meticulously restored high-quality vehicles and are fully operational. There are Duesenbergs, Packards, Cords, Auburns, Pierce-Arrows, the largest collection of Franklins in the world and more. There is a gift shop and the museum opens special exhibits every Memorial Day. Call for more information and special group admissions.

OLD RHINEBECK AERODROME
(Museum)
   44 Stone Church Rd.
   RHINEBECK, NY 12572
   (Halfway between New York City and Albany)

Phone: 845-752-3200
www.oldrhinebeck.org
Hours: *May 15 through Oct. 31* daily 10–5. Weekend air shows *mid–June to mid–Oct* at 2 and 4. Admission charged.

This unique museum complex is devoted primarily to displaying and flying antique airplanes from the 1900s to the late 1930s. The buildings of the complex are situated around a World War I-style aerodrome and every weekend in the summer air shows are performed over the aerodrome. Integrated into this unique scene are some 30 antique automobiles, several antique motorcycles and a World War I French Renault tank. Some of the vehicles take part in the air show. When not participating in the air shows, the planes and vehicles can be seen sitting around the field, or in

171

their hangars or in the museum. Old Rhinebeck has a gift and souvenir shop with many interesting items related to the museum's overall theme.

SARATOGA AUTOMOBILE MUSEUM
110 Avenue of the Pines
SARATOGA SPRINGS, NY 12866
(On I-87 30 miles north of Albany)
Phone: 518-587-1935
www.saratogaautomuseum.com
Hours: *Summer* daily 10–5, *winter* Tues.–Sun. 10–5.
Admission charged.

Here's a large automobile museum worth anyone's time. It is located on the grounds of the Saratoga Park Spa in a modern two-story building. On display are cars, trucks, carriages and other vehicles representing the automotive heritage of New York State and the world of motorized transportation. It is also the home of the New York State Stock Car Association Hall of Fame which honors stock car racing in New York state. The museum has many activities such as workshops, lectures and outdoor shows and there is a nice gift shop. Every May and September the museum is host to car festivals. Private and corporate events are also held at the museum. It's a great place for car clubs to visit.

KYKUIT, THE ROCKEFELLER ESTATE
SR 119
SLEEPY HOLLOW, NY 10591
(Tarrytown area)
Phone: 914-631-9491
www.hudsonvalley.org
Hours: *Late April–early Nov.*

W–M 10–3. Guided tours every 30 minutes. Admission charged.

This was the home to 4 generations of the Rockefeller family from 1913 when it was built by John D. Rockefeller, Jr. The mansion is open to the public and is appointed with antiques, fine art and memorabilia of the Rockefeller family. The terraced gardens are also open to the public and in the carriage house are 12 antique automobiles. The oldest is a 1907 Ford Model S. All of the cars were owned and driven by members of the Rockefeller family. Food is available. Tours not recommended for children under age 10.

INTERNATIONAL MOTOR RACING RESEARCH CENTER
610 S. Decatur St.
WATKINS GLEN, NY 14891-1613
(At the south end of Seneca Lake in the Finger Lakes district)
Phone: 607-535-9044
www.racingarchives.org
Hours: M–Sat. 9–5

This is a large research center and library devoted to the sport of motor racing. It is a world-class leader in the collection of materials representing the documentary heritage of amateur racing, highlighting Sports Car, Formula 1, NASCAR, and vintage and historic racing. The Center holds about 2,500 rare and reference books, hundreds of periodical titles, programs, manuscript collection, historic scrapbooks, posters, historic videos, fine art work and much more. A list of the Center's holdings is available. The Center is actively seeking additional documentation to enrich its material holdings such as driver's diaries, research notes on motor racing, team records, scrapbooks, etc. Would you have anything to offer?

HALL OF FAME AND CLASSIC CAR MUSEUM, D.I.R.T. MOTORSPORTS

1 Speedway Dr. (Adjacent to the Cayuga County Fairgrounds)
WEEDSPORT, NY 13166
Phone: 315-834-6667 or
315-834-6606
www.dirtmotorsports.com
Hours: *Apr.–Labor Day* M–Sat. 10–5, Sun. 12–7. *Sept.–Dec.* M–F 10–5, Sat.–Sun. 11–4, *Jan.–Mar.* closed. Admission charged.

This fine museum honors the sport of dirt track racing and the people associated with it. There are several race cars on display, several muscle cars and several dozen antique cars. The museum has a Finder's Network that assists people in locating, buying and selling antique cars. In the "Classic Corral", adjacent to the main building, are vintage cars for sale. The museum has a large gift and souvenir shop that offers a wide assortment of apparel, souvenirs and limited collector's items. Jack Speno is the museum's curator.

NORTH CAROLINA

▶ ASHEVILLE AREA

This is the Estes-Winn-Blomberg Antique Car Museum *and two of its fine old cars.*

**ESTES-WINN-BLOMBERG
ANTIQUE CAR MUSEUM**
Biltmore Homespun Shops/Grovewood Gallery
111 Grovewood Rd.
ASHEVILLE, NC 28804
(West-central part of state on I-40 and I-29)
Phone: 828-253-7651
www.grovewood.com
Hours: M–Sat. 10–5. Free.

This auto museum is part of the Biltmore Homespun Shops/Grovewood Gallery, a complex of buildings, adjacent to the luxurious Grove Park Inn. The Grovewood complex is housed in an historic woollen mill and was started by Mrs. George W. Vanderbilt in 1901 to preserve the Old World wool manufacturing skills of the local people. In the auto museum are some 20 cars dating from 1913. There are also a few carriages from the 1800s. In the complex is another museum displaying crafts of the mountain people and telling the history of the Grove Park Inn.

THE WINNING COLLECTION
(Dealer and storage)
10 New Bridge Parkway
PO Box 8669
ASHEVILLE, NC 28814
Phone: 888-533-RACE

174

www.winningcollection.com
Hours: M–F 9–5, Sat. 9–3

In this dealer's new and modern showroom, one will find collector cars, muscle cars, exotics, street rods and historic racing cars. They also offer climate-controlled storage for customers' vehicle. The Winning Collection takes trades, sells on consignment, will search for specific automobiles and assists in shipping and financing.

End of Asheville area

▶ CHARLOTTE AREA

If you like NASCAR racing, this is the place to be. Charlotte is the gathering place for NASCAR racing teams and many of the teams' shops are open to the public. These include *Hendricks Motorsports* (listed below), *Stavola Brothers Racing, Darrell Waltrip Motorsports, Bobby Allison Motorsports, Geoff Bodine Racing, Penske Racing South, Bahari Racing, Kranefuss/Haas Racing, Butch Mock Motorsports, NEMCO Motorsports, RPM Performance*, and *Joe Gibbs Racing*. Check locally for hours, locations and information.

HENDRICK MOTORSPORT MUSEUM & GIFT SHOP

4400 Papa Joe Hendrick Blvd.
(Directly west of the Charlotte Motor Speedway)
CHARLOTTE, NC 28262
(12 miles northeast of Charlotte)
Phone: 704-455-3400 or
877-467-4890 (toll free)
www.hendrickmotorsports.com
Hours: M–F 9–5. Free.

This large complex is the home of the Hendrick racing teams. The teams' shop is adjacent to the museum and a 40 Ft. window is provided in the dividing wall so that visitors to the museum can view the work in progress in the shop. The chassis shop, at another location, is also open to the public. In the museum are a number of race cars, race trucks, concept cars and movie cars. Technical displays tell of the working parts of a race car and an exploded display shows how the frame and body of race cars are constructed. There is a huge trophy display, uniforms, photographs and lots more. A 2,000 sq. ft. gift shop offers almost everything imaginable in the way of race-oriented souvenirs and gifts. The museum is also available for meetings, social events and other activities.

TOM MACK CLASSICS (Dealer)

231 Post Office Dr., Unit B-1
INDIAN TRAIL, NC. 28079
(13 miles east of Charlotte just off US 74)
Phone: 704-821-MACK or
888-TOM-MACK (toll free)
www.tommackclassics.com
M–F 9–5, Sat. 9–3

Tom Mack is real proud of this place. He has an 8,000 sq. ft. showroom packed with between 20 and 30 classic cars, muscle cars, special interest cars and fine

175

imports. And he's always on the lookout to buy top-of-the-line vehicles such as Mercedes, Lexus and other luxury imports. The company takes trades, helps with financing and delivery, provides appraisals and will pick you up at the airport.

End of Charlotte area ◄

The C. Grier Beam Truck Museum *of Cherryville, NC.*

C. GRIER BEAM TRUCK MUSEUM
111 N. Mountain St.
CHERRYVILLE, NC 28021
(30 miles northwest of Charlotte on SRs 150, 216, 274 and 279)
Phone: 704-435-3072
www.beamtruckmuseum.com
Hours: F 10–5 and Sat. 10–3. Free.

This unique truck museum was established by C. Grier Beam, founder of Carolina Freight Express, one of the nation's largest trucking firms. The museum has more than a dozen restored trucks on display, including a 1926 Chevrolet tractor, a 1935 International tractor, several White trucks and a 1947 Mack EF tractor with a 1946 Fruehauf trailer with a sleeping compartment in the front. These sleeping compartments were later discontinued for safety reasons. The museum has a small gift and souvenir shop. There aren't many truck museums around so this is worth your while to visit.

► CONCORD-MOORESVILLE AREA
(25 miles northeast of Charlotte on I-85)

BACKING UP CLASSICS (Museum)
4545 US 29 (Southwest from downtown Concord next to Lowe's Motor Speedway)
CONCORD, NC 28027
Phone: 704-788-9500
www.backingupclassics.com

Hours: M–Sat. 9–5, Sun. 10–5, *extended hours during racing events.* Admission charged.

Here's a large antique vehicle museum you will want to visit when you are in the area. There are some 50 vintage

The Memory Lane
Motorsports &
Historical
Automotive Museum
of Mooresville, NC

vehicles here; cars, muscle cars, race cars and motorcycles. Muscle cars from the 1950s and 1960s are a specialty. The cars on display rotate from time-to-time and some are for sale. There is an extensive display of country music memorabilia and a large gift shop offering NASCAR collectibles and automotive souvenirs. The museum is available for banquets, meeting and parties. Founded in 1988.

MEMORY LANE MOTORSPORTS & HISTORICAL AUTOMOTIVE MUSEUM

769 River Hwy. (SR 150)
MOORESVILLE, NC 28117
(12 miles northwest of
Concord off I-77 exit 36)
Phone: 704-660-6936 or
704-662-FORD
www.memorylaneautomuseum.com
Hours: *Summer* M–Sat. 9–5,
Dec.–Feb. same except closed Wed.
and Sun. Group tours available.
Admission charged.

If you like to see race cars, you gotta stop at this place. Memory Lane Museum has over 130 vehicles including the largest private collection vintage stock

cars in the U.S. Many of the stock cars are associated with famous NASCAR drivers and some have been used in movies. There are also collections of go-carts, soap box derby "racers" and bicycles. Another interesting feature at this museum is a display of wrecked stock cars with accompanying information on safety features built into the cars. Then too, you will see displays of automobile memorabilia and an antique farm tractor for two. There is a large souvenir shop and the museum is available for banquets and other events.

NORTH CAROLINA AUTO RACING HALL OF FAME

119 Knob Hill Rd.
MOORESVILLE, NC 28117
Phone: 704-663-5331
www.ncarhof.com
Hours: M–Sat. 9–5, Sun. 12:30–
4:30. Admission charged.

The mission of this fine museum is to celebrate and enhance the rich heritage of Motor Sports and to commemorate those who have made outstanding contributions to it. Those individuals so honored are,

NORTH CAROLINA

The North Carolina Auto Racing Hall of Fame *is easily accessible from I-77 north of Charlotte.*

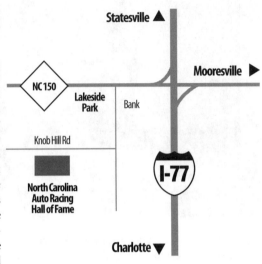

of course, highlighted in this museum. There are about 35 race cars on display representing all types of auto racing, some driven by Hall of Fame drivers. Other features of the museum are the Goodyear Mini-Theater and an Indy car simulator. An Art gallery displays works of some of the more famous motorsports artists; some of their works are on sale in the gift shop. Incorporated within the museum are race shops and a race-themed restaurant.

End of Concord-Mooresville area ◀

CARL SANDBURG NATIONAL HISTORIC SITE

Little River Rd.
FLAT ROCK, NC 28731
(22 miles south of Asheville)
Phone: 828-698-5627
http://www.nps.gov/carl/
Hours: Daily 9–5, closed Dec. 25. *June through Oct.* tours are given every 30 minutes, *rest of year* M–F at half-past the hour and on Sat.–Sun. every 30 minutes. Admission charged.

This is the home of the late poet-historian Carl Sandburg. Among his many belongings are two vehicles he owned at the time of his death in 1967, a 1951 Ford tractor and a 1962 Jeep. The Jeep was given to Sandburg as partial payment for writing the script of the movie *"The Greatest Story Ever Told."*

HAWKS HILL DEVELOPMENT COMMUNITY (Car collector community)

21 Eagle Ridge
1 Pheasant Run (Sales office)
LENOIR, NC 28645
(50 miles west of Winston-Salem near Pisgah National Forest)
Phone: 828-754-2328
www.hawkshill.com
Hours: Please phone.

Golfers cluster together in golfing communities, so why don't car collectors cluster together in car collector communities? Well, it is happening in North Carolina. They call it Hawks Hill Development Community, America's first community for the car collector. Instead of a golf course the community's center piece is an elegant garage/club house combination. In the garage part

Get out and get under—the easy way—at Hawk's Hill Development Community.

of the structure there's a lift, compressed air, welding facilities, tools and most everything it takes to service, and tinker with, old cars. In the club house there is a greatroom, fire place, full kitchen and guest rooms upstairs. The wooded lots are big with plenty of room for your own multi-car garage. The developers, Al & Pat Witt, long-time antique car buffs, have lots of car-buff neighbors now and plan further expansions of the development. To find Hawks Hill, proceed up SR 18 from its junction in Lenoir with U.S. 321, go past Cedar Rock Country Club (on the right), then three more miles to Hawks Hill (also on the right). Drive in and take a look.

WHEELS THROUGH TIME MUSEUM OF VINTAGE TRANSPORTATION

Hwy. 19 west
MAGGIE VALLEY, NC 28751
(on US 19 four miles east of the Cherokee Indian Reservation.)

Phone: 828-926-6266
www.wheelsthroughtime.com
Hours: *Apr.– Nov.* daily 9–6, *rest of year* 10–5, but closed on Wed. Admission charged.

This is the beautiful Great Smoky Mountain National Park area. You'll not only enjoy the scenery, but you can also enjoy this fine new 38,000 sq. ft. vintage transportation museum. The museum has an unusually large collection of motorcycles among their total collection of some 250 vehicles. Many of the motorcycles are pre-World War I models and very rare. There are also a number of military motorcycles. Most of the motorcycles and automobiles are in running condition and are driven regularly. That's why they call this place *"The Museum That Runs."* There are generous displays of memorabilia and art work and a well-stocked gift shop. You won't be disappointed by stopping here.

179

NORTH CAROLINA

The Spencer Shops of the Southern Railroad, built in 1907, are now a museum complex housing the North Carolina Transportation Museum.

MOORESVILLE (See Concord-Mooresville Area)

RICHARD PETTY MUSEUM

142 W. Academy St.
RANDLEMAN, NC 27217
(15 miles south of Greensboro)
Phone: 336-495-1143
www.pettyracing.com
Hours: M–Sat. 9–5. Admission charged.

This museum traces the racing careers of Lee Petty and his son, Richard Petty, from the late 1940s to the present. The walls of the museum are loaded with trophies, including Winston Cup trophies, won by this fascinating father and son racing duo. Also in the museum are several of Richard Petty's famous race cars along with many items of racing memorabilia. There is a mini-theater in which a 25-minute movie covering the racing career of Richard Petty is shown. Richard and his wife, Lynda, have loaned the museum their personal collections of dolls, watches, belt buckles, die cast models, guns, knives and other items. The museum has a gift shop with many racing-related items for sale.

NORTH CAROLINA TRANSPORTATION MUSEUM; SPENCER SHOPS NATIONAL HISTORIC SITE.

411 S. Salisbury St.
SPENCER, NC 28159 (35 miles south of Winston-Salem on I-85)
Phone: 704-636-2889
www.ah/dcr.state.nc.us/sections/hs/spencer/spencer.htm
Hours: *Apr. through Oct.* M–Sat. 9–5, Sun 1–5; *Nov. through Mar.* Tues.–Sat. 10–4, Sun. 1–4.
Donations accepted.

This is a large state-owned museum, housed in the buildings of the former repair shops of the Southern Railroad. Featured in the main museum building are displays of the various modes of transportation used through the history of North America from canoes, to Conestoga wagons, to railroads, to airplanes. Included, of course, are automobiles. In the car collection are fire engines, a depot hack and other utility vehicles, and a 1935 Ford Highway Patrol car. There is also a major display on the evolution of the automobile. An operating antique steam train takes visitors, for a small fee, on a tour of the complex, which includes a restored 37-bay roundhouse.

RICHARD CHILDRESS RACING MUSEUM

180 Industrial Dr.
WELCOME, NC 27374
(14 miles south of downtown
Winston-Salem on US 8)
Phone: 336-731-3389 or
800-476-3389 (toll free)
www.rcrracing.com
Hours: M–F 9–5, Sat. 9–3.
Guided tours available.
Free admission to museum.

This is the campus of the famous Richard Childress Racing Team. Located in the complex is this 47,000 sq. ft. museum displaying some of the team's famous race cars. In all, there are 46 race cars and 1 NASCAR race truck. These vehicles have been driven by some of the teams most famous drivers and have participated in NASCAR, NHRA and Indy car races. The museum is filled with trophies and memorabilia related to the Richard Childress Racing Team and to automobile racing in general. There are 16 video screens operating showing some of the highlights of the team's racing events. Also on display are some of Richard Childress's personal collection of hot rods. Visitors who take the guided tours are taken into the shop areas to see work in progress on the current racing machines. The museum has a large gift shop offering NASCAR souvenirs, clothing, posters and many hard-to-find items.

NORTH DAKOTA

WALKER'S GARAGE (Salvage)
SR 49 (3 miles north of Beulah)
BEULAH, ND 58523 (60 miles
northwest of Bismarck)
Phone: 701-873-4489
Hours: M–F 8–5, Sat. 8:30–3

This is one of the few salvage yards in the country with a significant number of Edsels. Walker's has over 200 of them among their total inventory of some 3,000 vehicles. Leroy Walker, the yard's proprietor, is known in some circles as the *"King of the Edsels".* He and his yard have been featured on ABC and CNN television shows. The other vehicles in the yard are mainly American-made cars, trucks, buses and tractors from 1946 to the present. There are a few pre-war vehicles and they also have whole cars, including Edsels, available for restoration or parts cars. Car clubs are welcome and visitors will be escorted through the yard. Walker's does repair work and some restoration. In business since 1962.

GREATER DAKOTA CLASSICS (Dealer)
903 3rd. Av. SE, PO Box 314
DEVIL'S LAKE, ND 58301 (85
miles west of Grand Forks on US 2)
Phone: 701-662-7222
www.greaterdakotaclassics.com
Hours: M–F 9–5

Here is the largest vintage car dealer in North Dakota. In their indoor show-room, one will find classic cars, muscle cars, street rods, custom cars and a generous display of automobilia, some of which is for sale. They also have a service department called the "Black Magic Rod and Custom Shop" which does restoration work, detailing, painting, etc. and can be viewed by visitors. Greater Dakota Classics takes trades, sells on consignment, searches for specific vehicles, aids in financing and shipping and offers cold or heated storage for customer-owned automobiles. Stan Orness is the owner.

DORY'S ANTIQUE AUTO MUSEUM
US 12 West, PO Box 7
MARMARTH, ND 58643
(Southwestern corner of the state
on US 12 five miles from the
Montana state line)
Phone: 701-279-5904
www.marmarth.org
Hours: *April to mid–Oct.* daily 9–5.
Admission charged.

J. D. VanHorn, a long-time car buff and restorer, started this museum—which is attached to his home—in 2002. During the good-weather months, he welcomes visitors and often gives them a personal tour. His museum contains about 40 cars, most of them restored, and ranging in age from 1901 to 1957. VanHorn's restoration facilities are also on the premises and visitors can watch work in progress. Out back is a mini-

These two Model A Ford replicas are side-by-side in the Bonanzaville *car museum. The car on the left is a Shay Reproduction and on the Right is a Classic Reproduction made in ND.*

junk yard with about 200 cars, mostly American-made and from the 1950s on down. And here's another surprise. The museum has an ice cream parlor. You won't find many museums like this in the country, so take the opportunity to stop by. Mr. VanHorn will be happy to see you and car clubs are welcome.

BONANZAVILLE, USA
(Museum complex)
    1351 W. Main St. (Junction of I-94, exit 343, and US 10)
    WEST FARGO, ND 58078 (Western suburb of Fargo)
    Phone: 701-282-2822 and 800-700-5317 (toll free)
    www.bonanzaville.com
    Hours: Village and museum open from *Memorial Day through late Sept.* M–Sat. 9–5, Sun. noon–5; *May 1–day before Memorial Day* M–F 9–5; *rest of the year* closed. Admission charged.

This large museum complex consists of 42 buildings on a 15-acre site. The Village is a reconstructed pioneer town representing life in North Dakota during the "Bonanza" farm era of the late 1800s-early 1900s. The museum has extensive exhibits on Indian culture and early pioneer life in the Red River Valley and the northern Great Plains. There is a train depot with a steam locomotive, railroad snowplow, coach car and caboose. Separate buildings house airplanes, telecommunications equipment, farm machinery, horse-drawn vehicles and antique cars. Some 80 antique cars and 40 pieces of farm machinery are on display. There are also displays of hubcaps, license plates, mechanic's tools and machinery and a small automotive library. An annual festival called *"Pioneer Review Days"* is held here during the third week in August. Bonanzaville has a large and well-stocked gift and souvenir shop.

OHIO

HASTY'S CAR COUNTRY (Dealer)
5051 Windsor Rd.
BLUE BALL, OH 45044
(Eastern suburb of Middletown, OH on I-75)
Phone: 513-424-4844
www.hastyscarcountry.com
Hours: M, Tues. & Thurs. 10–6, W and F 10–5

This energetic dealer has a 6,000 sq. ft. climate-controlled showroom full of classics, muscle cars, street rods and more. It's worth a stop. The company takes trades, sells on consignment, offers appraisals and aids in financing and shipping. Jim Hasty is the main man here and he started the business in 1986.

SNOOK'S DREAM CARS AUTOMOBILE MUSEUM
13920 County Home Rd. (Adjacent to US 6)
BOWLING GREEN, OH 43402-8670 (20 miles south of downtown Toledo on I-75)
Phone: 419-353-8338
www.snooksdreamcars.com

Hours: Daily 11–4.
Admission charged.

The first thing you will see as you approach Snook's Dream Cars Automobile Museum is a replica of a 1940s-era Texaco service station. Inside the museum, there's a lot more. Visitors will see a large collection of automobilia including such items as hood ornaments, window cranks, window curtains, seat covers, bug removers and back seat touring games. There's an operating four-bay mechanic's area and an area displaying amusement machines such as pinball machines, kiddies' rides and pedal cars. In the automobile showroom are vintage cars from the 1930s through the 1960s, all in running condition. Most are American made. The cars are displayed in period settings such as a 1930s general store, a 1940s scene of downtown Bowling Green, a 1950s diner, and a 1960s Sebring raceway pit lane. Keep an eye open for their gift shop. It's full of interesting stuff. Bill Snook and his son, Jim, won't be far away. The museum was founded in 2002.

▶ CANTON AREA
(Northeastern part of the state on I-77)

CANTON CLASSIC CAR MUSEUM
6th Street @ Market Ave. South (In downtown Canton)
CANTON, OH 44702 (20 miles south of Akron)

Phone: 330-455-3603
www.cantonclassiccar.org
Hours: Daily 10–5. Closed major holidays. Admission charged. Free parking.

Canton Marriott Hotel Lower Level
CANTON, ON 44702
Phone: 866-653-8900 (toll free)
www.motorcarportfolio.com
Hours: M–Sat. 9–5, Sun. noon–5,
open late Thurs. until 9.

This museum is on the historic Lincoln Highway in a 1915 Ford/Lincoln dealership building and has more than 45 restored vintage and classic cars. Some of the cars were made in Ohio and others are associated with celebrities and movies. Other displays include period memorabilia, fashions, displays of early advertisements, early police and fire department memorabilia, gasoline and steam engines, antique auto signs and post cards. There is also an automotive-oriented gift shop and the museum is handicapped accessible. You will walk out of this museum with a smile on your face.

The Canton Classic Car Museum of Canton, OH. and their 1929 Rolls Royce Silver Ghost. More than a bunch of old cars-Memorabilia antiques and more.

Here's an appropriate place for an antique car dealer—the lower level of the parking garage of the Marriott Hotel. Visitors can stay at the hotel and ride the elevator down to the dealership. There, they will find dozens of interesting machines and maybe a few surprises like an old camper trailer or two. Here's another surprise. They have a language translator and can converse with you in Spanish, French, German or Italian. Motorcar Portfolio takes trades, sells on consignment, will search for a specific vehicle, offers storage and helps find reasonable financing and shipping. Gary Brown and Bob Lichty run the operation.

MOTORCAR PORTFOLIO (Dealer)
320 Market Av. South

End of Canton area ◀

▶ CLEVELAND Area

CRAWFORD AUTO-AVIATION MUSEUM
10825 East Blvd. (at the Western Reserve Historical Society)
CLEVELAND, OH 44106
Phone: 216-721-5722

http://www.wrhs.org/crawford/default.asp
Hours: M–Sat. 10–5, Sun. noon–5. Admission charged.

Here is a very large museum that has

Part of the fine collection of antique and historic automobiles at the **Crawford Auto-Aviation Museum** *in Cleveland, OH.*

gift store. The museum is also available for business and social functions. At this same location is the Society's History Museum, Research Library and the magnificent Hay-KcKinney Mansion which is open to the public.

ROCK AND ROLL HALL OF FAME AND MUSEUM
E. 9th St. & N. Marginal Rd. at 1 Key Plaza.
CLEVELAND, OH 44114
Phone: 216-781-7625
www.rockhall.com
Hours: *Memorial Day–Labor Day* W and Sat. 10–9, rest of week 10–5:30. *Remainder of the year* daily 10–5:30 (Wed. 10–9). Admission charged.

about 200 cars of which some 80 are on display on a rotating basis. It is owned and operated by the Western Reserve Historical Society. The earliest vehicles are an 1897 Panhard et Levassor and an 1898 Winton Phaeton. They also have 1 of 4 "Chitty-Chitty-Bang-Bang" originals built in the 1920s that later inspired the movie car of the same name. Some of the cars on display were made in Cleveland. Other displays include aircraft, motorcycles, bicycles and other transportation-related items. The museum has an automotive library, a restoration shop in which visitors can watch restorations in progress, a turn-of-the-century cobblestone street of shops and an interesting

This is a very large museum and, as the name implies, honors individuals and groups who are well-known in the field of Rock and Roll music. Among the many items on display are several automobiles associated with famous Rock and Rollers. Several other cars are hanging from the ceiling with unique Rock and Roll histories of their own. Other vehicles belonging to Rock & Roll celebrities have been shown in the museum from time-to-time.

End of Cleveland area ◀

GRAVEYARD II AUTO PARTS
(Salvage)
   3383 Kuhn Rd.
   COLDWATER, OH 45828
   (East-central part of the state
   at the intersection of SRs 118 and

219 near the Indiana state line)
Phone: 419-586-1367
Hours: Normal business hours.

Need a part for your 1930 Mack tractor? This is the place to look. This interesting 35-acre salvage yard not only has a large selection of parts for every-day antique vehicles but a nice collection for big trucks and commercial rigs. That includes plenty of panel trucks, pickup trucks and a few hearses and buses. Joe Downey, the owner, has been collecting these vehicles since 1972. The place is hard to find, so you might phone first for directions.

▶ COLUMBUS Area

ARENA MOTOR SALES, INC. (Dealer)
2631 Morse Rd.
COLUMBUS, OH 43231
Phone: 614-418-5744
www.arenamotor.com
Hours: M–Tues. and Thurs. 10–7, W and F 10–6, Sat. 10–-5

How about a snappy yellow Mustang convertible or a maroon Corvette convertible or a tan and brown Ford Model A—or maybe a project car? You can see cars like this in Arena Motor's handsome showroom. They also offer a nice selection of motorcycles and street rods. The company takes trades, sells on consignment, leases cars, helps with shipping and can direct you to sources for financing. You will like what you see at Arena Motor Sales.

MOTORCYCLE HALL OF FAME MUSEUM
13515 Yarmouth Dr.
PICKERINGTON, OH 43147
(Eastern suburb of Columbus on SR 256, five miles south of I-70)
Phone: 614-856-2222
www.motorcyclemuseum.org
Hours: Daily 9–5.
Admission charged.
Directions: Exit I-70 at Pickerington exit 112A onto SR 256 south. Proceed to SR 204 and turn left, then turn left again at the first street, Yarmouth Dr., and proceed to the museum which is on your left.

This fine motorcycle museum is located on the campus of the American Motorcyclist Association and honors those individuals who have made significant contributions to the business and sport of motorcycling. Displays in the museum depict many domestic and international influences on motorcycling in America. Some of the museum's motorcycles are on loan so the displays are ever-changing. The museum is host to many activities and sponsors a major motorcycle event every two years called *"Motocross America."*

End of Columbus area ◀

▶ DAYTON Area

CARILLON HISTORICAL PARK
(Museum complex)
1000 Carillon Blvd.
DAYTON, OH 45409
Phone: 937-293-2841
www.carillonpark.org

Two of the buildings in **Carillon Historical Park** *include an early automobile dealership, left, and a 1924 Sun Oil Co. service station, right.*

Hours: *Apr. 1 through Oct. 31* Tues.–Sat. 9:30–5, Sun. noon–5. Admission charged.

In this large city park there is a collection of historic buildings and exhibits which trace the early history of Dayton and the progress of American transportation from the beginning of the 1900s. Buildings of interest to car buffs include a 1924 Sun Oil Co. service station, an early automobile dealership with vintage cars inside the showroom, and a replica of the Deeds Barn, the building in which Charles F. Kettering invented the automobile electric starter. His invention overcame one of the major problems of the early automobile industry, that of hand-cranking internal combustion engines. Before Kettering's invention, the need to hand-crank automobile engines put limitations on the size and compression of the engine so that the average man could turn the crank. Unfortunately not all men, and very few women, could crank a car. Kettering's invention eventually made the internal combustion engine the engine of choice for most automobiles. It also spelled the end of steam and electric-powered cars which had sold well because they did not require cranking. Other items of interest on display in the complex is a Concord stagecoach, an early steam locomotive and caboose, a trolley car, a restored 1905 Wright Brothers airplane, a replica of the Wright Brothers bicycle shop and a number of vintage cars, some of which were made in Dayton. Among the autos are Stoddard-Daytons and Xenia Cyclecars, both built in Dayton, and a vintage Cadillac which was the first car to be equipped with Charles Kettering's electric starter. There is a fine museum store with many auto-related items for sale.

THE CITIZENS MOTORCAR CO., AMERICA'S PACKARD MUSEUM
420 S. Ludlow St.
DAYTON, OH 45402
Phone: 937-226-1917

www.americaspackard-museum.org
Hours: M–F noon–5,
Sat.–Sun. 1–5

The Citizens Motor Car Co., America's Packard Museum *is convenient from either I-70 or I-75.*

This museum, near downtown Dayton, is in a building built in 1917 by the Packard Motor Car Co. as a branch office and a sales and service center. At that time, the center's name was "The Citizens Motorcar Company." The interior of the art deco building has been restored to look like a 1930s Packard dealership and has about 50 Packard vehicles on display. Along with the cars are several Rolls-Royce "Merlin" aircraft engines, built by Packard in large numbers during World War II under license from Rolls-Royce. There is considerable information and several displays on the Packard Motorcar Co. itself, including its original papers of incorporation and other documents which trace the company's history from its founding in 1899 to its demise in 1956. There is a museum store and the museum welcomes tour groups and is available for dinners, meetings and banquets. The Packard Automobile Classics (the national Packard club) is located at the museum. The museum was founded in 1992 by Bob Sigmon, a life-long Packard enthusiast.

End of Dayton Area ◀

BOB'S AUTO WRECKING AND RECOVERY, INC.

12602 SR 13 (Just north of Milan)
MILAN, OH 44846
(12 miles south of Sandusky
and just south of I-80/90)
Phone: 419-499-2005,
419-499-2415 and 419-499-4012
www.bobsautowrecking.com
Hours: M–F 8–5, Sat. 8–noon

There's some real treasure in this yard and it's worth a look-see. Bob's has about 5,000 vehicles ranging in age from the 1930s to the present on this 47-acre yard which was once the family farm. There is a general mix of cars and light trucks with most being American-made. Customers may browse the yard. In business since the 1960s—and they still remember their first car, a 1948 Mercury for which they paid $35.00.

OHIO

PHIL STALLING CLASSIC CARS. LTD. (Dealer)

2525 Mt. Vernon Rd.
(SR 13 north)
NEWARK, OH 43055
(33 miles east of downtown Columbus on SR 13 and SR 16)
Phone: 740-745-1147
www.phils-classics.com
Hours: M–F 9–5, Sat. 9–3

You'll find 25 or more very nice vintage vehicles in this dealer's showroom, which is decorated with wheel covers, antique signs and other automobilia. Most of the cars are American-made but there will also be an MG or a Rolls-Royce or two. Phil Stalling Classic Cars, Ltd. takes trades, sells on consignment, offers appraisals and aids in financing and shipping. They also do service work. Drop by; you'll like what you see.

The **Welsh Jaguar Classic Car Museum,** *Steubenville, OH.*

MERSHON'S WORLD OF CARS (Dealer)

201 E. North St.
SPRINGFIELD, OH 45503 (20 miles northeast of Dayton on I-70)
Phone: 937-324-8899 and 800-220-9249 (toll free)
www.mershons.com
Hours: M–Thurs. 9–7, F 9–6, Sat. 9–5

This is a large dealer of collector cars specializing in all years of Corvettes. Up to 60 vehicles can be seen in their spacious, carpeted and air conditioned indoor showroom with additional cars on their adjacent lot. Other makes of cars are offered with heavy emphasis on muscle cars, sports cars and collector cars. Financing, leasing and shipping can be arranged and the company takes trades. The owner is Dan Mershon.

WELSH JAGUAR CLASSIC CAR MUSEUM and THE JAGGIN' AROUND RESTAURANT AND PUB

Corner of 5th & Washington Sts., PO Box 4130
STEUBENVILLE, OH 43952
(Eastern edge of the state on the Ohio River opposite Weirton, WV)
Phone: 614-282-1010 and 800-875-5247 (toll free)
http://www.classicar.com/museums/welshjag/welshjag.htm
Hours: Thurs.–Sun. 11–4.
Admission charged.

This privately-owned museum houses over 20 Jaguars and muscle cars from the early days of Jaguar to the present. Several car-related murals can also be found in the museum and the Jaggin' Around Restaurant and Pub. In both establishments one will find generous displays of Jaguar and other automobilia. The museum also sells NOS and used parts for Jaguars. All car clubs and other interested organizations are welcome. The museum has a gift shop offering local arts and crafts, souvenirs and Jaguar memorabilia. William E. Welsh is the museum's founder who says his museum is a *"Celebration of the Glory Days of the Jaguar."*

▶ TOLEDO Area

When approaching the **Toledo** area from the north on I-75 one can see the old *Willys* manufacturing plant off to the east. In the old brick smoke stack the word *"Overland"* is still clearly visible. In the nearby area are *Jeep Boulevard* and *Willys Boulevard*.

NATIONAL PACKARD MUSEUM
1899 Mahoning Ave. NW
(SRs 5 and 82 south)
WARREN, OH 44483
(Northeastern corner of the state just northwest of Youngstown)
Phone: 330-394-1899
www.packardmuseum.org
Hours: Tues.–Sat. noon–5, Sun. 1–5. Admission charged.

The famous Packard Motor Car Company was founded in Warren, OH in 1899 and operated there until it moved to Detroit in 1903. The local citizens of Warren have never forgotten this and have erected this grand museum in honor of the company and its founders, James and William Packard. A second company, the Packard Electric Co., is

The entrance to the **National Packard Museum** *in Warren, OH is shaped like the famous grill design of the Packard automobiles.*

also remembered in the museum. It was founded by the Packard brothers here in Warren and remained a part of their industrial empire until 1932 when it was acquired by General Motors. Inside the museum are shining examples of vintage Packards which were top-of-the-line motorcars in their day. Cars are rotated from time-to-time, so additional visits are very much in order. The museum honors members of the Packard families, Packard's employees, and Packard's customers and hosts an annual car show. The museum's library contains many original documents from the companies and there is a nice museum shop.

WORLD WAR II VEHICLE MUSEUM AND LEARNING CENTER

5959 W. Liberty St. (SR 304)
HUBBARD, OH 44425
(Northeastern suburb of
Youngstown on US 62 and SR 304)
Phone: 330-534-8125
www.wwiivehiclemuseum.com
Hours: M–F 9–noon and 1–5.
Admission charged.

Here is a very unique museum which specializes in the collection and display of World War II vehicles. Mixed in with the tanks, mobile artillery pieces, tank retrievers, etc. is a generous assortment of trucks, Jeeps, ambulances, staff cars, trailers, motorcycles, motorscooters and amphibious vehicles. All of the vehicles have been restored to their wartime new condition. This 52,000 sq. ft. museum also has large displays of small arms, uniforms, tents, medals and personal equipment used by the GIs. Throughout the year the museum is host to military vehicle swap meets, flea markets, vehicle shows and WW II reenactment activities.

NATIONAL ROAD/ ZANE GREY MUSEUM

8850 East Pike (US 40)
NORWICH, OH 43767
(10 miles east of Zanesville)
Phone: 740-872-3143 and
800-752-2602 (toll free)
http://www.ohiohistory.org/places/natlroad/
Hours: *May 28–Sept. 5* W–Sat. 9:30–5, Sun. noon–5; *Sept. 6–May 27* closed. Admission charged. Group tours available. Handicapped accessible.

Much of this large museum is devoted to the history of the "National Road", the first federally-funded road in the US. Funded by Congress in 1806, the road began at Cumberland, MD, passed through Zanesville, and ran to Vandalia, IL. It was built by animal and human power and was instrumental in opening up the Northwest Territory and the areas beyond until railroads took over that task. Over the years, most of the National Road was converted into modern-day US 40. One of the main displays in the museum is a glass-encased diorama showing the evolution of the National Road. There are also recreations of early roadside services such as a tavern and a wheelwright shop, and antique artifacts such as covered wagons and restored antique automobiles. Another part of the museum honors Zane Grey, the famous writer of western novels, who was born in Zanesville. One of Grey's favorite themes was the opening of the west beyond the National Road. His best-known work was "Riders of the Purple Sage". Also, Zane Grey's great-grandfather, Ebenezer Zane, was a well-known road builder. He built the first public road in Ohio known as Zane's Trace, which is in the Zanesville area.

OKLAHOMA

Oklahoma is one of several states that has made a concerted effort to preserve portions of the famous **Route 66** that runs through their state. Route 66 was the main road from America's heartland to the west coast for many years in the early part of the twentieth century. Oklahoma has over 400 driveable miles of the original route 66, more than any other state. Cities and towns along the route have cooperated in preserving historic and unique landmarks relative to the highway. The State of Oklahoma prints a very informative brochure on the highway entitled *"Get Your Kicks on Oklahoma Historic Route 66"* that is available from the Oklahoma Tourism and Recreation Department, PO Box 60789, Oklahoma City, OK 73146-0789, phone: 405-521-2406. The route is also well-marked with distinctive brown and white signs.

DARRYL STARBIRD'S NATIONAL ROD & CUSTOM CAR HALL OF FAME MUSEUM

55251 E. SR 85A
AFTON, OK 74331
(Northeastern corner of the state off the Will Rogers Turnpike)
Phone: 918-257-4234 and
918-257-8073
http://www.darrylstarbird.com
Hours: *March–October*
W–Sun. 11–5, closed *rest of year.*
Admission charged.
Directions: Take the Afton exit off the Will Rogers Turnpike and go south to SR 59. Then take a right on SR 125 to SR 85A.

This is a new and modern 40,000 sq. ft. lake-front museum with a very unique mission. It is the only museum in the world dedicated to the preservation and display of classic hot rods and custom cars while honoring the vision, craftsmanship and tenacity of the men who built them. There are some 40 such cars on display—cars like you've never seen before. The walls of the museum are covered with photos and other memorabilia related to the profession of custom car building. And, of course, the men who have been instrumental in this field are duly honored in the hall of fame. Visiting this museum is an experience you will never forget. Don't leave without visiting their gift shop.

BUD'S AUTO SALVAGE

SR 8, PO Box 9
ALINE, OK 73716 (North central part of state 40 miles west-northwest of Enid. Aline is two miles east of SR 8)

OKLAHOMA

Phone: 580-463-2204
Hours: M-F 8-5:30.

Look for the 40 foot lumberjack with the ax in his hand. This is Bud's Auto Salvage on the plains of rural Oklahoma. Beneath the ax-man is 20 acres of antique cars dating mostly from the 1950s and 1960s. Actually, Bud's has 60 acres of cars and some 6,000 total, but only those below the ax-man qualify as antiques. Cars from the 1950s and 1960s are plentiful and there are several rows of restorable cars. Bud's is a good source for early factory and add-on air conditioning parts. It gets real hot in this part of the country in the summertime. Ask for Rocky. He is the man that knows the antique stuff. Customers may remove their own parts. The yard was started in 1967.

OKLAHOMA ROUTE 66 MUSEUM

2229 W. Gary Blvd.
CLINTON, OK 73601
(West central parts of the state on I-40 and US 183)
Phone: 580-323-7866
www.route66.org
Hours: *May–Aug.* M–Sat. 9–7, Sun. 1–6, *Feb.–April and Sept.–Nov.* M–Sat. 9–5, Sun 1–5, *rest of year* Tues.–Sat. 9–5.
Admission charged.

The museum tells the story of Route 66 as well as the history of transportation from the 1920s through the 1970s. There are many displays on the Route 66 theme, a replica of a roadside diner and a number of vintage cars. The museum has a gift shop selling many Route 66-related items including books and audio/videos. Items can be mailed. They say that Clinton, OK is where the east meets the west.

NATIONAL ROUTE 66 MUSEUM

US 66, PO Box 5
ELK CITY, OK 73648 (Western part of the state on I-40)
Phone: 580-225-6266
http://www.elkcitychamber.com/route66.asp
Hours: M-Sat. 9-5, Sun. 2-5. Admission charged.
Directions: Leave I-40 at exit 32 and travel five miles along old US 66. Watch for the museum—it's on the north side of the road.

You can get your kicks at this museum which highlights the famous and historic US 66 highway. The museum is part of the Old Town Museum complex in Elk City and has extensive exhibits on the famous "Mother Road," its route through eight states, and many of the sites along its way. One unique display is an old Oklahoma gas station complete with one pump and an ice cooler for soda pop. Audio kiosks provide recordings of personal accounts and general history regarding the road. Several antique cars are also in the museum. The museum gift shop has an extensive selection of merchandise concerning the road and many books and audio tapes on the highway.

KEEPSAKE CLASSIC CARS (Dealer)

6320 N. SR 74C
GUTHRIE, OK 73044 (28 miles north of Oklahoma City on I-35)

Phone: 405-282-6238
www.keepsakecars.com
Hours: M-F 9-5, Sat. 9-3

They start in the 1930s and go up to the 1970s. That's the vintage of cars you will see in this dealer's showroom. There are classic cars and trucks, custom hot rods, muscle cars, sports cars and vintage Corvettes. Keepsake Classic Cars sells on consignment, takes trades, helps with financing and shipping and will search for the vehicle of your dreams. Browsers are always welcome here. You'll enjoy Guthrie, too. It's a pretty and historic town.

HUDSON'S SALVAGE YARD

US 62 east
HARRAH, OK 73045 (Eastern suburb of Oklahoma City)
Phone: 405-964-2347
Hours: Tues.-Sat. 8:30-5:30

You'll find lots of interesting old cars here including a number of orphans. The yard also has a generous number of pickups. Most of the vehicles are from the 1950s, 1960s and 1970s and some are whole and restorable. The yard was started in 1980 by Bill Hudson and is now run by his lovely daughter, Lesa. She says that her prices are very reasonable. Mind your manners, though, when

you come here. There's a sign on the door that says *"No Cussin'."*

HAUF AUTO SUPPLY (Salvage)

US 177 (three miles south of town)
STILLWATER, OK 74076 (35 miles north-northeast of Oklahoma City)
Phone: 405-372-1585
www.haufauto.com
Hours: Tues.-F 8-5

Hauf's is a 30-acre salvage yard with about 1,500 cars and trucks from 1930 to the present, with a high concentration of cars and trucks from the 1940s through the 1970s. Whole cars are available for parts cars or rebuilding. Customers may browse the yard. In business since 1946 as a 4th-generation family business. The current generation is Gene and Jo Hauf.

COURT HOUSE/CITY HALL

Downtown
TULSA, OK.

Buried on the Courthouse/City Hall lawn is a brand new 1957 Plymouth. The car was donated by a local Chrysler Plymouth dealer and was buried there in 1957 in a waterproof chamber along with several drums of gasoline. It is to be exhumed in 2007. Until then a plaque marks the site.

OREGON

▶ AURORA AREA
(22 miles south of Portland just east of I-5)

AURORA WRECKERS & RECYCLERS
21111 SR 99e NE
AURORA, OR 97002
(22 miles south of downtown
Portland just east of I-5)
Phone: 503-678-1107
Hours: M–Sat. 9–5

Old cars and trucks—that's what you will find here at Aurora Wreckers & Recyclers. They date from the 1930s through the 1960s. A high percentage of the vehicles are Chrysler products, but other American makes are well-represented. Some cars and trucks are whole and suitable for restoring. Company personnel remove all parts and customers may browse the yard with supervision.

BIRD BRAINS (Dealer)
12184 Ehlen Rd. NE
AURORA, OR 97002
Phone: 503-678-5599
www.birdbrains.net
Hours: M–F 8–5:30

The people here at Bird Brains really aren't bird brains, they are Ford Thunderbird lovers. They specialize in restored, driveable and nice original 1955-57 Thunderbirds—although—you might see a Hupmobile or two in their handsome black and white tiled showroom. Bird Brains also sells a complete line of new and used Thunderbird parts. They take trades, offer appraisals and technical advice, help with financing and can arrange shipping. In business since 1987.

End of Aurora area ◀

PACIFIC NORTHWEST TRUCK MUSEUM
Brooklake Rd. (PO Box 9281)
BROOKS, OR 97305-0281 (Northern suburb of Salem just off I-5)
Phone: 503-537-4040 and *Sat.–Sun. May through Sept.* 503-463- 8701
www.pacificnwtruckmuseum.org
Hours: *April 1 to Oct. 1* M–F 10–4:30. Admission charged.

Directions: Leave I-5 at exit 263 and travel west on Brooklake Rd. two miles to *Antique Powerland*, which is on the north side of the road. The truck museum is in the lower lever of Antique Powerland.

Have You ever seen a 1917 Gersix Model G truck? You will see one here and it is believed to be the only one left in the world. This truck, and about 100 other Gersixs, were made in Oregon. This truck is symbolic of the museum which endeavors to keep alive the memory of the heavy trucks and vehicles used here in the Northwest during a greater part of the Twentieth Century. Some of the trucks were modified by their owners to cope with the longer distances and rough terrain of the Northwest. In total, there are over 50 trucks, all of them restored. The museum was founded by, and is operated by, a group of dedicated antique truck buffs.

ANTIQUE MOTORCYCLE AND AUTO MUSEUM

1235 Oregon St. (US 101),
PO Box 751
PORT ORFORD, OR 97465
(On the southern coast of Oregon and US 101)
Phone: 541-332-0523 and
541-290-4552
www.antiquemotorcyclemuseum.com
Hours: *Apr. 1 through Oct. 29*
Thurs.-M 10–5:30, *rest of year*
F–M 10–5. Admission charged.

This is a beautiful part of the Oregon coast and in this museum one will also see another beautiful sight—about 30 vintage motorcycles and several vintage cars. Motorcycles, of course, are highlighted, with the oldest one being an 1896 model. Some of the cycles are rare and there are several one-of-a-kind models. Still others are associated with famous people. There are additional displays of antique musical instruments, radios and victrolas. The museum's owner is Stan Dishong, a well-known racer and motorcycle aficionado.

WILDCAT AUTO WRECKING

46827 S.E. Wildcat Mountain Rd.
SANDY, OR 97055
(25 miles east of Portland on US 26)
Phone: 503-668-7786
www.wildcatmopars.com
Hours: Tues.–F 9–6, Sat. 10–6.
Open on Tuesdays, but they
do not answer the phone.

Walter P. Chrysler never saw this place but he would smile if he ever had. There's eight acres of his automobiles here, some 800 of them. They date back several decades—to the 1940s—and some of them are still in one piece ready to be restored. Customers may pull their own parts with permission, otherwise yard personnel do the job. This is beautiful mountain country with lots of wildlife about. Enjoy the hummingbirds and wild ducks, but don't get too close to the elk. Ed Yost is the owner and he started the company here in "God's country," as he calls it, in 1993.

PENNSYLVANIA

Within Pennsylvania are two of the nation's most historic roads, the **National Road** and the **Lincoln Highway**. Segments of both have been preserved.

The National Road, which traversed southwestern Pennsylvania from *Cumberland, MD* to *Wheeling, WV* is now a 75-mile-long state park designated by the state as the **NATIONAL ROAD HERITAGE PARK**. Modern-day US 40 parallels the old road. Along the old National Road many sites have been preserved such as inns, mile markers, toll houses, bridges, gas stations, cabin camps and various buildings. Several period restaurants are also located in the Park/Road. For information about the road and a detailed map contact the park's headquarters at 61 E. Main St. *Uniontown*, PA 15401, phone: 412-430-1248.

The Lincoln Highway is much longer than the National Road and traverses the entire state from the Philadelphia area to Pittsburgh and the Ohio state line. Segments of the road have been preserved and they too contain many historic sites and building. Modern-day US 30 parallels most of the road.

▶ ALLENTOWN AREA

AMERICA ON WHEELS (Museum)
5 North Front St. PO Box 590
ALLENTOWN, PA 18105-0950
Phone: 610-432-4200
www.americaonwheels.org

This is a museum-to-be that will open in the summer of 2006. It will be large and have a sizeable number of vintage vehicles. The museum's mission is to provide a glimpse of the past, present and future of our nation's over-the-road motor transportation. It is part of a larger community project which will revitalize the famous *Lehigh Landing* of Allentown.

MACK TRUCKS HISTORICAL MUSEUM
997 Postal Rd.
(From US 22 exit Airport Rd. North. In an industrial park adjacent to the Allentown Airport.)
ALLENTOWN, PA 18103
Phone: 610-266-6767
www.macktrucks.com
Hours: M, W and F 10–4. Free.

This is the Mack Truck Corporation's company museum. On display are about two dozen trucks and vehicles associated with the company. There is a 1900 open-air, 27-passenger Mack touring

There are more than two dozen antique trucks on display at the Mack Trucks Historical Museum *in Allentown, PA.*

bus, a 1910 Brockway motor wagon, a nicely restored Model AB Mack tank truck, a 1918 Mack Model AC 5¹/₂ ton fire truck fully equipped as it was when it was in service in the city of Baltimore, and many other interesting vehicles. The museum has a library of some 80,000 photographs of historic trucks. Don Schumaker and Snowy Doe are the museum's co-curators.

End of Allentown area ◄

JEM CLASSIC CAR MUSEUM
SR 443, Box 120C
(10 miles west of Lehighton)
ANDREAS, PA 18211 (20 miles
northwest of Allentown)
Phone: 717-386-3554
www.fieldtrip.com/pa/73863554.htm
Hours: *June through Sept.* M–F 9–4,
Sat.–Sun. noon–4. *Oct. through May*
M–F 9–4. Handicapped accessible.
Admission charged.

This privately-owned 18,000 sq. ft. museum is nestled in the beautiful Pocono Mountains and displays about 40 antique cars. The vehicles range in age from 1902 to the 1960s. Most of the cars are American-made and some are very rare. The museum also has a nice collection of motorcycles and large-scale model airplanes. A bubble juke box plays oldies but goodies as visitors tour the museum. There is a gift shop, a snack bar and inside and outside picnic tables. Car clubs and groups are always welcome.

BOYERTOWN MUSEUM OF HISTORIC VEHICLES
85 S. Warwick St.
BOYERTOWN, PA 19512
(30 miles east of Reading)
Phone: 610-367-2090

PENNSYLVANIA

www.boyertownmuseum.org
Hours: Tues.–Sun. 9:30–4.
Closed major holidays.
Admission charged.
Directions: Proceed from SR 100
to Jct. of SRs 73 and 562, then two
blocks south to Warwick St.

This museum, in the heart of the
Pennsylvania Dutch country, displays
many types of vehicles, many of which
are associated with the local area. There
are more than 50 vehicles to be seen.
The museum building is part of an
original factory complex where some
of the vehicles on display were built
between 1872 and 1990. Some of the
vehicles built by local Pennsylvania
Dutch craftsmen sport names such as
Duryea, SGV, Daniels, Middleby, Boss,
Dile and Fleetwood. Other exhibits
include electric vehicles, motorcycles,
carriages, sleighs, bicycles, children's
vehicles, license plates, tools and other
transportation-related items. The museum sponsors an annual auto show
and flea market called "Duryea Days".
There is an orientation theater, research
library and a gift and souvenir shop
which offers many auto-related items.
Founded in 1965.

GRICE CLEARFIELD
COMMUNITY MUSEUM

119 N. 4th St.
CLEARFIELD, PA 16830 (15 miles
northeast of Allentown on SR 512)
Phone: 814-768-7332
Hours: *June through Sept.* M–Sat.
10–4, Sun. noon–4. Closed *rest of
year.* Free.

There's lots of interesting stuff in this
community museum including about 60

antique cars. The collection consists of a
variety of makes and models, US-made
and imports. In addition to the cars, visitors will see mounted wild game and fish
and other items of interest. There is a gift
shop and car clubs are always welcome.
The museum's founder is Lynn Grice.

AUTO TOY STORE/NEMACOLIN
WOODLANDS RESORT & SPA
(Museum & dealer)

1001 LaFayette Dr.
(Off US 40—watch for signs)
FARMINGTON, PA 15437
(In southwestern Pennsylvania
on US 40)
Phone: 724-329-8555 and
800-422-2736 (toll free)
www.nemacolin.com
Museum hours: 10–5 daily. Free

The Nemacolin Woodlands Resort
& Spa is a very large resort and at the
heart of it all is the Auto Toy Store which
consists of a collection of more than
a dozen cars, plus a few motorcycles.
Some of the cars are restored. All of the
vehicles can be viewed or purchased.
Actually, the Toy Store is considered to
be a part of a much larger art collection
on display at the resort. The museum
is handicapped accessible and there is
ample free parking. If it's winter time,
bring your skis; if it's summer, bring
your bathing suit.

EISENHOWER NATIONAL HISTORIC
SITE (Historic Home)

Adjacent to Gettysburg National
Military Park
GETTYSBURG, PA 17325
(40 miles southwest of Harrisburg
near the Maryland state line)
Phone: 717-338-9114

www.nps.gov/eise/
Hours: Daily 9–4. Site accessible by shuttle bus from National Park Visitor Center on SR 134. Admission charged.

This was the home and 230-acre farm of President and Mrs. Dwight D. Eisenhower. On the grounds are a visitor center, with exhibits on Eisenhower's life, and the home itself in which the Eisenhowers lived during his Presidency and retirement years. Several out-buildings hold and display the personal belongings, awards, gifts, paintings, farm equipment and other memorabilia of the Eisenhower family. In the large garage, which was once a chicken house, is a modified Crosley runabout, jokingly called by Eisenhower the "surrey with the fringe on top". The President used the Crosley to take visitors around the farm. Some of the world's most famous people, including Winston Churchill, Nikita Khrushchev and Charles De Gaulle, rode in this little car. Also in the garage is the chauffeur's quarters and a walk-in cooler for meat storage.

EPERTHENER'S AUTO WRECKING
(Salvage)
683 Teiline Rd.
GROVE CITY, PA 16127
(25 miles east of Youngstown, OH on PA SRs 58 and 173)
Phone: 814-786-7173
Hours: M–F 9–5, Sat. 9–noon

Did you ever see a 1937 Chevrolet full of hub caps? You will see one here at Eperthener's (that's French by the way). You will also see hundreds of old cars and trucks dating back to the 1940s. Eperthener's also has some NOS parts and a nice selection of old manuals dating back to the 1930s. And how about an antique snowmobile? You can get new and used parts for all makes of snowmobiles here. The Eperthener family was, at one time, a dealer for the Polaris snowmobiles. Visitors may browse the yard with permission, but company personnel remove all parts. This is a family-run business. The person who answers the phone will probably be one of the Eperthener's. They started the yard in 1957.

 # HARRISBURG AREA

ROLLS-ROYCE FOUNDATION'S RESEARCH LIBRARY AND EDUCATIONAL MUSEUM
189 Hempt Rd.
MECHANICSBURG, PA 17050
(8 miles southwest of downtown Harrisburg on I-76)
Phone: 877-795-4050
www.rollsroycefoundation.com
Hours: M, W & F 10–2. Other times by appointment. Free

This exclusive museum, which opened in 2004, is part of the Rolls-Royce Foundation's headquarters complex. About eight to ten Rolls-Royce and/or Bentley automobiles are on display at all times. Some are associated with famous people. A number of the vehicles are on loan from private collectors so the display changes from time-to-time. The research library is extensive and is one of the best sources in the US for information on Rolls-Royce and Bentley automobiles. Seminars and other functions are held here and there is a museum store.

STATE MUSEUM OF PENNSYLVANIA

300 North Third St.
HARRISBURG, PA 17108
(South-central part of the state on I-81, I-76 and I-83)
Phone: 717-787-4979 and 717-783-9899 (direct to curator of automobile display)
www.statemuseumpa.org

Hours: Tues.–Sat. 9–5, Sun. noon–5, closed holidays. Free.

This is the official museum of the state of Pennsylvania with displays on a wide variety of topics concerning the history, industry, natural resources, arts and people of the state. There are about half a dozen antique autos in the museum, most of them pre-World War I and some of them made in Pennsylvania. The museum has an automotive library containing literature, periodicals, etc. and is available to the public by appointment.

End of Harrisburg area ◀

▶ HERSHEY AREA (12 miles east of Harrisburg)

ANTIQUE AUTOMOBILE CLUB OF AMERICA LIBRARY AND RESEARCH CENTER

501 W. Governor Rd.
HERSHEY, PA 17033
Phone: Library 717-534-2082,

National Headquarters 717-534-1910
www.aaca.org
Hours: M–F 8:30–3:45

This is a large library created and operated by the Antique Automobile Club

The Antique Automobile Club of America Library and Research Center, *Hershey, PA, was founded in 1981 and is open to visitors and researchers.*

of America and is open to visitors and researchers. The library has a wealth of information on antique cars including books, periodicals, catalogs, sales literature, ads, brochures, owner's manuals, shop manuals, parts books, color charts and chips, photographs, sheet music, postcards, calendars, jokes, cartoons and company annual reports. Materials may not be taken from the library but library personnel will photocopy or otherwise provide working copies for borrowers and researchers. Individuals seeking research information should request a Research Request Form from the Library in order to facilitate the research process. Fees are charged for research work done by library personnel.

The Antique Automobile Club of American Museum *in* Hershey, PA.

ANTIQUE AUTOMOBILE CLUB OF AMERICA MUSEUM

161 Museum Dr. PO Box 234
HERSHEY, PA 17033
Phone: 717-566-7100
www.aacamuseum.org
Hours: *Daily* 9–5. Admission charged.

The Antique Automobile Club of American is one of the guiding lights in the world of antique automobiles. These diligent folks have put together this excellent 70,000 sq. ft. three-story museum on 25 acres of land to display the fruits of their labor. The museum relates the history of the automobile from its inception to the present day. Some 90 restored vehicles are on display in period settings that give visitors a feel for the automotive days of old. Additional vehicles are in storage so the vehicles on display rotate. The museum is available for banquets, weddings, meetings, receptions, trade shows and other events. Food and bar services can be provided. The museum also has an interesting gift shop.

THE MUSEUM OF BUS TRANSPORTATION

161 Museum Dr.
HERSHEY, PA 17033
Phone: 717-566-7100 ext. 119
www.busmuseum.org
Hours: *Memorial Day through Labor Day* M–Sun. 9–5, *Labor Day through Memorial Day* W–Sun. 9–5. Admission charged.

This museum is part of the Antique Automobile Club of American Museum that, as the name implies, specializes in busses. There are more than 20 antique busses on display, some owned by the museum and some on loan. Each bus is clearly identified by make, year of manufacture and purpose. There are over-the-road buses, city busses, school buses and tourist buses. They range in age from pre-WW I models to the 1980s. Maybe you rode on one of them.

End of Hershey area ◀

SWIGART MUSEUM

US 22 East (4 miles east of Huntingdon)
HUNTINGDON, PA 16652
(22 miles east of Altoona)
Phone: 814-643-0885
www.swigartmuseum.com
Hours: *Memorial Day through Oct.* daily 9–5, closed *rest of year.*
Admission charged.

This is the oldest antique car museum in America—started in 1920—and it has one of the foremost and most diverse collections of antique cars in the country. There are some 200 vehicles in the collection including two—count them—Tuckers. The museum's founder, the late W. Emmert Swigart, started the museum in order to preserve a portion of Americana that was, in 1920, rapidly disappearing—automobiles. As a result, there is a large collection of pre-World War I vehicles with long-forgotten names as well as vehicles powered by one and two cylinder engines. There are vehicles here, too, with more familiar names: Pierce-Arrow, Packard, Duesenberg, Cord and others. Some of the vehicles are associated with famous people. Other exhibits include the world's largest collection of license plates as well as automobile name plates (there were some 5,000 makes of automobiles produced in the US). Other items on display are bicycles, brass horns, lights, toys, post cards and period clothing. The museum has a library which is open to researchers. William E. Swigart, Jr. is the owner.

GREBLE AUTO PARTS (Salvage)

988 Houtztown Rd.
MEYERSTOWN, PA 17067
(Midway between Harrisburg and Reading on US 422)
Phone: 717-933-4818
Hours: M–F 8–4, Sat. 8–noon.

The Swigart Museum *of Huntingdon, PA is the oldest antique car museum in the US.*

No tall weeds in this 30-acre salvage yard thanks to a unique landscaping service—sheep. Customers can walk freely among the 3,000 or more vehicles—and the sheep—hunting for their parts or just looking. Browsers are welcome here. Most of the cars are American-made and ranging in age from the 1940s to the present. The heaviest concentration is in the 1960s and 1970s. All cars can be easily located by row and car numbers. Visitors can get a map at the office. This clean and well-organized yard is owned by Daniel Pohronezny who started it in 1976.

STEWART CRISWELL AND SON'S SALVAGE YARD

13 Roberts Rd.
NOTTINGHAM, PA 19362
(On US 1 and SR 272 south of Lancaster near the Maryland state line.)
Phone: 717-529-2612
Hours: M–Sat. 8–5
Directions: Proceed west on SR 272 out of Nottingham for 5 miles and watch for Lloyd's Road. Turn north onto Lloyd's Rd. and the yard is 50 feet ahead.

"We never crush the old stuff." That's what Alan Criswell, the yard's operator, will tell you—and it's music to the ears of an old car buff. Beneath 18 acres of trees, there are some 2,500 cars ranging in age from the 1930s and up. The majority of the cars are from the 1950s through the 1970s. Also available is a nice collection of light trucks as well as complete cars for parts cars or restoration. Visitors may browse the yard and pull their own parts. Criswell's also installs auto glass. In business since 1945.

FREE LIBRARY OF PHILADELPHIA AUTOMOBILE REFERENCE COLLECTION

1901 Vine St.
PHILADELPHIA, PA 19103
Phone: 215-686-5404
www.library.phila.gov
Hours: *Automobile Collection* M–F 9–5. *Library* M–W 9–9, Thurs.–F 9–5, Sat. 9–5, Sun. October through June, 1–5. Closed on Sun. rest of year. Free.

This is a large city library with one of the largest collections of automotive literature in the country. The Automotive Reference Collection is open as noted above. The library's staff welcomes phone inquiries. No browsing is permitted.

THE FRICK ART AND HISTORICAL CENTER

7227 Reynolds St.
PITTSBURGH, PA 14208
Phone: 412-371-0600
www.frickart.com
Hours: Tues.–Sun. 10–5.
Admission charged.

This is the restored estate of the late industrialist Henry Clay Frick. The main building was the home of the Frick family and is an example of fine Italian Renaissance architecture. Inside the mansion are works of art and bronzes by many famous artists, as well as examples of rare and exquisite tapestry and Chinese porcelains. There is also a concert hall which hosts musical events, lectures, etc. On the grounds, several of the outbuildings have been converted into a quality antique car museum known as *"The Car and Car-*

riage Museum." On display are some 20 vehicles including several cars owned by the Frick family. Most of the motor cars are pre-World War I. An award-winning video entitled *"Pittsburgh and the Automobile"* is shown at various times throughout the day. Other videos and films are also shown. If you get hungry, there is a cafe on the premises.

TYRED WHEELS MUSEUM

1164 Russell Corner Rd.
(Rt. 2, Box 302)
PLEASANTVILLE, PA 16341
(60 miles south of Erie)
Phone: 814-676-0756
Hours: *Memorial Day weekend through and including Labor Day — Sat., Sun., Mon. 1–5.*
Other times by appointment.
Admission charged.

This museum is in the heart of Pennsylvania oil country and has some 5,000 miniature vehicle models on display. There are Danbury and Franklin Mint

Here is how to get to Tyred Wheels Museum.

miniatures, dealer promotional models, miniature tractors and trains. In addition to the miniatures there are some 25 antique automobiles plus airplanes, motorcycles, old radios, bicycles, pedal cars, doll houses and tin toys. This is a family-owned museum run by Gene, Cora and Gene Burt.

JERRY'S CLASSIC CARS AND COLLECTIBLES MUSEUM

394 S. Centre St.
POTTSVILLE, PA 17901
(Midway between Harrisburg and Allentown on US 209 and SR 61)
Phone: 570-628-2266 and 570-622-9510
www.jerrysmuseum.com
Hours: *April 1 through Dec. 31,* Sat.–Sun. noon–5. Admission charged.

Jerry and Janet Enders love collecting old cars and lots of other stuff. Visitors are invited to see the fruits of their labor by visiting their museum. There are some 20,000 items on display including about a dozen antique cars, many of them from the 1950s and 1960s. The walls of the museum are lavishly decorated with murals depicting automotive scenes, including a drive-in movie theater and an old Atlantic Oil Company service station. Other attractions in this interesting museum are a soda fountain, a barber shop, a library, a huge record collection, musical instruments and lots of automobilia. The building itself is an automotive relic having been a Studebaker dealership in the 1920s and later a Morgan dealership. If you get hungry, there is a snack bar. Jerry and Janet opened the doors in 1997.

GAST CLASSIC MOTORCARS EXHIBIT
(Museum & dealer)
    421 Hartman Bridge Rd.
    (On SR 896 just north of town)
    STRASBURG, PA 17579 (8 miles
    southeast of Lancaster)
    Phone: 717-687-9500
    www.classicar.com
    Hours: Daily 9–5, closed Jan 1,
    Easter, Thanksgiving, Dec 24 and
    25. Admission charged.

This is a beautiful exhibit of approximately 50 restored and fine original vehicles with many of the cars for sale. Because of this, the cars on display are constantly changing. Some of the vehicles are associated with famous people. And who knows, you might find the car you had in high school or drove on your honeymoon. Gast's has a large gift shop called the *"Car Buff's Gift Shop"* which offers a generous assortment of automotive-oriented gifts, books, posters, jewelry, etc. You won't be sorry you stopped here.

ENGLER'S USED AUTOS & PARTS
(Salvage)
    1768 Stairville Rd.
    WAPWALLOPEN, PA 18660
    (On SR 239 and the Susquehana
    River 7 miles northwest of the
    junction of I-80 and I-81)
    Phone: 570-868-3990
    Hours: M, Tues., Thurs., F 8:30–5,
    W and Sat. 8:30–noon.

Planning a trip to the Poconos? Here's a place to put on your itinerary. Engler's has some real oldies in their well-kept 30-acre yard dating back to the 1930s with a large number of 1940s and 1950s vehicles. There is also a generous selection of 1950s and 1960s models. Bob Engler, who runs the yard, likes to hold on to the oldies. Engler has some 3,000 vehicles in the yard and visitors may pull their own parts. In business since 1950.

TEE-TO-TUM MUSEUM
    US 6 in Wysox
    WYSOX, PA 18848 (50 miles
    northwest of Scranton on US 6)
    Phone: 570-265-5505 or
    570-265-8272
    Hours: *April through Nov.*
    Tues.–F 10–4. *Rest of year,* F 10–4.
    Admission charged.

This is a privately-owned museum displaying over 40 antique cars from 1897 to WW II, but mostly pre-1915. All are in restored, original or "as found" condition. There are a number of very unique cars such as the Grant and the Brough. In addition to the cars, there are displays of engines, accessories, advertising, and oil company advertising. Other items to be seen in the museum include antique dolls, toys, firearms, railroad memorabilia, tools and many other American antiques. The museum is operated by Howard and Dietland Crain and there is a small antique shop on the premises.

AGRICULTURAL AND INDUSTRIAL MUSEUM OF YORK COUNTY
    480 E. Market St.
    YORK, PA 17403
    Phone: 717-852-7007
    www.fieldtrip.com/pa/78527007.htm
    Hours: Tues., Thurs. and Sat. 10–4.

PENNSYLVANIA

Closed major holidays. Admission charged.

This is a large county-owned museum with two locations that trace the history of York County from just before the Civil War through World War I. Exhibits highlight industrial equipment, agricultural items and products used and made in York County. Many of the exhibits are hands-on for additional educational

Visitors will see Pullman automobiles like these, which were made in York County, at the Agricultural and Industrial Museum of York County. *Left is a 1909 Pullman touring car; right, a 1910 Pullman touring car.*

appeal. In the E. Market St. location is a collection of antique vehicles including several made in York County such as the Pullman automobile, the Bell Car and a Mayflower Huckster Wagon. The museum also has a collection of horse-drawn vehicles, antique farm equipment, engines (some made in York County), an old machine shop, weaving equipment, boats, a locomotive, railroad cars, a grist mill and displays on various automobile components made in York County over the years. There is a gift shop, a meeting room which can be rented, a children's area and a garden.

EASTERN MUSEUM OF MOTOR RACING

100 Baltimore Rd. (At the Latimore Valley Fairgrounds)
YORK SPRINGS, PA 17372
(Midway between Harrisburg and Gettysburg on US 16 and SR 94)
Phone: 717-528-8279
www.emmr.org
Hours: *April through Dec.* Sat.–Sun. 10–4. Closed *rest of year.* Donations accepted.

If racing is your thing, you will want to see this museum. As its name implies, it highlights racing in the eastern part of the US. On display is an outstanding collection of vintage race cars and artifacts as well as a research library of rare books, documents and photos pertaining to the sport of auto racing. Included in the collection are Indy cars, dirt track racers, sprints, midgets, NASCAR vehicles, drag racers, stock cars and a number of racing motorcycles. Some of the restored race cars participate in an exhibition race at the Latimore Valley Fairground each year in June. There is also a nice gift shop.

RHODE ISLAND

GOLD'S AUTO WRECKING
  113 Fenner Av.
  MIDDLETOWN, RI 02842
  (On SR 138 just north of Newport)
  Phone: 401-846-0399
  Hours: M–F 9–5. Sat. 9–3

They go back to 1947 in this 4-acre 800-car salvage yard. Most of the vehicles are American-made and there are light trucks and some muscle cars. Customers may pull their own parts if they wish. Otherwise, company personnel will do the job. When you walk into the office you will probably hear golden oldies on the radio, see a large collection of license plates from all 50 states, and enjoy a large aquarium - not many salvage yards have an aquarium. Be on the lookout, though,

for "Spike," the yard's watchcat. He can be mean. The yard is run by Charlie Laurine and his lovely wife, Betty.

ARNOLD'S AUTO PARTS (Salvage)
  1484 Crandall Rd. (SR 81)
  TIVERTON, RI 02878 (5 miles
  southwest of Fall River, MA)
  Phone: 401-624-6936
  Hours: M–F 8–5, Sat 8–3

This salvage yard, with about 1,000 vehicles, specializes in cars and trucks of mixed makes from the 1930s to the 1990s. Most are domestic. Arnold's also offers a towing service and customers may browse the yard. Car clubs are always welcome. In business and run by the Waite family since 1952.

SOUTH CAROLINA

NMPA STOCK CAR HALL OF FAME— JOE WEATHERLY MUSEUM

US 52 and 401 and, SRs 34 and
151 West (adjoining the
Darlington Raceway)
DARLINGTON, SC 29532
(10 miles northwest of Florence)
Phone: 803-395-8821
www.americanracefan.com
Hours: Daily 9–5.
Admission charged.

CLOSED

This hall of fame and museum honors famous individuals in the sport of stock car racing. For three decades the National Motorsports Association (NMPA) has strived to promote professionalism and fellowship among journalists, writers, photographers, broadcasters and corporate leaders who are devoted to the field of motorsports. NMPA bestows a number of awards through the year for excellence in the various fields of motorsports racing. In the museum are pictures and plaques of those who have been honored in the Hall of Fame and the museum displays a collection of history-making stock cars. Many of the cars are associated with famous race drivers. Also included in the museum are racing engines and an interesting collection of illegal racing parts removed from race cars at actual racing events. The museum has a gift and souvenir shop offering stock car-related merchandise.

LOW COUNTRY CLASSICS OF SOUTH CAROLINA (Dealer)

3113 S. Fraser St.
GEORGETOWN, SC 29440
(On the coast 30 miles
south of Myrtle Beach)
Phone: 843-545-8191
www.lowcountryclassics.com
Hours: M–F 9–6, Sat. 9–3

Classics and muscle cars can be found in this seaside dealer's showroom. They normally carry about 50 cars in inventory and most are in the affordable category. Low Country Classics buys cars, sells cars, takes trades, offers appraisals, helps with financing and shipping and can provide mechanical and body work with pick-up and delivery available. Warranties are also offered. In business since 1987.

AMERICAN LaFRANCE MUSEUM

8500 Palmetto Commerce Parkway
LADSON, SC 29456 (Northern
suburb of Charleston on I-26)
Phone: 843-486-7400 or
888-253-8725 (toll free)
www.americanlafrance.com
Hours: M–F 9–5

If you like to see big old trucks, you'll be happy here. This is the company museum of the famous American LaFrance Corp. which has made multi-purpose trucks and a broad line of fire trucks for over 170 years. The museum displays a wide range of trucks and fire apparatus, some horse-powered, some steam-powered and some human-powered. American LaFrance is a part of Freightliner, LLC which is owned by DaimlerChrysler. Tours of their plants are available upon request.

ANTIQUES HAVEN (Museum)

517 Flat Rock Rd. (Corner of SR 35 and Flat Rock Rd., 3 miles east of downtown Liberty)
LIBERTY, SC 29657 (15 miles west of Greenville just north of US 123)
Phone: 864-843-6827
Hours: W–Sat. 11–5, Sun. 1–5.
Donations accepted.

This interesting museum has the largest varied antique collection in the southeast. Browse through an early barber shop, a traveling dentist office (fillings are 25 cents), a general store, a tavern, a 7-room house and an early Auto Supply Store. Some twenty vehicles are on display most of them are pre-World War I and some of them are the three-wheeled variety. There are also several very old motorcycles. Guided tours can be provided for one or a dozen visitors with a guarantee you will see things you have never seen before. Some of the vehicles are for sale and there is a large antique shop on the premises. Car clubs are always welcome. The museum was started by Remy Baker who collected his first car in 1944.

BMW ZENTRUM MUSEUM

Intersection of I-85 and SR 101 west of Spartenburg, PO Box 11000
SPARTENBURG, SC 29304-4100
(Northwestern part of state)
Phone: 888-TOUR-BMW
(888-868-7269) (toll free)
www. bmwzentrum.com
Hours: Tues.–Sat. 9:30–5:30.
Admission charged.

This is the BMW company's museum and visitor center attached to their large manufacturing plant just west of Spartenburg. The 28,000 sq. ft. museum traces the history of the company and highlights many of its contributions to the automotive, aircraft and motor-cycle industries. Several historic and antique BMW automobiles, race cars and motorcycles are on display. Another display highlights the company's work in innovative aircraft engines and engines designed to use alternative fuels. The museum has an extensive art gallery with paintings of auto-related subjects by world-famous artists. There is also a 230-seat multi-screen *"Experience Theater,"* a gift shop and a cafe. To reach the BMW facility take exit 60 from I-85 South, proceed north and then west at the first stop light. Watch for signs leading to the facility.

SOUTH DAKOTA

B & B AUTO SALVAGE
County Rd. 69
BELLE FOURCHE, SD 57717
(West central part of the state 10
miles from the Wyoming border
on US 85 and US 212)
Phone: 605-892-3248
www.buyusedparts.net
Hours: M–F 9–6, Sat. 9–1
Directions: Leave I-80 at exit 10
and go north of US 85 into the
town of Belle Fourche. Then go
west on county Rd. 69 about 1
mile. B & B will be on the left.

Here on the South Dakota grasslands
is a large salvage yard with hundreds of
vintage cars, both American-made and
imports. Included in their inventory
are Willys, De Sotos, Morris Minors,
Renaults, Packards, Hudsons and Studebakers. Some of their vehicles are in
rebuildable condition. If you collect
license plates, B & B has tons of them.
Jason Eisenberger is the yard's manager.

▶ MITCHELL AREA
(65 miles west of Sioux Falls on I-90)

DAKOTA SALVAGE
2421 W. Havens St.
MITCHELL, SD 57301
Phone: 605-996-8204
Hours: M–F 8–5, Sat. 8–noon
Directions: Leave I-90 at exit 332 and
head into Mitchell. In a very short
distance, look for a Holiday Inn. At
that intersection is West Havens St.
Proceed half a mile west on West
Havens and Dakota Salvage will be
on the south side of the road.

"Look! Behind that bush! A 1949
Chevy four-door fastback!" That's what
you might say when you visit this yard.
The bushes are tall and the cars are old.
There are a few 1930s and 1940s models,
but a lot of 1950s, 1960s and 1970s
models. There are also some light trucks.

A large storage facility holds much of
the good stuff. Customers may browse
the yard, but yard personnel remove all
parts. This is a family business run by
Florence, Fred, Bob and Randy Shank.
Founded in 1950.

**TELSTAR MUSTANG-SHELBY-COBRA
RESTORATIONS AND MUSEUM**
1300-1400 S. Kimball St.
MITCHELL, SD 57301
Phone: 605-996-6550
www.telstarmotors.com
Open: *Mid-May through mid-Sept.*,
or any time by appointment.
Admission charged.
Guided tours available.

This is the first Shelby and Mustang
museum in the USA. The current mu-

This is only part of the vehicles on display at the Telstar Mustang-Shelby-Cobra Museum *in Mitchell, SD.*

seum opened to the public in 1990 and has dozens of Cobras and Shelbys on display. All have been restored by Telstar technicians. Every year of the Shelby Mustang is represented here and all of their titles have been autographed by Carroll Shelby. As you tour the climate-controlled museum, muscle-car music will be playing softly in the background.

Several restored high-performance engines are on display for close inspection.

Telstar offers full restoration services for their own vehicles and for those of customers and can bring a Shelby or Cobra back to original manufacturers' standards. The owners of the collection are Jerry and Mavis Regynski.

End of Mitchell Area ◀

PIONEER AUTO MUSEUM AND ANTIQUE TOWN

Junction of I-90 and US 16/83
MURDO, SD 57559 (South-central part of the state on I-90)
Phone: 605-669-2691
www.classicar.com
Hours: *June through Aug.* daily 8am–9pm. Hours in *April–May and Sept.–Oct.* vary. Admission charged.

This is a very large museum complex of 39 buildings, most of which comprise an Antique Town. Of interest to old car buffs is the museum's unusually large collection of antique cars—nearly 250. Plus, there are motorcycles, antique tractors and pieces of antique farm equipment.

Watch for the unique Pioneer Auto signs on your way to Pioneer Auto Museum and Antique Town.

Some of the cars are of pre-World War I vintage and there are numerous vehicles from the 1920s and 1930s. Some of the cars and motorcycles are associated with famous people. Visitors will also see large collections of music boxes, antique toys, ladies fashions, dishes and glassware, and an outstanding collection of gems, fossils and rocks. The museum has a snack shop and a large and interesting gift shop.

▶ RAPID CITY AREA
(Southwest corner of the state on I-90)

MOORE'S AUTO SALVAGE
    1761 Country Rd.
RAPID CITY, SD 57701
Phone: 605-348-4926
www.mooresautosalvage.com
Hours: M–F 9–5, Sat. 9–noon

You'll find a lot of rebuildable vehicles here—more than usual for a salvage yard of this size. Moore's specializes in cars and truck from the 1920s to the 1980s and has over 2,000 vehicles on their 20-acre spread. This is a low-rust part of the country so the vehicles are in pretty good shape. And guess who runs the yard—that's right—the Moore family. They started the business in 1988. When you walk in the door, one of them will probably greet you. Tell them the *"Tour Book"* sent you.

MOTION UNLIMITED MUSEUM AND ANTIQUE CAR LOT
(Museum and dealer)
    6180 S. SR 79
RAPID CITY, SD 57701
Phone: 605-348-7373
www.motionunlimitedmuseum.com
Hours: M–F 9–6, Sat. 9–4.

Here is a place that shows 'em and sells 'em. The best vehicles are, understandably, in the 13,000 sq. ft. showroom, where some are for sale and some are not. Owners Bill and Peggy Napoli do complete vehicle restorations so many of the vehicles on display are the products of their labor. When you visit, they will probably have 5 or 6 vehicles being restored and you can see how they do it. Altogether, there are some 100 vehicles on display and for sale. Motorcycles are plentiful here, too, along with childrens' pedal cars, tractors, signs, gas pumps and other memorabilia. Vehicles constantly change so this is a place you can visit often.

End of Rapid City area ◀

STURGIS MOTORCYCLE MUSEUM & HALL OF FAME
    Main and Junction Sts. in downtown Sturgis, PO Box 602
STURGIS, SD 57785 (On I-90, 28 miles from the Wyoming border)
Phone: 605-347-2001
www.sturgismotorcyclemuseum.org
Hours: Open daily. Closed major holidays. Admission charged.

Ask anyone who has a motorcycle about Sturgis, SD and they'll tell you that this city is the geographic center of motorcycledom. This is due partly to the fact that the huge *Sturgis Motorcycle Rally*, one of the country's largest motorcycle events, is held here each year. At the center of this activity is the Sturgis Motorcycle Museum and Hall of Fame. This museum has some 100 motorcycles and motorscooters on display along with many other motorcycle-related memorabilia. Some of the motorcycles are on loan so the display changes from time-to-time. Its Hall of Fame pays tribute to those people who have contributed to the role of motorcycling in terms of industry, transportation, recreation and competition. One of the displays in the museum highlights the Sturgis Motorcycle Rally and its international appeal and grandeur. The museum has a gift shop offering many rally souvenirs and official logo products. The museum opened in 2001.

MUSEUM OF WILDLIFE, SCIENCE & INDUSTRY

US 12 (1 mile west of jct. with SR 25) *WEBSTER*, SD 57274
(10 miles west of Waubay on US 12)
Phone: 605-345-4751
www.sdhsutiry.org/soc/Hist_Orgs/muswildsciindNESD.htm
Hours: M–F 9–5, Sat.–Sun. 1–5.
Donations accepted.

This is a large museum complex consisting of 25 buildings replicating a South Dakota village of the late 1800s and displaying the attributes and historical assets of this part of South Dakota. Within the museum are more than a dozen antique automobiles plus antique tractors, farm equipment, tools and mounted animals. In the village, one will find a jail, barber shop, school house, post office, railroad depot, church and country store. The museum has a large collection of period clothing including some 10,000 shoes.

TENNESSEE

INTERNATIONAL TOWING AND RECOVERY MUSEUM AND HALL OF FAME

3315 Broad St.
(in downtown Chattanooga)
CHATTANOOGA, TN 37408
Phone: 423-267-3132
www.internationaltowingmuseum.org
Hours: *Apr. 1 through Nov. 1*
M–Sat. 9–5:30, Sun. 11–5; *rest of
year* M–Sat. 10–4:30, Sun. 11–5. It
is suggested that travelers phone
before visiting the museum.
Admission charged.

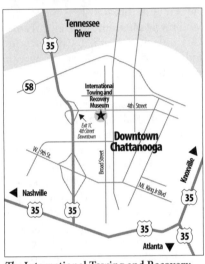

The International Towing and Recovery
Museum *is located just northwest of
downtown Chattanooga.*

This is the world's only tow truck
museum. For years one of the country's
major towing equipment manufacturers,
the Ernest Holmes Company, was located in Chattanooga and this museum
honors the memory of that company as
well as the unique nature of the vehicle
towing and recovery business. Many
restored tow trucks are on display dating back to the pre-World War I years.
Displays also tell the history of vehicle
towing and recovery. The vehicles on
display rotate, so multiple visits are
advisable. The walls of the museum are
generously covered with photos, paintings, prints and other memorabilia related to towing. The Hall of Fame honors
those individuals who have made major
contributions to this unique industry.
There is a nice gift shop offering collectibles, toy tow trucks, souvenirs and
other interesting items. The museum
was founded in 1995.

▶ KNOXVILLE/SMOKY MOUNTAIN AREA

HOLLYWOOD STAR CARS MUSEUM

914 Parkway
(Next to the Convention Center)
GATLINBURG, TN 37738

Phone: 865-430-2220
www.gatlinburg.com/starcars/
Hours: Daily 10 A.M.–9 P.M.
Admission charged.

Here is a very unique car display–cars used in, and sometimes made for, Hollywood movies and TV shows. Most of the 30 cars on display were created by the famous car designer, George Barris of Hollywood. One of the delights that can be seen is the world's

Floyd Garrett's Muscle Car Museum *displays more than 90+ such cars.*

only stone-age automobile, the Flintstone-mobile. Other vehicles include the Dukes of Hazard's *"General Lee"*, the Monster's *"Drag-u-la"* and cars from the Beverly Hillbillies, Jurassic Park, Knight Rider and other memorable films. There are some celebrity cars here too, cars which belonged to Frank Sinatra and Elvis. Stop in, you will have fun. Charles Moore is the general manager.

FLOYD GARRETT'S MUSCLE CAR MUSEUM

320 Winfield Dunn Parkway (Hwy. 66)
SEVIERVILLE, TN 37876
(23 miles east of Knoxville near the western entrance to the Smokey Mountain National Park)
Phone: 865-908-0882
www.musclecarmuseum.com
Hours: Daily 9–6 except Thanksgiving and Dec. 25.

Muscle car lovers usually smile from ear-to-ear when they walk into this museum. There are 90+ muscle cars to savor—over five million dollars worth. Some of the cars once belonged to famous people and all are American-made. Also on display are rare engines and other mechanical wonderment as well as

automotive memorabilia and NASCAR souvenirs. The museum was opened in 1996 and is the personal collection of trucking magnet, Floyd Garrett.

SMOKY MOUNTAIN CAR MUSEUM

2970 Parkway (US 441),
PO Box 385
PIGEON FORGE, TN 37868-0385
(Near the western entrance to Smoky Mountain National Park)
Phone: 865-453-3433
Hours: *May through Oct.*
daily 10-6, *rest of year* please inquire. Admission charged.

There are about 30 cars in this museum and some of them are associated with famous, and infamous, people. Some were used in movies. Other displays include gas pump globes, radiator emblems and other automotive memorabilia. For sale in the museum are automotive books, posters and post cards.

SPECIALTY AUTOWORKS, INC.

(Replica builder)
4601 Mill Branch Lane, Suite 3
KNOXVILLE, TN 37938
Phone: 865-925-2500
www.specialtyauto.com
Hours: M–Sat. 8:30–5:30

TENNESSEE

You've probably seen those kit car ads but, like many people, felt you did not have the wherewithal to put them together. Well, here's a company that will do it for you–and they have been at it since 1981. They can build just about any vehicle that's available in kit form: Jaguars, Cobras, Ferraris, Lamborghinis, MGs, Mercedes, Porsches, etc. They also build hot rods and other street machines. Visitors can see some of their finished cars in their showroom and visit the shop and watch work in progress. If you buy a car from these guys, you can rest assured you'll have the only one in the neighborhood.

End Knoxville/Smokey Mountain Area ◀

DAVID GREENE'S CLASSIC CARS
(Dealer)

> 901 E. Broadway
> **LENOIR CITY**, TN 37771
> (22 miles southwest of downtown Knoxville, just off I-75)
> Phone: 865-988-4828
> www.greenesclassic.com
> Hours: M–F 9–5, Sat. 9–noon

You will find quite a variety of vintage machines in this dealer's showroom and on his lot. Greene's offers classics cars, muscle cars, street rods, and cars like your father used to drive.

Wheels and chrome accessories are also available as is detailing, mechanical repairs, painting and restorations. The company takes trades, sells on consignment, aids in shipping and can provide appraisals.

ELVIS PRESLEY
AUTOMOBILE MUSEUM

> 3764 Elvis Presley Blvd. (across from Graceland Mansion at the south end of Graceland Plaza)
> **MEMPHIS**, TN 38116
> Phone: Graceland 800-238-2000, Corporate Office 901-332-3322.

www.elvis.com
Hours: *March through Oct.*
M–Sat. 9–5, Sun. 10–4. *Rest of year* W–M 10–4, closed Jan. 1, Thanksgiving and Dec. 25.
Admission charged.

Here's where they keep Elvis's "toys". It's across the street from his Graceland mansion. Every Elvis fan knows that the "King" liked cars, motorcycles, and other motorized toys. The Elvis Presley Automobile Museum displays many of those items for the public to see. There are cars, including one of his famous pink Cadillacs, motorcycles, a pink Jeep, jet skis, dunes buggy, golf carts, a snowmobile and other possessions he collected during his fascinating but short life. Also on display are many of Elvis's automotive-related personal belongings, such as his black leather jacket, biking gear, a pedal car, gas credit cards and his driver's license. In the museum is a simulated 1970s drive-in movie where visitors sit in 1957 Chevy seats and listen to the original videos being shown on old drive-in movie speaker boxes. The Graceland complex is one of the most popular tourist sites in Tennessee.

▶ NASHVILLE AREA

LANE MOTOR MUSEUM

702 Murfreesboro Pike (US 40/70S)
NASHVILLE, TN 37210
Phone: 615-742-7445
www.lanemotormuseum.org
Hours: Thurs.–Mon. 10–5.

This is a big antique vehicle museum. There are some 100 automobiles and motorcycles on display, many of which are not typically seen in the U.S. Some of the vehicles are on loan, so the displays change. The museum is divided into several areas; the Main Floor, the Clyde Wing (motorcycles), the Play Area, and a nice gift shop. Automobilia is displayed on the walls and in other locations throughout the museum and the museum has an interesting art gallery. Lane Motor Museum is always in the market for unusual cars to purchase. Keep that in mind when you go to sell your vintage car.

MUSIC VALLEY CAR MUSEUM

2611 W. McGavock Pike
(Across from Opryland Hotel)
NASHVILLE, TN 37214
Phone: 615-885-8020
Hours: June–Aug. daily 8 A.M.–10 P.M., *rest of year* daily 9–5. Closed Thanksgiving and Dec 25. Admission charged.

This museum displays about 50 vehicles, many of which belonged to famous country and western music performers such as Dolly Parton, Hank Snow, Chet Atkins, Randy Travis, Tom T. Hall, Ronnie Stoneman, George Jones, Hank Williams, Jr., Joe Don Baker and Elvis Presley. Most of the other cars are antiques and special interest vehicles and some are for sale. The displays at the museum change weekly. There is a gift shop offering a wide variety of items related to the country music scene and the Grand Ole Opry.

End of Nashville Area ◀

DIXIE GUN WORKS/
OLD CAR MUSEUM

1412 W. Reelfoot Av. (US 51 South),
PO Box 130
UNION CITY, TN 38261
(Northwestern corner of the state)
Phone: 731-885-0700 and
800-238-6785 (toll free)
www.dixiegunworks.com
Hours: M–F 7–5, Sat. 8–noon. Closed holidays. Admission charged to the car museum.

Visitors to this museum will see 36 antique and classic cars, dating from 1908 through the 1940s. Included in the collection are some 20 Fords and a 1912 Cadillac, the first production car equipped with a Kettering self-starter. Other displays include steam engines, steam whistles, headlights, bulb horns and farm equipment. The Dixie Gun Works is a firm that specializes in selling and supplying parts for antique guns and rifles. Dixie has a display of over 1,000 antique guns on display and a replica of an early American gunsmith's shop.

TEXAS

Like other states that were served by famous US 66, Texans have taken steps to preserve their segment of the old road. Route 66 crossed the Texas panhandle in the same general area as present-day I-40. Along the old route, visitors will see preserved buildings, restaurants, motels, motor courts, service stations, historic markers, signs, etc. In *Amarillo* there is a mile-long **Historic Route 66 District** on 6th Av. between Georgia and Western. At *McLean*, 35 miles west of the Oklahoma border, travelers can visit the **TEXAS OLD ROUTE 66 MUSEUM** and two other interesting sites, a World War II Prisoner-of-War Camp and a World War II camp for enemy aliens.

FM 600 WRECKING

9402 W. Lake Rd.
ABILENE, TX 79601 (140 miles west of Ft. Worth on I-20)
Phone: 915-672-2597
www.fm600wrecking.com
Hours: M–F 8–6, Sat. 8:30–1.

Here is one of the best places in the world for a salvage yard. The land is flat with sparse vegetation (no trees growing behind bumpers) and the weather is dry. That's what Janet and Ronny Tutt thought when they started the business in 1975. Now, they have some 8,000—that's 8,000—vehicles. Most of the cars are from the 1950s through the 1970s with a smattering, here and there, of cars from the 1940s and 1930s. FM 600 Wrecking is a good place to search for Chevy parts—they have lots of them. Customers may browse the yard and remove their own small parts.

Here's what an 8,000-vehicle yard looks like. This is **FM 600** *Wrecking of Abilene, TX.*

▶ AMARILLO AREA
(In the center of the Texas panhandle)

PANHANDLE-PLAINS HISTORICAL MUSEUM
2503 4th Av. (On the campus of West Texas A&M University) *CANYON*, TX 79016 (15 miles south of downtown Amarillo)
Phone: 806-651-2244
www.panhandleplains.org
Hours: June through Aug. M–Sat. 9–6, Sun. 1–6, rest of year M–Sat. 9–5, Sun. 1–6. Closed Jan. 1, Thanksgiving and Dec. 25. Admission charged.

This is the oldest and largest state-owned museum in Texas. It has major displays on the history, economy, geology, Indians and pioneer settlers of northwestern Texas. Also, there is a reconstructed turn-of-the-century pioneer town with shops, homes and other buildings filled with artifacts of the period. The museum has a large transportation display with horse-drawn vehicles, sleighs and about a dozen antique cars. One vehicle of interest is a 1903 Ford Model A, serial number 28, which is believed to be the oldest surviving assembly-line-manufactured car in the world. The museum has a large transportation library with an extensive automotive section, a snack area and a gift and souvenir shop.

UP-ENDED CADILLACS (Curiosity)
On I-40 West of town on the south side of I-40 between mile markers 61-62. *AMARILLO*, TX

Driving along I-40 west of Amarillo one will note on the south side of the highway 10 Cadillacs from the 1950s up-ended and partially buried in the ground. This is a pop-art sculpture, in a working grain field. It is the brain child of local millionaire Stanley Marsh III and is designed to pay homage to the extravagant automobile tail fins of that era. The site is best viewed from the access road that parallels I-40. There is a parking area there where visitors may stop and view the sculpture. Other "artists" have added their talents to the site—the cars are covered with graffiti and on a hot day, one can see cattle enjoying the shade created by the cars. Locally the site is known as the *"Cadillac Ranch."*

End of Amarillo Area ◀

LYNDON BAINES JOHNSON LIBRARY AND MUSEUM
2313 Red River St.
AUSTIN, TX 78705
Phone: 512-721-0200
www.lbjlib.utexas.edu
Hours: Daily 9–5, closed Dec. 25. Free

This is the presidential library and museum of the late President Lyndon B. Johnson. It chronicles the life and presidency to the man known to millions as "LBJ." Of interest to antique car buffs are two vehicles in the museum used by LBJ. There is his 1968 Lincoln limousine used during his presidential years and a Model T Ford that Johnson owned and used on his ranch. The Model T was given to Johnson by Henry Ford and was a copy of the Model T Ford Johnson's father owned when Johnson was a youth.

SAM RAYBURN HOUSE MUSEUM
US 82 West
(2 1/4 miles west of town)
BONHAM, TX 75418
(60 miles northeast of Dallas near the Oklahoma state line)
Phone: 903-583-5558
www.thc.state.tx.us/samrayhouse/
srhdefault.html
Hours: Tues.–F 8–5, Sat. 9–5.
Closed state holidays. Free.

This was the 12-room farm home of the famous Democrat politician Sam Rayburn, Speaker of the US House of Representatives at various times during the 1930s, 1940s and 1950s. Rayburn served in that capacity longer than any other man in history and was one of the major political figures of his day. The home contains many of the Rayburn family furnishings and belongings. In the garage are three cars, a 1945 Dodge pickup truck used around the farm, a 1947 Plymouth Savoy 4-door sedan which belonged to Sam's sister and a fully restored 1947 Cadillac Fleetwood which was acquired by Rayburn in the following manner. After one of the national elections the Republicans won control of the House of Representatives

and Rayburn, being a Democrat, had to step down as Speaker. His Democrat colleagues offered to give him a new Cadillac as a show of their appreciation for his leadership through the years. Rayburn declined the offer, but let it be known that he would accept personal checks from his colleagues no larger than $25 each which would be used toward the purchase of a new Cadillac. His colleagues obliged and Rayburn was able to buy the car. Some of the canceled $25 checks are displayed in the museum.

CLASSIC & ANTIQUE CARS (Dealer)
4112 Hwy. 2147
COTTONWOOD SHORES,
TX 78657 (55 miles northwest of Austin just west of US 281)
Phone: 830-693-7224
www.classic-automobiles.com
Hours: M–F 9–5, Sat. 9–1

Here's a dealer located in the beautiful hill country of central Texas just outside the popular Horseshoe Bay Resort on Lake LBJ. They have dozens of vintage vehicles in their showroom of mixed makes and manufacture. Included are classics, exotics, trucks, vans and other unique vehicles. The company has a highly-trained sales staff and sells many cars on consignment. They also will sell you a list of individuals wishing to sell their cars. The list includes informa- tion on the cars and instructions how you can contact the owners direct and negotiate your own purchase. Classic & Antique Cars takes trades, offers appraisals, provides storage and has a repair service.

▶ DALLAS/FORT WORTH AREA

CTC AUTO RANCH, INC. (Salvage)
3077 Memory Lane/I-35 north
DENTON, TX 76207-4919 (33 miles north of downtown Ft. Worth)
Phone: 940-482-3007 and 800-482-6199 (toll free)
www.ctcautoranch.com
Hours: M–F 9–5, Sat. 9–1.
Directions: *Going north on I-35*, exit at the 474 mile marker (Cowling Rd.), stay on service road. *Heading south on I-35*, exit at the 473 mile marker (Milam Rd.), go up & cross the overpass & circle around by Love's, then get on the service road heading north.

There are some 1,300 vehicles on this 28-acre salvage yard. Most of them are American-made vehicles and range in age from the 1940s through the 1970s with a high concentration in vehicles from the 1950s through the early 1970s. Emphasis is also placed on muscle cars from the 1960s and 1970s and there are project cars available. CTC Auto Ranch carries many ready-to-ship sheet metal parts purchased from other yards. This is a very clean yard with the vehicles in neat rows and grass and weeds are kept under control. It's also a rust-free area for old cars. In business since 1985.

PATE MUSEUM OF TRANSPORTATION
18501 US 377 (3 miles north of Cresson, TX)
CRESSON, TX 76035 (Southwestern suburb of Ft. Worth on US 377)
Phone: 817-332-1161
Hours: Tues.–Sat. 10–5, Sun 12–5
Free—donations accepted.

Here is one of the foremost attractions in the Southwest. This is a large museum with airplanes, helicopters, railroad cars, a Navy minesweeper and other forms of transportation including about 30 antique cars. The oldest car is a 1903 Cadillac Tonneau. There is also an automotive library, with 1,500 pieces, which is open to the public. Longhorn cattle can be seen grazing near the museum and the Pate Museum is the home of the annual Pate Swap Meet, one of the largest automotive swap meets in the country.

SARGENT AUTO SALVAGE
4729 Mansfield Hwy.
FT. WORTH, TX 76119
Phone: 817-536-5811
Hours: M–Sat. 8–6

Here's a very unique salvage dealer. The yard is small, but the warehouse is big and full of restorable cars. Some 200 vehicles, mostly American-made and mostly from the 1960s and 1970s, are in storage awaiting the loving hands of a restorer. There is a goodly selection of muscle cars available and a few light trucks. Contact Tonie Hewitt for information about the cars.

TEXAS

SOUTHWEST GALLERY OF CARS
(Dealer)

6333 Denton Dr., Suite 700
(Near southwest corner of
Love Field Airport)
DALLAS, TX 75235
Phone: 214-350-9636 or
214-443-1212 (Voice Mail)
www.southwestgallerycars.com
Hours: M–Sat. 8–5

Gary Walker, the owner of this dealership, offers the public a very nice selection of muscle cars, sports cars and special interest cars. Most are from the 1940s through the 1970s. On average, about 60 cars are on display in their showroom. The company takes trades, sells on consignment, provides appraisals and offers long-term storage. Car clubs are welcome.

End of Dallas/Fort Worth Area ◄

LAWRENCE MARSHALL ANTIQUE CAR MUSEUM (Museum and dealer)

52294 US 290 West
HEMPSTEAD, TX 77445 (50 miles northwest of Houston on US 290)
Phone: 979-921-2277 and
877-353-2277 (toll free)
www.marshallantiquecars.com
Hours: Tues.–F 8–5, Sat. 8–3.
Small admission charged.

CLOSED

This organization is both a museum and a dealer. There are about 150 antique, custom, muscle, and special-interest cars in their brightly-lit showroom including street rods, and a few classic trucks and military vehicles. The company buys and sells antique vehicles, takes trades, sells on consignment, and will aid in shipping and financing. Since this company is a dealer, the inventory turns frequently making it a museum that can be visited many times. Car clubs are most welcome. Founded in 1999, Spanish spoken.

► HOUSTON AREA

AUTO COLLECTORS GARAGE
(Dealer and restorer)

9848 Southwest Freeway (US 59)
HOUSTON, TX 77074
Phone: 713-541-2281
www.autocollectorsgarage.com
Hours: M–F 9–5
Directions: Located one mile from the intersection of US 59 and beltway 8 in SW Houston.

If you like exotics and muscle cars, here's a dealer that will serve your needs. Auto Collectors Garage deals in quality classic automobiles and rare American-made and imported top-of-the-line vehicles. British cars are usually plentiful and the company has extensive knowledge of Maseratis. The company also does restorations and service work. They take trades, offer appraisals, sell on consignment and can aid in financing and shipping. The owners count 40 years of experience in the field.

NATIONAL MUSEUM OF FUNERAL HISTORY

415 Barren Springs Dr.
HOUSTON, TX 77090
Phone: 281-876-3063
www.roadsideamerica.com/attract/TXHOUfuneral.html
Hours: M–Sat. 10–4, Sun. noon–4.
Admission charged
Directions: Leave I-45 north at exit 63—Airtex (by the airport). Make a right U-turn over the overpass, then right onto Ella St., then 2 blocks, take a right onto Barren Springs and watch for #415.

Here's a one-of-kind museum. This is a 20,000 sq. ft. museum dedicated to the history of funerals and the undertaking profession. It is the country's largest museum of its type. Of interest to antique car buffs is the sizeable collection of hearses and other funeral vehicles. There are both conventional and custom-made hearses on display, including a gaudy Japanese hearse custom-made from a 1972 Toyota Crown station wagon and a 1916 Packard funeral bus designed to hold the coffin, pallbearers and up to 20 mourners. Some of the vehicles on display have conveyed famous people to their resting places. The museum offers group tours and there is a gift shop which can provide a catalog of the items it sells. Some of the gift items display the museum's motto "Any day above ground is a good day."

STREET DREAMS (Dealer)

12810 Jess Pirtle Blvd.
SUGARLAND, TX 77478 (Southwestern suburb of Houston on US 59)
Phone: 281-242-1957
www.streetdreamstexas.com
Hours: Tues.–F 10–6, Sat. 1–4.

Here's a nice big dealer's showroom full of beautiful classic street rods and muscle cars. Street Dreams normally carries dozens of vehicles in stock, many of them in cherry condition. The company takes trades, sells on consignment, locates specific vehicles, and helps with financing and shipping. These people really try to make your street dreams come true.

End of Houston area

KING RANCH MUSEUM

405 N. 6th St.
KINGSVILLE, TX 78363 (30 miles southwest of Corpus Christi)
Phone: 361-595-1881
www.king-ranch.com
Hours: M–Sat. 10–4, Sun. 1–5, closed holidays. Admission charged.

The King Ranch Museum is housed in the Henrietta Memorial Center, a renovated ice factory near downtown Kingsville, and displays many antique and historic items from the local area and its famous namesake ranch. Included in the collection are several vintage cars including a customized 1949 Buick Eight used as a hunting car. There are also several horse-drawn vehicles including buggies and carriages. Another popular display at the museum is the collection of award-winning photographs by Toni

A customized hunting car on display at the King Ranch Museum.

Frissell who describes life on the King Ranch in the early 1940s. The museum has a gift shop and car clubs are always welcome.

THUNDERBIRDS SOUTHWEST (Dealer)

4635 E. SR 71
LA GRANGE, TX 78945
(Midway between Houston and San Antonio just north of I-10 on US 77 and SR 71)
Phone: 979-249-4200
www.thunderbirdsouthwest.com
Hours: M–F 9–5, Sat. 9–1.

Thunderbirds, Mustangs, Fords, Thunderbirds and more Thunderbirds—that's what you'll find in this vintage car dealer's showroom. They have dozens of the aforementioned cars from 1949 up. The showroom is worth seeing in its own right in that it is decorated in a 1950s motif, including life-sized cutouts of 1950s movie stars, and a 1950s-era soda fountain. The company also supplies a complete line of parts, takes trades, sells on consignment and will search for the vehicle of your dreams. Adjacent to their facility is a grass landing strip, so if you are a pilot you can drop by in your airplane or helicopter.

AUTOMANIA (Dealer)

6401 I-35 South
NEW BRAUNFELS, TX 78130
(25 miles northeast of San Antonio on I-35)
Phone: 830-629-4843,
210-389-1281 and 210-389-1282
www.automaniacs.com
Hours: M–Sat. 9–6

This company has one of America's premiere classic, collectible and exotic car collections. Several dozen vintage autos and light trucks are on display and offered for sale in their 28,000 sq. ft. showroom. Project cars and motorcycles are also offered as are some late model vehicles. Automania provides service and restoration work, sells parts and can add air conditioning units to vintage cars. The company takes trades, sells on consignment, offers appraisals and will search for specific vehicles. Browsers are always welcome.

CENTRAL TEXAS MUSEUM OF AUTOMOTIVE HISTORY

2502 SR 304 North

The Sterling McCall Old Car Museum *at Round Top, TX—a place to behold.*

(12 miles south of Bastrop)
ROSANKY, TX 78953 (30 miles southeast of Austin on SR 304)
Phone: 512-237-2635
www.ctmah.org
Hours: April 1 through Sept. 30 W–Sat. 10–5, Sun. 1:30–5. Rest of year F–Sat. 10–5, Sun. 1:30–5. Admission charged.

This is a large museum—40,000 Sq. Ft—with over 100 vintage cars, many of them classic and historic vehicles and some associated with important and well-known individuals. The museum's mission is to collect, restore and preserve historic automobiles, accessories and related items. Displays include old gas pumps, license plates, automotive signs, photos, antique furniture and a reconstructed Texaco gas station. The museum has an extensive library and an interesting gift shop. Every fall, the museum holds a large, well-attended swap meet. The museum was founded in 1980.

STERLING McCALL OLD CAR MUSEUM

4212 SR 237
ROUND TOP, TX 78954 (Midway between Austin and Houston just south of US 290 on SR 237)
Phone: 979-249-5089
http://www.oldcarcountry.com
Hours: Thurs.–F 11–4, Sat.–Sun. 10–5. Admission charged.

Down here, deep in the heart of Texas, you will find a very interesting—and large—old car museum. There is a variety of some 130+ domestic and imported vehicles in the collection and a truck or two as well as a collection of automobilia. These people like company and have a large outdoor pavilion for picnics and catered events. Car clubs, school groups, etc. are always welcome. The vehicles are all the personal property of Sterling McCall, a long-time car collector. The museum started up in the late 1990s.

TEXAS TRANSPORTATION MUSEUM
11731 Wetmore Rd.
SAN ANTONIO, TX 78247
Phone: 210-490-3554
www.txtransportationmuseum.org
Hours: Thurs, Sat. & Sun. 9–4.
Admission charged.

This is the former headquarters of the Longhorn & Western Railroad and now primarily a railroad museum. There are several buildings in the complex displaying locomotives, a large variety of railroad cars, electric rail vehicles, model trains, and about a dozen antique cars, several antique trucks and fire trucks. There is also antique farm equipment and horse-drawn vehicles on display. The museum offers train rides which leave and return to an old restored railroad station. The museum is available for parties, meetings and other functions and holds an annual Christmas extravaganza called *"Santa's Holiday Depot."* The museum was founded in 1964.

ACTION AUTO RECYCLERS (Salvage)
SR 36, PO Box 352
TEMPLE, TX 76503 (Between Waco and Austin on I-35)
Phone: 254-773-6201
Hours: M–F 8–5, Sat. 8–noon.
Directions: Leave I-35 at exit 299 and go east on Loop 363 for 6 miles. Watch for Action Auto Recyclers on the right hand side at SR 36.

Everybody in these parts knows that Charles Pehl is a Ford man. He has more than 600 of them in his 1,200-car, 8-acre salvage yard. Many of them are whole and restorable and some of them go back to the 1940s. The yard has a generous selection of Mustangs. The non-Ford cars and light truck are all American-made vehicles with many Chevys in the mix. Pehl has a personal collection of Fords, so you might see him drive up in one of his favorites. Pehl's yard has been in operation since the end of World War II.

UTAH

▶ SALT LAKE CITY AREA

UNION STATION/BROWNING KIMBALL CAR MUSEUM

2501 Wall Av.
OGDEN, UT 84401
(30 miles north of Salt Lake City)
Phone: 801-629-8444
www.theunionstation.org/museums/autos/carmuseum.html
Hours: *Memorial Day to Labor Day*
M–Sat. 10–5, Sun. 11–3. *Rest of year*
M–Sat. 10–5, closed Sun.
Admission charged.

The Browning Kimball Car Museum at Ogden's Union Station

The city of Ogden has converted its old union station into a number of attractions and museums including the Browning Kimball Car Museum. This is a small but elegant display of about a dozen cars which are part of a larger collection. The cars on display rotate every 6 months. All are classics, each with its own unique history. A guide is usually in attendance to walk visitors through the museum and narrate the history and details about each car. There are three other museums in the Union Station building; Utah State Railroad Museum, the Natural History Museum and the Browning Arms Museum. In addition, there is an art gallery, restaurant, train and gift shop and an information center.

SALT LAKE CITY AREA CLASSIC CAR MUSEUM

355 West 700 South St.
SALT LAKE CITY, UT 84101
Phone: 801-322-5509 or
801-582-6883
www.classicarmuseumsales.com
Hours: M–Sat. 8:30–4:30.
Donations requested.

This is a collection of some 200 vehicles with only a part of the collection on display at this location. The other cars in the collection are regularly rotated. All of the cars have been restored and some are for sale. There are classics, special interest cars, show cars, cars of movie stars and other famous people. The museum will also search for specific cars for buyers. The museum is owned by Richard and Stacy Williams.

CLASSICS AND MORE (Dealer)
854 S. Main St.
SALT LAKE CITY, UT 84101
Phone: 801-364-2572 and
877-365-2572 (toll free)
www.classicsandmore.com
Hours: M–F 9–5, Sat. 9–1

Looking for an antique car under $10,000? Here's where you might find it. That's the mission of this dealer. Classics and More can provide driveable, presentable, clean and rust-free cars and trucks ranging in age from the 1940s to the 1970s. Most of their vehicles in their showroom are American-made. They also service what they sell and now and then have vehicles over $10,000. The company will search for vehicles you may want at the price you want to pay. The company takes trades, sells on consignment, offers appraisals and aids in shipping and financing. Ben Crass is the owner and has had some 15 years in the business.

End of Salt Lake City area ◀

VERMONT

▶ BENNINGTON AREA
(Southeastern corner of the state)

BENNINGTON MUSEUM
75 Main St.
BENNINGTON, VT 05201
Phone: 802-447-1571
www.benningtonmuseum.com
Hours: Jun.–Oct. daily 9–6. Rest of
year daily 9–5. Closed Thanksgiving, Dec. 25 and Jan. 1. Admission
charged.

This museum displays items of early
Americana, a large collection of locally
made pottery, paintings by Grandma
Moses and one antique automobile—a
very special automobile. It's a 1924
Martin-Wasp made in Bennington. This
is the last of only 20 large and luxurious,
hand-made Martin-Wasps made from
1920 to 1924. It was made primarily of
aluminum and had mahogany trim and
red leather. In its day it sold for $10,000
making it one of the most expensive cars
in America. The museum has a gift and
souvenir shop and is within walking
distance of Hemmings Publishing Co.,
publisher of *Hemmings Motor News*.

HEMMINGS PUBLISHING COMPANY
(Antique car publications)/**VEHICLE
DISPLAY/SUNOCO FILLING STATION/
CAR LOVER'S STORE**
200 block on Main St.
(Near the Bennington Museum)

BENNINGTON, VT 05201
Phone: 800-447-9580 (toll free)
for visitor information
Phone: 800-227-4373 (toll free)
Ext. 654 for Sunoco Filling Station
www.hemmings.com
Hours: *Publishing company operations and tours*, M–F 8–5; *Vehicle
display May through Oct.* M–F
10–10:30 A.M. and 2– 2:30 P.M.,
rest of year by appointment; *Sunoco
Filling Station and Car Lover's Store*
daily 7 A.M.–7 P.M.

This is the home of *Hemming's
Motor News*, the "bible" of the antique
car hobby. The magazine is published
monthly and is distributed world-wide.
It lists thousands of vehicles for sale and
many activities and functions within the
antique car hobby. Tours of the publishing facilities are available. Hemmings
has a display of about 25 vehicles on
the lower level of the publishing house
and many automobilia items are also on
display. There is no charge to see this
display. Next door to the publishing
house is a restored and fully functional
Sunoco Filling Station whose personnel give prompt and courteous old
fashioned service. They pump your gas,
check your oil, wash your windshield,
headlights, rear windows and taillights

VERMONT

and have the cleanest restrooms in Vermont. Parked on the station's premises, weather permitting, is an ever-changing display of about half a dozen vintage vehicles. Inside the station is a *"Car Lover's Store"* full of books, models and other collectors items. It is a perfect place to shop for gifts for your car crazy friends and relatives. Inside the Car Lover's Store is a replica of an old roadside diner decorated in a 1950s motif.

During June–July–August each year the company holds a well-attended "Cruise-In" every other Thursday in which car owners from the surrounding area are invited to display their vehicles on the company's premises. Many trophies and awards are given for a variety of categories. Hemmings is a favorite destination for car clubs and groups and will make special arrangements to accommodate such visitors.

End of Bennington area ◄

THE WESTMINSTER MG CAR MUSEUM

US 5
WESTMINSTER, VT 05158 (17 miles north of Brattleboro)
Phone: Summer 802-722-3708, winter 603-756-4121
www.vmga.org/windham/westminmg.html
Hours: *Memorial Day–Labor Day* Sat.–Sun. 10–5. Closed *rest of year*.
Admission charged.

Twenty seven MGs, many of them very rare models, are on display at this museum devoted solely to that marque. Included in the collection is a rare 1927 14/28 Tourer Flatnose 4-seater, one of only 6 known to exist and thought to be the oldest MG in the US. Many MG artifacts are also on display. The museum has a library and a gift shop with many MG-related items for sale. Founded in 1984. On the first Sunday in October, the museum sponsors a well-attended British Car Day.

CLOSED

VIRGINIA

FRED'S CAR MUSEUM
SR 24, PO Box 809
APPOMATTOX, VA 24522 (20
miles east of Lynchburg on US 460)
Phone: 434-352-0606
www.appomattox.com/htm/
car_museum.html
Hours: M–Sat. 10–5, Sun. 1–5.
Admission charged.

~~CLOSED~~

Here, in this very historic part of
America, is a fine antique car museum
with a stunning exhibit of over 65 vintage cars and trucks. Many of the cars
are pre-World War I and some are
very rare. Also on display are toy cars,
metal cars, cast iron cars including
some Corgi cars. Elsewhere around
the museum visitors will find generous
displays of automobilia. Their gift shop
is big and has selections of books, hats,
flags, Coca-Cola items, teddy bears,
figurines, toys, and—since this is an
important Civil War area—Civil War
memorabilia. The famous Appomattox
Court House Historical Park is just up
the road a piece.

W W MOTOR CARS & PARTS, INC.
(Restorer and dealer)
132 Main St.
BROADWAY, VA 22815 (in north-
western Virginia near the West
Virginia state line 13 miles north of

Harrisonburg and just off I-81)
Phone: 540-896-8243
www.wwmotorcars.com
Hours: M–F 9–5

Everyone in Broadway, VA knows
what W W Motor Cars & Parts does.
They restore cars, display them in their
showroom and sell them. There are
usually more than 30 vehicles in the
showroom which is a former Chevrolet
dealership. Additional cars are stored
elsewhere. The company offers full or
partial restoration services for customers' cars as well as their own. Visitors will
see work in progress and Mustangs are
something of a specialty. As a dealer, W
W Motor Cars & Parts sells on consignment, takes trades, provides appraisals
and indoor storage and aids in shipping
and financing. Some automobilia is for
sale and they have a research library.
Jack and Libby Wenger own and operate
the company and have been here since
1986.

**ROARING TWENTIES ANTIQUE
CAR MUSEUM** (and antique store)
1445 Wolftown-Hood Rd.,
PO Box 576 (On SR 230
between US 29 and US 33)
HOOD, VA 22723-9802
(About 25 miles north-
northeast of Charlottesville)

VIRGINIA

Phone: 540-948-6290 and
540-948-3744
www.roaring-twenties.com
Hours: M–F 9–1, by appointment
and by chance. Admission charged.

This interesting museum—the largest family antique car collection in Virginia—has about 32 vehicles, mostly from the 1920s and 1930s. The oldest car in the collection is a 1904 Carter Electric Motorette and the latest model is a 1948 Playboy. Other displays include horse-drawn vehicles, stationary engines, hood ornaments, radiator caps, period advertising signs, glassware, and a myriad of relics. The Roaring Twenties Museum opened in 1967 and its curator is John Dudley. The same folks have a large antique store at a nearby location.

DAVE'S FERNCLIFF AUTO PARTS
(Salvage)
3088 Three Notch Rd. (US 250)
LOUISA, VA 23093 (22 miles east of Charlottesville on I-64)
Phone: 434-589-3642
www.ferncliffauto.homestead.com
Hours: M, Thurs. & F 9–5, Sat.–Sun. 9–2
Directions: Leave I-64 at the Ferndale Exit (SR 208). Turn south on SR 208 and proceed one-half mile to its intersection with US 250. Turn east on US 250, go one-half mile and the yard is on the north side of the road.

When you see the old red fire truck and sign you'll be at Dave's Ferncliff Auto Parts. This 20-acre yard specializes in Pontiacs in general and in Pontiac Fieros in particular. But you'll find other makes here too. The yard has over 500 vehicles and—surprisingly—some used airline ground equipment. Dave Winding and his mother run the yard and Dave used to work at the Dulles International Airport near Washington, DC. He knows the value of those airline equipment parts. There are some complete cars available and the company does engine and transmission work.

CAR AND CARRIAGE CARAVAN OF LURAY CAVERNS (Museum)
970 US 211 West (1 mile west of Luray at entrance to Luray Caverns)
LURAY, VA 22835 (In the Shenandoah Valley 25 miles northwest of Harrisonburg on US 211)
Phone: 540-743-6551
www.luraycaverns.com
Hours: *Mar. 15 through June 14* daily 9–6, *June 15 through Labor Day* 9–7, *after Labor Day through Oct. 31* daily 9–4 *rest of year* M–F 9–4, Sat.–Sun. 9–5. Admission charged.

This large antique vehicle museum is part of the famous Luray Caverns complex, one of the most famous cave systems in the US. In the museum are about 75 restored vintage cars along with carriages, coaches, buggies and other modes of transportation dating back to 1725. Some of the vehicles are associated with famous people. There is a large gift shop offering a wide variety of items and the complex has its own restaurant.

PHILBATES AUTO WRECKING, INC.
(Salvage)
SR 249, PO Box 28 (¹/₂ mile west of junction with SR 33)

NEW KENT, VA 23124 (25 miles east of downtown Richmond)
Phone: 804-843-9787 and 804-843-2884
Hours: M–F 9–5, Sat. 9–2

This is a very large salvage yard with some 6,000 vehicles on more than 100 acres of land. All American-made makes are represented and most are between 1940 and 1982 with the majority between the late 1940s and 1960s. Muscle cars are well represented. A parts locating service is offered, as is a towing service. Customers may browse the yard. In business since 1955.

▶ NORFOLK/NEWPORT NEWS/ HAMPTON ROADS AREA

The Chrysler Museum, *Norfolk, VA.*

CHRYSLER MUSEUM (Art museum)
245 Olney Rd. (at Mowbray Arch)
NORFOLK, VA 23510
Phone: 757-664-6200
www.chrysler.org
Hours: W 10 A.M.–9 P.M., Thurs.– Sat. 10–5, Sun. 1–5. Closed Jan 1, July 4, Thanksgiving and Dec 25. Admission charged.

This is the city art museum of Norfolk named after the late Walter P. Chrysler,

General MacArthur's staff car, a 1950 Chrysler Imperial limousine, is displayed at the MacArthur Memorial. He used it both in Japan and the US from 1950 until his death in 1964.

GENERAL DOUGLAS MacARTHUR MEMORIAL
MacArthur Square,
Bank St. & City Hall Av.
NORFOLK, VA 23510
Phone: 757-441-2965
www.macarthurmemorial.org
Hours: M–Sat. 10–5, Sun. 11–5. Free.

This is the former city hall of Norfolk which has been turned into a museum honoring one of America's most famous World War II commanders, General Douglas MacArthur. Among the many displays of personal belongings, maps, murals, photographs, models, etc., is the General's staff car, a 1950 Chrysler Imperial. It is on display in the gift shop.

Jr., son of the founder of the Chrysler Corporation. In 1970 Walter P. Chrysler, Jr. agreed to move his large and valuable art collection from Provincetown, MA to this museum in Norfolk, his wife's home town. In gratitude, the city named the museum after him. The Chrysler Museum is considered to be one of the top 20 art museums in the country and contains works from ancient Greece and Rome, pre-Columbian works from America, works of European and American masters, and an 8,000-piece glass collection considered to be one of the finest in the world. Walter P. Chrysler, Jr. had a long and successful career at Chrysler Corporation as founder and head of the Air-Temp Division, which developed the first air conditioning systems for automobiles.

US ARMY TRANSPORTATION MUSEUM
300 Washington Blvd., Besson Hall
FORT EUSTIS, VA 23604 (West of, and adjacent to, Newport News)
Phone: 757-878-1115
www.transchool.eustis.army. mil/museum/museum.html
Museum hours: Tues.–Sun. 9–4:30, closed Federal holidays. Free.

Fort Eustis is the home of the US Army's Transportation Corps and this museum, which is just inside the main entrance to the base, displays many of the motorized and horse-drawn vehicles used by the Corps from Colonial days to the present. This includes many antique trucks and Jeeps, including several prototype

Tour Book for Antique Car Buffs

Displayed at the U.S. Army Transportation Museum *is the Bantam Motor Car Company's version of the Jeep, which was presented to the Army for evaluation.*

Jeeps produced by various manufacturers in the early 1940s when the Army was developing that vehicle. There are displays of captured enemy equipment and amphibious vehicles. Other displays include aircraft, trains, marine craft, experimental vehicles, models of various vehicles, dioramas, photos, uniforms, medals, weapons and many other items used by the Corps. There is a gift and souvenir shop in the museum.

End of Norfolk/Newport News/Hampton Roads Area ◀

VIRGINIA MUSEUM OF TRANSPORTATION
303 Norfolk Av.
ROANOKE, VA
24016 (In western Virginia on I-81)
Phone: 540-342-5670
www.vmt.org/Default.htm
Hours: M–F 11–54, Sat. 10–5, Sun. 1–5. Admission charged.

This city-owned museum displays steam, electric and diesel locomotives, railroad cars, horse-drawn vehicles, a Canadian dog sled, miniature circus vehicles, a railroad station building, a telegraph office and has about a dozen antique

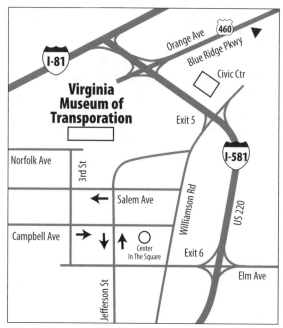

The Virginia Museum of Transportation *is near the junction of I-81 and I-581.*

cars and trucks. Included is a 1927 White truck, a 1930 Chevrolet stake truck, a 1938 Cadillac fire truck and a 1926 Studebaker taxi. The museum has a picnic area and a gift shop offering many items related to the field of transportation.

WOODROW WILSON BIRTHPLACE AND MUSEUM

18-24 N. Coalter St., PO Box 24
STAUNTON, VA 24401-0024
(30 miles north-northwest of Charlottesville on I-81 and I-64)
Phone: 540-885-0897 and
888-496-6376 (toll free)
www.woodrowwilson.org
Hours: *March through Oct.*
M–Sat. 10-5, Sun. noon-4.
Rest of year M–Sat. 9-5. Closed Jan. 1, Thanksgiving and Dec. 25. Admission charged.

This is the birthplace and boyhood home of President Woodrow Wilson who was born here in 1856. The home was the manse of the First Presbyterian Church where his father, the Rev. Joseph Ruggles Wilson, was pastor. It has been restored to appear as it did at the time of Woodrow's birth. Among the many family belongings and displays is a Pierce-Arrow limousine used by Wilson when be became President.

LOWREY'S SEAFOOD RESTAURANT

528 Church Ln.
TAPPAHANNOCK, VA 22560
(40 miles northeast of Richmond on the Rappahannock River)
Phone: 804-443-2800 and
804-433-4315
www.lowreysrestaurant.com
Hours: M–Thurs. 11 A.M.–9 P.M., F–Sat. 8–10:30 A.M. and 11 A.M.–9:30 P.M., Sun. 8–10:30 A.M. and 11 A.M.– 9 P.M. Closed Dec. 25.

This fine restaurant has a couple of antique cars on display inside their dining room. They are a 1910 Cadillac and a 1926 Chrysler touring car. Upon occasion, additional antique cars are parked outside. There is also automobile memorabilia inside the restaurant and a gift shop. Car clubs are welcome. Contact William Lowrey, co-owner.

WASHINGTON

WHOOP-N-HOLLER MUSEUM
1 Whitmore Rd.
BICKLETON, WA 99322
(43 miles south of Yakima)
Phone: 509-896-2344
http://www.ohwy.com/wa/w/
whooholl.htm
Hours: *Apr. 1 through Sept. 30*
Tues.–Sun. 9–5.
Admission charged.
Directions: Proceed 12 miles south
of Bickleton on East Rd. or 11 miles
north on Roosevelt and East Rd.
and watch for Whitmore Rd. Then
follow the signs to the museum.

This is a privately-owned museum
consisting of several buildings containing a wide variety of pioneer artifacts
from the earliest days of settlement in
the area. Most of the items have been
collected by Lawrence and Ada Ruth
who own the museum and are descen-
dants of homesteaders who first settled
here. There are displays of hand-carved
doll furniture, home remedies, pioneer
clothing, musical instruments including
a pipe organ, Coke cans from around
the world and a collection of some 30
antique vehicles. The vehicles range in
age from pre-World War I to post-World
War II. In the auto collection one will
see Studebakers, a Maxwell, a Republic
truck, an old fire truck, a Ford Model
T and two Edsels. There is also a picnic
area and playground for the kids.

THE VINTAGE MOTORCYCLE MUSEUM & HOTEL WASHINGTON GRAND ROOM
545 N. Market Blvd.
CHEHALIS, WA 98532
Phone: 360-748-3472
www.antiquemotorcycles.net
Hours: M–F 9–1
Directions: Leave I-5 at Exit 77 and
proceed east on Main St. through
town. Main St. dead ends at Market
Blvd. Turn north on Market Blvd.
and watch for the museum on the
west side of the street.

Where were you in 1916? The motorcycles you will see here were all put-put-
ting around America at that time. The 40
or more cycles on display are all pre-1916
models and are good originals or fully restored models. They have names like Thor,
Sears, Reading Standard, Pierce, Indian
and Harley-Davidson. Visitors will also
see an interesting collection of ancient bicycles, some dating back to the early 1800s
and some made of wood. Next door to the
museum is the restored Washington Hotel
which is associated with the museum. The
hotel provides space for meetings, parties
and other social events associated with the
museum. Also in the hotel are shops and
a restaurant. The museum and hotel are
the works of Frank Mason, a local builder
and motorcycle lover. Frank has restored
several other building around town.
He's quite a guy.

The Lynden Pioneer Museum of Lynden, WA has a sizeable collection of antique cars.

ANTIQUE CAR & TRUCK MUSEUM

17812 SR 21 N (three miles south of Curlew, watch for the old truck atop their sign)
CURLEW, WA 99118 (Northeastern corner of the state on SR 21)
Phone: 509-779-4204
Hours: *Memorial Day through Labor Day weekends* F–M 11–5.
Donations accepted.

Here, in big timber country just a few miles south of Canada, is an antique vehicle museum that's worth your time. Antique Car and Truck Museum has about 50 vehicles under roof and another collection of vehicles outside. The good stuff, of course, is inside. On display are cars, trucks, motorcycles, steam engines, farm and industrial equipment, and many other items of interest. There is a small gift shop and car clubs are always welcome. The museum was founded in 1990 and is associated with the Ansorge Hotel Museum in downtown Curlew.

LYNDEN PIONEER MUSEUM

217 W. Front St.
LYNDEN, WA 98264 (8 miles northeast of Bellingham near the Canadian border)
Phone: 360-354-3675
www.lyndenpioneermuseum.com
Hours: M–Sat. 10–4, Sun. 1–4 (from Memorial Day to Labor Day 1–5). Admission charged.

This is a large museum of some 29,000 sq. ft. housed in a former John Deere dealership. It has displays on early pioneer life, Indians, agricultural machinery, military items from the Spanish-American War to the present and other displays pertaining to the history of the local area. There are a large number of horse-drawn vehicles including a large collection of buggies. The museum also has a sizeable antique auto collection. Many of the cars are Chevrolets and date back to the pre-World War I era. The museum has a gift and souvenir shop. Founded in 1976.

▶ SEATTLE AREA

AMERICAN CLASSICS AUTO SALES
(Dealer)
>   1036 Central Av. South
>   *KENT*, WA 98032 (A southern
>   suburb of Seattle on SRs 167 & 516)
>   Phone: 877-877-2200
>   www.franksclassics.com
>   Hours: M–F 9–5, Sat. 9–1

A.C.A.S. has the largest classic Mustang inventory in the United States and the owner, Frank Kuhn, has had over 25 years of experience working with Mustangs. The company does superior body work on Mustangs—theirs or yours—and provides the best paint job that can be had. Every vehicle they sell, unless otherwise stated, has been painted by A.C.A.S. In their showroom one will normally find between 30 and 40 vehicles, mostly Mustangs but also an assortment of other makes and models. Some of the vehicles sold here have been upgraded to increase their value and all have been road tested for 100 miles. The buyer also gets a complete description of the vehicle he purchases and a warranty. The company takes trades, sells on consignment, provides testimonials, and will arrange shipping and aid in financing.

COSMOPOLITAN MOTORS (Dealer)
>   2030 8th Av.
>   *SEATTLE*, WA 98121
>   Phone: 206-467-6531
>   www.cosmopolitanmotors.com
>   Hours: M–F 9–5, Sat. 9–1

"…From the practical to the extravagant," that's what the people at Cosmopolitan Motors say of the cars they sell. That covers a wide range of vehicles and that's what you will find in their spacious showroom. Then, there's a surprise—Bugatti replicas. Cosmopolitan Motors is the American distributor of the beautiful Pur Sang Bugatti replicas that are hand crafted in Argentina. Most of the parts of these automobiles are interchangeable with the original and the cars have been tested by famous race driver, Phil Hill. The company takes trade-ins, sells on consignment, does service work, offers appraisals and aids in shipping and financing.

KOMPACT KAR KORNER (Dealer)
>   17510 SR 99
>   *LYNNWOOD*, WA 98037 (A northern suburb of Seattle on SR 99)
>   Phone: 425-745-1660
>   www.kompactkarkorner.com
>   Hours: M–F 9–5, Sat. 9–1

Classics, street rods, Corvettes, vintage, muscle cars—they are all here at Kompact Kar Korner—and more. Several dozen vehicles will be on display in their comfortable showroom. If you don't see what you want, the company has an auto locator service to help you find it. And, they can also locate parts. The company takes trades, sells on consignment, helps with financing and shipping and can provide appraisals. Car clubs are welcome to come and visit.

End of Seattle Area ◀

▶ TACOMA AREA

THE LeMAY MUSEUM

423 152nd St. East
TACOMA, WA 98445
Phone: 253-779-8490, 253-536-2885 or 877-902-8490 (toll free)
www. lemaymuseum.org
Hours: Tues.–Sat. 10–3

Here is one of the largest projects afoot in all of antique cardom. Harold E. LeMay made a fortune in collecting garbage and put a lot of his money into collecting antique vehicles. His collection rose to over 3,000 vehicles and was the largest privately-owned collection in the world. This was confirmed by the fact that his collecting was listed in the Guinness Book of Records. Now, that collection is to be displayed in this centerpiece museum for all to see. About 150 cars will be displayed at any one time on a rotating basis. The facility is scheduled to open in 2007.

PREMIUM MOTORS (Dealer)

102 Puyallup Av.
TACOMA, WA 98421
Phone: 253-272-5293 and 253-988-7750 (mobile)
www.premium-motors.com
Hours: M–F 9–6, Sat. 10–5

Premium Motors refers to itself as "the premium source for classic and custom automobiles." They back it up by offering a generous selection of classics, street rods, muscle cars, sports cars and special-interest cars at honest prices. Visitors will find about 40 vehicles in their two handsome showrooms at all times. The company buys cars, takes trades, sells on consignment, and assists in financing and shipping.

USA OF YESTERDAY CO. (Dealer)

445 St. Helens Av.
TACOMA, WA 98402
Phone: 253-627-1052
www.collectorcar.com/usa.htm
Hours: M–Sat. 10–5:30

This dealer of antique cars is located in a spacious old building built in the 1940s as a Buick dealership. They carry between 40 and 50 vehicles in stock at all times and specialize in American-made cars from the 1930s through the 1970s. The company takes trades, sells on consignment, offers appraisals, rents storage space and welcomes car clubs. They have an annual open house in July or August each summer. There is a large gift and souvenir shop associated with the company called Wheel World that carries models, kits, apparel and other automobilia. USA of Yesterday has a big 1950s-style banquet facility which is available for parties and special occasions.

End of Tacoma area

ALL AMERICAN CLASSICS, INC.
(Salvage)

15209 NE Fourth Plain Rd.
VANCOUVER, WA 98682
(Southeastern Washington across the
Columbia River from Portland, OR)
Phone: 360-254-8850 and
800-955-4999 (toll free)
www.allamericanclassics.com
Hours: Tues.–F 8:30–5, Sat.
8:30–3:30

This is a neat and well-kept sal-
vage yard of 20 acres with some 2,500 vehicles. And, as the company name
implies, they are all American-made.
Some cars date back to the 1930s, but
most are post-war to the early 1970s. All
American has a computerized inventory
system and offers a nation-wide locator
service. They will ship any part, large or
small. Customers may browse the yard,
but company personnel will remove all
parts. All American also carries NOS
and reproduction parts and there are a
few whole vehicles suitable for restoring.
In business since 1989. The lot is owned
and operated by the Toedtli family.

WISCONSIN

C.L. CHASE USED AUTO AND TRUCK PARTS (Salvage)

W10416 County Rd. C West
CAMP DOUGLAS, WI 54618
(48 miles east of LaCrosse on I-90/94)
Phone: 608-427-6734
Hours: Daily 8–6
Directions: Leave I-90/94 at Exit 55 and look for the C. L. Chase sign on the side of a big semi. Then follow signs to the yard.

There are some 5000 cars and trucks in this salvage yard dating from the teens to the present. Trucks range from pickups to semis. Chase offers a towing service with both light and heavy-duty wreckers and has a 100-ton crane. Customers may browse the yard. Car clubs are welcome. In business since 1968.

WISCONSIN AUTOMOTIVE MUSEUM

147 N. Rural St. (Downtown Hartford)
HARTFORD, WI 53027
(35 miles northwest of Milwaukee)
Phone: 262-673-7999
www.wisconsinautomuseum.com
Hours: *May 1 through Sept. 30*
M–Sat. 10–5, Sun. noon–5; *rest of year* closed on M, Tues. and major holidays.
Admission charged.

This museum is the largest antique auto museum in Wisconsin and has a noteworthy collection of Kissel au-tomobiles and trucks. Kissels were made in Hartford from 1906 to 1931 and only about 200 still exist today out of some 36,000 manufactured. The museum is also the home of the Kissel Kar Klub. Other makes of vintage cars are displayed making a total of about 90 cars altogether. Included in the display are many cars from the 1960s and a good variety of trucks and fire trucks. The museum displays more than a dozen Nashes which were made in nearby Kenosha, WI. There are also Nash-related art and memorabilia on display. Other exhibits include gas & steam engines, gasoline pumps and related automobilia. The museum has a gift shop, a banquet hall and an automo-tive library.

JIM CARLSON'S AUTO CENTER (Dealer)

N6411 Holmen Dr., PO Box 98
HOLMEN, WI 54636-0098
(4 miles north of LaCross on I-90 and the Mississippi River)
Phone: 608-526-3358
www.autocenterusa.com
Hours: M–Sat. 8–5

Jim Carlson and his crew specialize in Chevrolets, but also have a nice selection of other makes in their well-appointed showroom. Normally, there are more than two dozen vehicles to choose from here and in other locations. The vehicles range from fixer-uppers to those ready for the car show. The company buys cars, takes trades, arranges financing and transportation, offers appraisals, leases cars, rents storage and searches for specific vehicles. Furthermore, the company sells restoration supplies for all makes and models and has an inventory of rust-free used parts. Jim Carlson, a former race car driver, knows cars very well and has been at this location since 1976.

▶ MILWAUKEE AREA

VALENTI CLASSICS, INC.
(Dealer and restorer)
355 South US 41 (Parallels I-94. Valenti can be seen from I-94)
CALEDONIA, WI 53108
(A southern suburb of Milwaukee)
Phone: 262-835-2070
www.valenticlassics.com
Hours: M–F 9–6, Sat. 9–5

This dealer, on the south side of Milwaukee, carries a large inventory of classic and collectible automobiles in their new and modern showroom and adjacent lot. Available are affordable antique cars and top-of-the-line collectible cars. They carry from 50 to 75 vehicles in inventory at all times. Valenti has a full restoration service, does repair work and service work, sells cars on consignment, searches for vehicles upon request, takes trades and provides appraisals. There is a large selection of gas station memorabilia available for sale and the company has a sizeable gift shop.

End of Milwaukee area ◀

DEXTER'S CLASSIC CARS (Dealer)
3711 W. Mason St.
ONEIDA, WI 54155 (Western suburb of Green Bay on SR 54)
Phone: 920-499-2080
www.dextersclassiccars.com
Hours: M–F 9–5, Sat. 9–1

You will find more than 20 beautiful old cars on the black and white checkerboard tile floor of this dealer's showroom. They are of mixed makes and models and all worthy of note. Dexter's also carries a huge inventory of antique car parts and has a service department. The company takes trades, sells on consignment, provides testimonials and aids in financing and shipping.

Mark Wilson and his lovely wife own and operate the business. In business since 2003.

JACK'S AUTO RANCH (Salvage)
6848 N. Island View Rd.
WATERTOWN, WI 53094
(Midway between Milwaukee and Madison on SR 26)
Phone: 920-699-2521
www.jacksautoranch.com
Hours: M–F 8–5, Sat. 8–noon

To get to Jack's, take the Sullivan exit off I-94, go south one mile to Hwy. B and follow the signs. When you arrive you'll find some 3,500 vehicles on Jack's 40-acre lot dating back to the

WISCONSIN

1930s. Most of the cars are GM, Ford and Chrysler, but there are a respectable number of orphans and a large selection of Cadillacs. The yard is neat and orderly and the various makes are grouped together. Jack's specializes in engines and transmissions and keeps an inventory of between 250-300 on hand at all times. This is a family operation run by the Bender family. The company was founded in 1964.

This 1969 Camaro Indy 500 Pace Car is on display at the **Dells Auto Museum.**

DELLS AUTO MUSEUM

591 Wisconsin Dells Parkway
(US 12 and SR 23 on the "Strip")
WISCONSIN DELLS, WI 53965
(40 miles northwest of Madison
on I-90/94)
Phone: 608-254-2008 (Summer)
and 608-221-1964 (Winter)
Hours: *May 15 through Labor Day* daily 9–9, *after Labor Day to Oct. 1* Sat. & Sun. 9–5, *rest of year* by appointment. Admission charged.

This museum exhibits about 25 of its 200 vehicles on a rotating basis on the museum floor. Many of the cars are convertibles and there is a goodly number of Indy 500 pace cars. Some of the cars displayed in the museum are for sale. Other displays include license plates, antique dolls, toys and period clothing. There is an automotive library and a souvenir shop with many antique car-oriented items.

WYOMING

Wyoming is another state that has preserved parts of the old **Lincoln Highway** and some of the historic sites along the way. The highway ran from *Cheyenne* westward to *Salt Lake City*, UT and parallels current I-80.

WYOMING CLASSIC CARS (Salvage)
12200 Poison Spider Rd.
CASPER, WY 82604 (East central part of the state on I-25)
Phone: 307-322-3365
www.wyomingclassiccars.com
Hours: M–F 9–5, Sat. 9–1

It's dry and grassy in this part of the country and an ideal spot for a salvage lot. Arranged in neat rows on 15 acres of prairie land, visitors will see about 1,600 vehicles waiting to serve. There are about 260 mid-1950s Chevrolets and a good selection of other GM makes. And still other vehicles, ranging from Anglias to Willys, are available as are some cars from the 1930s. Whole cars are also available for restoration. Many parts are in storage in the company's building and a complete listing of Wyoming Classics Cars is on their web site. Customers may remove their own parts or have them removed by company personnel. Cold drinks are available on hot days. Frank Jones is the man behind it all.

BLACK HILLS ANTIQUE AUTO
(Salvage and dealer)
Hwy. 16 (12 miles east of town)
NEWCASTLE, WY 82701
(Northwestern edge of the state near the South Dakota state line on US 16 and US 85)
Phone: 605-749-2242
www.bhantiqueauto.net
Hours: M–F 8–5

They go back to the 1920s in this salvage yard and up to the late 1960s. Most of Black Hills' 1200 vintage salvage cars comprise a general mix of makes and models and there are whole cars suitable for restoring. Customers may browse the yard with permission. The company also buys and sells street rods and good originals and has them displayed on a lot at the front of their property. They normally carry some 50+ vehicles for sale. They sell on consignment, will assist in shipping and will search for specific vehicles. In business since 1970.

HERITAGE AND RESEARCH CENTER
OF YELLOWSTONE NATIONAL PARK
PO Box 168
YELLOWSTONE NATIONAL PARK, WY 82190 (northwestern corner of the state)
Phone: 307-344-2563 or
307-344-2267 or 307-344-2565
www.nps.gov/yell/technical/

museum/closure.htm

Hours: Vary due to weather and other conditions.

Here's another reason why everyone should see Yellowstone National Park at least once in their lifetime. This magnificent park has wonders that can't be seen anywhere else. One of the latest additions to the park is this heritage and research center that informs visitors on the many fascinating features in the park such as its wild life, biology, ethnology, geology, archeology and more. Of interest to antique car buffs is a collection of some 30 horse-drawn and motorized vehicles which include early stage coaches, early tour busses, touring cars, service trucks, fire engines, motor scooters and human-powered vehicles including fire hose carts, handcarts and "Mollys" used by hotel maids and bellboys.

CANADA

ALBERTA

SOUTH PEACE CENTENNIAL MUSEUM

Hwy. 34 North 2 Km
BEAVERLODGE, AB T0H 0C0
(West-central part of the province
28 miles west of Grande Prairie)
Phone: 780-354-8869
http:www.geocities.com/Heartland/
Plains/2894/
Hours: *Mid-May through Sept. 31*
daily 10–6. Admission charged.

This fine museum displays pioneer artifacts, equipment and furnishings from the early 1900s. There is a pioneer home, c1928; a fully stocked general store; a flour mill; a schoolhouse; an Anglican church; a railway caboose; farm machinery and a collection of about 20 antique cars and trucks. Some of the vehicles on display include a 1927 Chevrolet truck, a 1929 Graham-Paige, a 1955 Oldsmobile and several Ford Model As. The museum has a well-supplied gift and souvenir shop. They also have an old-time clay baking oven in working order and from time to time sell freshly baked bread.

HOMESTEAD ANTIQUE MUSEUM

901 N. Dinosaur Trail
(Hwy. 838 ½ mile west of Hwy. 9)
DRUMHELLER, AB T0J 0Y0
(60 miles northeast of
Calgary on Hwy. 9)
Phone: 403-823-2600
http://www.virtuallydrumheller.com

Hours: *Mid-June through Labour Day* daily 10–8, *mid-May through mid-June* and *day after Labour Day-second M in Oct.* daily 10–5. Admission charged.

Pioneer and Indian artifacts are highlighted in this museum including clothing, home furnishings, clocks, musical instruments, gramophones, radios, horse-drawn vehicles, farm equipment, steam-powered tractors, a 1919 catalog-ordered house and several antique cars and trucks. Cars and trucks displayed include a 1919 Ford Model T, a 1914 Ford 4-door touring car, a 1919 Chevrolet roadster and a 1920 Canadian-built Gray-Dort pickup truck. All of the cars and trucks are in running order. There is an interesting gift and souvenir shop in the museum as well as a teahouse.

This is the entrance to the Homestead Museum *of Drumheller, AB.*

ALBERTA

HANNA MUSEUM AND PIONEER VILLAGE

Pioneer Tr. and 4th St.
HANNA, AB (100 miles northeast of Calgary on Hwy. 9)
Phone: 403-854-4224
http://www.hanna.ca/museum.htm
Hours: *June–Aug.* daily 10–6, *May and Sept.* 1–5 by appointment, *rest of year* closed. Admission charged.

You will be pleasantly surprised when you arrive in Hanna. This town of only 3,000+ souls have put together a magnificent pioneer village and museum to celebrate the town's past. It is located on the east side of town - and they have antique cars on display. The cars, though, are only a part of the bigger show, which includes hundreds of thousands of artifacts displayed in the museum's complex of buildings. There's old railroad equipment, steam engines, farm machinery, blacksmithing items, an old school house, a dental office, a ranch house and much more. You will have fun here in Hanna, Alberta.

ALDON AUTO SALVAGE, LTD.

Hwy. 831
LAMONT, AB T0B 2R0
(30 miles northeast of Edmonton)
Phone: 780-895-2524
Hours: M–F 8–5:30, Sat. 8:30–3

This is a large salvage yard of some 4,000 cars and light trucks. Aldon specializes in North American-made vehicles and has vehicles ranging in age from 1940 to the present. Some whole cars are available for restoration. Customers may browse the yard. Additional services offered include towing, engine rebuilding and parts locating. Car clubs are welcome. In business since 1971.

SMITHSON INTERNATIONAL TRUCK MUSEUM

5620 51st St. Box 813
(Pas-Ka-Poo Historic Park)
RIMBEY, AB T0C 2J0 (about halfway between Edmonton and Calgary on Hwy. 20)
Phone: 403-843-2004
www.paskapoopark.cm/truckmuseum.htm
Hours: Daily 10–6.
Admission charged.

This museum displays a collection of 19 restored International half-ton trucks. There is one example for each model change during the life of the truck from 1935 to 1974. The trucks were restored by Ken Smithson, a local IHC enthusiast, and purchased by the town of Rimbey. There are several other vehicles in the collection other than International trucks. The museum has antique farm equipment, a collection of IHC signs and other company memorabilia. Tours are available. There is a gift shop offering souvenirs and other collectibles.

A 1935 C-1 International Truck is one of the many International half-ton trucks on display at thr Smithson museum.

▶ WETASKIWIN AREA
(45 miles southwest of Edmonton)

REYNOLDS MUSEUM/REYNOLDS AVIATION MUSEUM
4119 57th St. (Hwy. A2)
WETASKIWIN, AB T9A 2G1
Phone: 800-661-4726 (toll free)
www.albertaheritage.net/museums/
display.php?institution=272
Hours: Daily 9-5 except Sept.-May
closed M and extended hours
during summer to 7. Admission
charged.

Don't confuse this museum with the Reynolds-Alberta Museum. They are two different entities and both are big. Here, visitors will see not only antique cars and trucks but aircraft, military equipment, steam engines, fire trucks and farm equipment. A large selection of transportation memorabilia is on display along with many other items. Car clubs are most welcome. Stanley G. Reynolds is the President.

REYNOLDS-ALBERTA MUSEUM
Hwy. 13 west
WETASKIWIN, AB T9A 2G1

Phone: 780-361-1351 or
800-661-4726 (toll free)
www.reynoldsalbertamuseum.com
Hours: *May 14 through Sept. 5*
daily 10-5 with extended hours
to 6 from *July 1 to Sept. 5.*
Rest of the year Tues. through Sun.
10-5. Handicapped accessible.
Admission charged.

Here is a large provincially-owned museum with air craft, military vehicles, farm equipment, steam engines, industrial equipment, horse-drawn vehicles, musical instruments, household appliances, weapons and antique cars and trucks. Altogether there are about 350 vehicles on display made in both North America and imported. A large part of the automobiles are from the pre-World War I era. Vintage car and aircraft rides are available. The museum also houses Canada's Aviation Hall of Fame and there is a reference center with thousands of pieces of literature. Food is available and there is a gift shop. The museum opened in 1992.

End of Wetaskiwin area ◀

BRITISH COLUMBIA

COOMBS CLASSIC ROADSTERS
(Restored and dealer)
2458 Alberni Hwy. Box 508
COOMBS, BC V0R 1M0
(On Vancouver Island
80 miles north of Victoria)
Phone: 250-248-1072 and
877-448-1072 (toll free)
www.classic-roadsters.com
Hours: M–Sat. 10–5

The drive up from Victoria on Hwy. 1 is magnificent. At the end of this delightful journey, car buffs will find this very interesting establishment in the small town of Coombs. Coombs Classic Roadsters restores vintage automobiles, vans and light trucks and offers some of them for sale. You know you are in the right place when you see their old-time service station out front with two manually-operated gas pumps. The company buys cars for resale and restoration, sells on consignment, restores customer's vehicles and helps with shipping and financing. All of their cars are rigorously tested and serviced and extended warranties are available. They do service work, collision repairs, sell parts and accessories, offer temporary storage and will rent space to do-it-yourself restorers.

TREV DEELEY MOTORCYCLE MUSEUM
13500 Verdun Place
RICHMOND, BC V5M 4W5
(Eastern suburb of Vancouver)
Phone: 604-273-5421
www.trevdeeley.com
Hours: M–F 10–4. Free

This is one of the oldest Harley-Davidson dealers in Canada. They started in business in 1917. In recent years, the company has established a magnificent motorcycle museum with a total of some 260 vintage bikes on display. They say on their website that their collection is "quite possibly the finest collection of rare and antique motorcycles in the world." So, it's well worth your time to visit. Being a dealer, the company sells new and used bikes, does service work and participates in racing events and other motorcycle-oriented activities.

MANITOBA

MANITOBA AGRICULTURAL MUSEUM

Hwy. 34 South
(1.6 miles south of Jct. Hwy 34
and TransCanada Hwy. 1)
AUSTIN, MB R0H 0C0
(78 miles west of Winnipeg)
Phone: 204-637-2354
www.ag-museum-mb.ca
Hours: *Mid-May through Sept. 30*
daily 9–5. Admission charged.

This is a large agricultural museum consisting of several buildings displaying antique tractors, various types of old farming equipment, a large collection of steam engines, an old railway station and several railroad cars. There is also an assortment of about 20 antique cars, trucks and fire trucks in the collection. The annual Manitoba Threshermens' Reunion and Stampede is held here in late July. The museum has a gift and souvenir shop, a campground and an airstrip. Associated with the museum is a reconstructed Homesteaders' Village consisting of historic buildings and furnished in a period motif.

MANITOBA AUTOMOBILE MUSEUM FOUNDATION

TransCanada Hwy. #1 East
ELKHORN, MB R0M 0N0
(Southwestern corner of the
province 10 miles from the
Saskatchewan border)
Phone: 204-845-2161
www.mbautomuseum.com
Hours: *May 1 through late Sept.*
daily 9–9. Admission charged.

This is Manitoba's oldest antique auto museum having opened in 1967. It has about 75 vintage autos and trucks, most of them in running condition. Included in the collection are many pre-WW I cars and a nice selection of Canadian-made McLaughlins. There is a 1909

The Manitoba Agricultural Museum *is easy to reach from the TransCanada Highway by going 1.6 miles south on Hwy. 34.*

MANITOBA

Hupmobile personally restored by the museum's founder, Isaac "Ike" Clarkson and is one of the oldest Hupmobiles in existence. Other displays include agricultural equipment, Indian and pioneer artifacts, china, license plates and other memorabilia. The museum has a small gift and souvenir shop.

WATSON CROSSLEY COMMUNITY MUSEUM
405 Railway Av. (West side of town at the sports ground)
GRANDVIEW, MB R0L 0Y0
(West-central part of province on Hwy. 5)
Phone: 204-546-2040 (*summer*)
and 204-546-2764 or
204-546-2661 *rest of year*)
http://www.museumsmanitoba.
com/dir/parkland/35.html
Hours: *Mid-June through early Sept.* daily 10–6, *rest of year* by appointment. Admission charged. Handicapped accessible.

This interesting museum displays many artifacts of local history, a miniature lumber mill, a restored homesteaders cabin, farm equipment including a large number of antique tractors and about 15 vintage cars and trucks. In the car collection is a 1915 Ford half-ton Model T truck, a 1916 Overland, a 1926

Essex and a rare 1952 Dodge style-side truck. There is also a restoration shop and visitors may watch restoration work in progress.

ARCHIBALD HISTORICAL MUSEUM
S.E. 17-49 Pembina Municipality (Hwy. 3 East 4 miles west of Manitou)
LA RIVIERE, MB R0G 1A0
(South-central part of the province near the US border)
Phone: 204-242-2825
http://www.rmofpembina.com/
museum.html
Hours: *Mid-May to Labour Day*
F–Tues. noon–8 P.M.
Admission charged.

Antique furniture, household items, farm machinery, tools, buggies and several vintage cars can be seen in this nice local museum. One of the main exhibits is a log house built in 1878 which was the residence of Canadian authoress Nellie McClung from 1890 to 1891, and a second frame home, fully furnished, where Nellie and her husband, Wes McClung, lived in Manitou from 1904 to 1911. La Riviere's old Canadian Pacific Railroad station and other historic buildings have also been relocated to the museum and are furnished with period items and antique furniture.

NEW BRUNSWICK

ANTIQUE AUTOMOBILE MUSEUM

35 Principale St. (On TransCanada Hwy. 2 in Saint-Jacques)
EDMUNDSTON, NB E0L 1K0 (Northwestern corner of the province on the northern border of Maine)
Phone: 506-735-2525 and 506-735-2637
http://www.tourismnewbrunskick.ca/Cultures/en-CA/Products/Museum/2A20F77B-385D
Hours: *Late June through Labour Day* daily 10–8. Admission charged. Limited wheelchair accessibility.

This museum, at the entrance of *de la Republique* Provincial Park, exhibits about 20 vintage cars and related automobilia. Of interest in the collection is a 1910 Detroit Electric, a 1929 Stutz Black Hawk, a 1928 Willys Knight, a 1933 Rolls-Royce limousine, a 1937 Diamond T fire truck, a 1956 Corvette and a 1942 Plymouth 45-ton locomotive. There are also displays of early steam engines and bicycles. The museum was founded in 1976.

ONTARIO

RM CLASSIC CAR EXHIBIT
(Exhibit and restorer)

1 Classic Car Dr.
BLENHEIM, ON N0P 1A0
(45 miles east of Detroit, MI
on Hwy. 401)
Phone: 519-352-9024 or
877-523-2684 (toll free)
www.cktourism.com
Hours: April–Nov. daily 9–5,
admission charged.
Directions: Leave 401 at Exit 90
(Hwy. 40) and follow signs to
the exhibit.

At this interesting establishment, they restore 'em and show 'em. Several dozen vehicles are on display in their well-appointed showroom. Many of the vehicles are top-of-the-line models and some are for sale. Guided tours are offered through the restoration facility for visitors interested in seeing how they do it.

THE GUILD OF AUTOMOTIVE RESTORERS (Dealer and restorer)

44 Bridge St., PO Box 1150
BRADFORD, ON L3Z 2B5
(30 miles north of Toronto
on Hwys. 11 and 88)
Phone: 905-775-0499
www.theguildofautomotive
restorers.com
Hours: M–F 9:30–5, Sat. 9:30–1

The Guild is a large restoration facility where everything from light tune ups to full Concourse restorations are performed. The company has a large showroom where vintage automobiles, hot rods, classics and other vehicles are offered for sale. Various items of automobilia are on display. There is also a large and well-stocked gift shop and a speed shop. Visitors may tour the restoration facility upon request. The company takes trades, sells on consignment, offers appraisals and helps with financing and shipping. Car clubs are welcome.

CANADIAN VINTAGE MOTORCYCLE MUSEUM

347 Greenwich St., Bldg. #19
BRATFORD, ON N3T 5W5
(25 miles west of Hamilton)
Phone: 905-627-4185
www.cvmg.on.ca/museum.php
Hours: *April through Sept.*
Tues.–Sun.10:30–4:30, *rest of
year* Tues.–F 1–4:30, Sat.–Sun.
19:30–4:30. Admission charged.

They call it CVMM and it is housed in the Canadian Military Heritage Museum, so both museums can be seen in one visit. CVMM is a federally-registered foundation with the mission to preserve Canada's rich motorcycling history. Over 30 motorcycles are on display, most of which are on loan from museum members and associates, so

This is the Silvester Collector Car Store *in Brigden, ON.*

the collection changes from time-to-time. The motorcycles on display are unrestored originals or partially or fully restored models and some are Canadian-made while others are military models. Motorcycling artifacts and memorabilia are also on display. In the Military museum, visitors will see a number of antique military vehicles. CVMM opened in 1994.

SILVESTER COLLECTOR CAR STORE
(Dealer and restorer)
3026/3037 Brigden Rd.
BRIGDEN, ON N0N 1B0 (12 miles southeast of Sarnia/Pt Huron, MI)
Phone: 519-864-1646
www.silvestercollectorcars.com
Hours: M–F 8–5, Sat. by appointment.

This is a restorer that also offers cars for sale in an indoor museum-like showroom. Silvester's is a full-service restoration shop that offers service work and repairs on old cars. In their showroom they carry about a dozen North American-made affordable antique vehicles for sale, some restored, some as-is. They will sell cars on consignment, do appraisals and take trades. Car clubs are welcome. The owner is Ernie Silvester.

SOUTHWESTERN ONTARIO HERITAGE VILLAGE (Museum)
County Rd. 23/Arner Town Line
(10 minutes south of Essex)
KINGSVILLE, ON N0R IG0
(25 miles southeast of the Detroit/Windsor on Lake Erie)
Phone: 519-776-6909
www.swoheritagevillage.ca
Hours: July through Aug. daily 10–5, April through June and Sept. through Nov. W–Sun. 10–5. Admission charged.

This is a large museum complex with 12 buildings which date from 1826 to 1930. There is an old time general store, a church, a one-room schoolhouse, a barber/shoe shop, a train station, several homes, a gift shop and a transportation building housing some 30 vintage automobiles along with other modes of transportation. Some of the automobiles are very rare. A portion of the cars are on loan from local collectors so the collection changes periodically. Guided tours of the museum are available. The museum hosts several antique car events during the year and has a gift shop and picnic facilities.

ONTARIO

MINAKER'S AUTO PARTS (Salvage)
3073 County Rd. 10
MILFORD, ON K0K 2P0 (20
miles southeast of Belleville)
Phone: 613-476-4547
www.groups.msn.com/
minakersautoparts
Hours: M–F 9–5, Sat. 9–4.
Closed Thurs. at noon.

This salvage yard of approximately
3,000 vehicles specializes in North
American-made cars from 1930 to 1980
with about half the cars and trucks being
pre-1970. There is a good selection of
sedans from the 1940s and light trucks
from the 1950s. They also offer NOS and
NORS parts including suspension parts
and thousands of brake shoes, master
wheel cylinders and wheel cylinders.
Some whole cars are offered for sale.

Customers may browse the yard and car
clubs are welcome. Founded in 1925.

CLASSIC IRON MOTORCYCLE MUSEUM
5743 Victoria Av.
NIAGARA FALLS, ON L2G 3L6
Phone: 905-374-8211
www.classiciron.ca
Hours: Daily 10–10.
Admission charged.

Classic Iron Motorcycle Museum
offers a collection of custom and vintage
motorcycles from the beginning of the
era to the present. The oldest motorcycle
dates from 1916. Also on display are
antique toys, rare motorcycle art and
motorcycle memorabilia. Check out
their gift shop for unique licensed
products.

▶ OSHAWA AREA
(15 miles east of Toronto on Lake Erie)

Oshawa is the center of Canada's automobile industry and there are several
historic sites in the area related to that industry. The city's largest employer had
long been *General Motors of Canada* which was formed in Oshawa in 1918
with the merger of the *McLaughlin Carriage Co.* and the Canadian branch
of *Chevrolet*. One-third of the population of Oshawa was employed in the
automotive industry and its related services.

CANADIAN AUTOMOTIVE MUSEUM
99 Simcoe St. South
OSHAWA, ON L1H 4G7
Phone: 905-576-1222
www.oshawa.ca/tourism/can_mus.
asp
Hours: M–F 9–5, Sat.–Sun. 10–6.
Closed only on Dec. 25.
Admission charged.

The Canadian Automobile Museum is,
as its name implies, Canada's premier auto
museum. It is a large museum with some
65 vehicles and has the largest collection
of Canadian-made vehicles in the world.
It is located in an old 1920s automobile
dealership building where Chevrolets,
Pontiacs and Oaklands were once sold.
Integrated into the auto displays are

The **Canadian Automotive Museum** *of Oshawa, Ontario, has the world's largest collection of Canadian-built vehicles.*

other items of the same period, such as trucks, motorcycles, bicycles, washing machines, printing presses, etc., to give the displays an historic perspective. Other exhibits include spark plugs, model cars, automotive lighting components, pinball machines, jukeboxes, and stoves. There is a very large automotive library open by appointment and an impressive gift shop. The museum was founded in 1961.

PARKWOOD ESTATE & GARDENS
(Historic Home)
    270 Simcoe St. North
    OSHAWA, ON L1G 4T5
    Phone: 905-433-4311
    www.parkwoodestate.com
    Hours: *June through Aug.* Tues.–
Sun. 10:30–4, *rest of year* Tues.–Sun.
1:30–4. Admission charged.
Directions: Exit #417 from Hwy. 401 eastbound, or exit # 418, westbound onto Simcoe St. North. Watch the street number.

This National Historic Site was once home to Col. R. S. "Sam" McLaughlin (Founder of General Motors of Canada). He and his family lived here during the latter part of the 1800s and the early 1900s. The family consisted of Sam, his wife and five daughters. The 55-room mansion has an indoor pool, bowling alley, a squash court, an elevator, a grand Conservatory and is furnished with period furnishings, trappings and decorative art from the years 1918 through 1939. There is also a 12-acre garden which is magnificently landscaped and several greenhouses still in operation. The McLaughlin family was very wealthy and subsequently became one of Canada's greatest philanthropists. On the grounds is a gift shop, a tea room, a conference center in the carriage house and facilities for meetings, banquets, weddings and other events. Guided tours are available.

End of Oshawa area ◀

ONTARIO

CANADA SCIENCE AND TECHNOLOGY MUSEUM

1867 St. Laurent Blvd.
OTTAWA, ON
K1G 5A3
Phone: 613-991-3044
www.sciencetech.
technomuses.ca
Hours: *May 1 to Labour Day* daily 9–5, *rest of year* Tues. through Sun. 9–5. Admission charged.

The Canada Science and Technology Museum *is just south of Queensway East on St. Laurent Blvd.*

This is one of Canada's largest and finest museums. It has numerous exhibits on science and technology illustrating the paths from which we have come and the points to where we are going. Located in a 35-acre garden-like park setting, the museum contains 140,000 sq. ft. of exhibit space divided into galleries. Displayed in the transportation collection are automobiles, carriages, sleighs, motorcycles and bicycles. The museum's automobile collection consists of about 90 cars and trucks, many of them Canadian-made, but only about a dozen are on display at any one time. The museum maintains a large automotive library which is open to the public. There is a gift shop, cafe and picnic facilities.

▶ TORONTO AREA

CANADIAN MOTORSPORT HALL OF FAME

Exhibition Place, Hall of Fame Bldg.
TORONTO, ON M6K 3C3
Phone: 416-263-3223
www.cmhf.ca
Hours: Tues.–Sat. 10–5, donations accepted.

Here is Canada's first and largest motorsport museum. It covers all disciplines of motor car racing including oval track racing, drag racing and Indy-type racing. The Hall of Fame honors Canadians and others who have made significant contributions to the sport of auto racing and there is a sizeable collection of vintage race cars. Racing and automotive memorabilia such as trophies, photographs, etc. can also be seen. There is a large archives collection and the *Hall of Fame* is run by a board of governors from all over Canada.

LEGENDARY MOTORCAR COMPANY, LTD. (Dealer)
8242 Fifth Line
HALTON HILLS, ON L7G 4S6
(A western suburb of Toronto less than two minutes off Hwy. 401. Watch for signs)
Phone: 905-875-4700
www.legendarymotorcar.com
Hours: M–F 9–5, Sat. 10–3

This is Canada's largest antique car dealer with some 40,000 sq. ft. of floor space. In their spacious showroom, visitors will find a large assortment of interesting and affordable vintage vehicles. The company has a large restoration facility and some of the cars they restore are for sale. Visitors can visit the restoration facility and view work in progress. The company takes trades, provides appraisals, aids with financing and shipping, sells parts, offers rentals and storage and has a nice gift shop. And, here's a surprise. They are also in show Biz. They are the home of the popular TV show *"Dream Car Garage."* Nick Smith is the man to contact here and if you e-mail him he will answer you promptly.

End of Toronto area ◄

PRINCE EDWARD ISLAND

CAR LIFE MUSEUM

TransCanada Hwy.
BONSHAW, PE (13 miles
southwest of Charlottetown)
Phone: 902-675-3555
www.gov.pe.ca/visitorsguide/
search/display.php3?number=359
Hours: *July–Aug.* daily 9–7, *May–
June and Sept. 1 through mid- Sept.*
daily 10–5. Admission charged.

This is a very nice museum in one of the most picturesque areas of North America. On display are many antique agricultural vehicles, tractors and about 20 antique cars. The cars range in age from 1898 to 1959. Car Life Museum also has one of Elvis Presley's cars, a 1959 pink Cadillac. All vehicles on display are restored. There is a gift shop and a picnic area.

SPOKE WHEEL CAR MUSEUM

(Museum, restaurant and lounge)
RR 3
DUNSTAFFNAGE, PE C1A 7J7
Phone: 902-629-1240 and
902-629-1796
www.2hwy.com/pe/s/shcumsfe.htm
Museum hours: *June-Sept.* daily 10-7.

Here's a unique establishment where you can have a really good time; a car museum, a restaurant and a lounge. What more could anyone ask for? In the museum is a private collection of about 35 cars (and growing) ranging in age from 1916 and up. Most of the automobiles are North American-made. Car clubs and other interested groups are always welcome.

QUEBEC

MUSEE GILLES VILLENEUVE
(Museum)
960 Avenue Gilles Villeneuve
BERTHIERVILLE, QC J0K 1A0
(45 miles northeast of Montreal on
Hwy. 40 and the St. Lawrence River)
Phone: 450-836-2714 or 800-639-
0103 (toll free)
www.gilles.villeneuve.com/english/
a_propos_e.htm
Hours: daily 9–5
Directions: Leave Hwy. 40 at
exit #144 and watch for signs.

In Berthierville, race car driver Gilles
Villeneuve is a local hero. So much so
that they have build a museum honoring
his life and times. Inside the museum
visitors will see vintage race cars and a
considerable amount of race memorabilia including personal items owned
and used by Gilles. There is a racing pit,
a race track ambulance, steel guardrails,
racing flags and more. Visitors can try
their hand at racing in a unique Ferrari-
like virtual reality racing simulator. The
museum has several annual activities
including a golf tournament and a
benefits banquet.

AUTO DENIS CONNOLLY (Dealer)
58, Route 116 Road E., CP Box 453
DANVILLE, QC J0A 1A0
(25 miles east of Drummondville
on Hwy. 116)
Phone: 819-839-2861 and
819-352-1495 (cell)

www.adcautos.com
Hours: M–F 9–5

Si vous coulez en connaltre plus par
rapport a nos voitures, communiquez
avec nous des aujourde'hui! Don't be
alarmed, they speak English here, too.
That simply means "If you want more
information on our cars, contact us
today." If you do contact them, you
won't be disappointed. This company
has a nice selection of between 15 and
20 vintage vehicles in their multi-win-
dowed showroom. The cars range from
fine originals to fully restored show cars.
Denis and his crew take trades, sell on
consignment, help with shipping and
welcome car clubs. In business since
1992.

MUSEE ANTIQUE VICTOR BELANGER
(Museum village)
1080 route Kennedy
SAINT-COME-LINIERE,
BEAUCE, QC G0M 1J0
(18 miles northwest of the border
with Maine on Hwy. 73)
Phone: 418-685-2302,
418-685-3866 and 418-685-3869
www.museevbelanger.com/
museum.html
Hours: *May 15–Sept. 15* daily 9–5,
rest of year by appointment.

This is the reconstruction of an early
Quebec village and consists of several
buildings including a log school, a rail-

QUEBEC

way station, a Canadian-style home, an Indian camp, a general store, a saloon, a sugar house and more. Within the village are over 30 antique cars and trucks. Visitors will also see a large collection of old telephones, toys, clocks, lamps, dolls and more. There is a gift shop selling items and handicrafts related to the theme of the village. French and English are spoken here.

SASKATCHEWAN

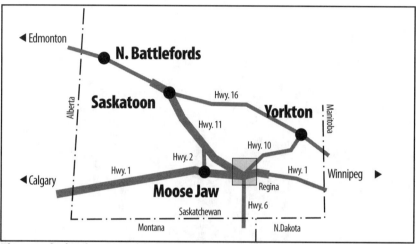

These are the four locations of the Western Development Museum *of Saskatchewan.*

The **Western Development Museum of Saskatchewan** consists of four separate museums, one each in **Moose Jaw, North Battleford, Saskatoon** and **Yorktown**. Each portrays a different theme. All four have antique cars, but the majority of cars are in Moose Jaw and Saskatoon. All of the Western Development Museums can be accessed on their web site www.wdm.ca.

BARR COLONY HERITAGE CULTURAL CENTRE

On Hwy. 16E at 45th Av.,
Weaver Park
LLOYDMINSTER, SK S9V 0T8
(In the west-central part of province on the Saskatchewan/Alberta line)
Phone: 306-825-5655
www.city.lloydminster.ab.ca
Hours: *Mid-May to mid-Sept.* daily 9–8, *rest of year* W–F noon–5, Sat.–Sun. noon–5. Admission charged.

In Weaver Park there are a number of new and restored buildings marking the spot where the Barr colonists first settled this part of Saskatchewan in 1903. Some of the buildings that visitors will see are Lloydminster's first church, a schoolhouse circa 1906, a log cabin furnished in the style of 1906-1915, an old-time filling station and the Barr Colony Heritage Cultural Centre. In the Centre is a display of about a dozen vintage vehicles which include Lloydminster's first fire truck, a 1924 Model T one-ton truck, a 1925 Hudson Brougham, a 1930 Durant and several Edsels. Other attractions in the Park consist of an art gallery, a wildlife display, an oil refinery display, a gift shop, a picnic area and a camp ground.

▶ MOOSE JAW AREA (40 miles west of Regina)

This is the auto museum at the Sukanen Ship Pioneer Village and Museum.

SUKANEN SHIP PIONEER VILLAGE AND MUSEUM

Hwy. #2 (8 miles south of town)
MOOSE JAW, SK S6H 5V0
Phone: 306-693-7315
www.sukanenmuseum.ca
Hours: *Mid-May through mid-Sept.*
M–Sat. 9–5, Sun. noon–8.
Admission charged.

This is a village museum with more than 30 historic buildings, and at the entrance, the very unusual Sukanen ship. The ship is a hand-made vessel built locally by an eccentric Finnish im-migrant, Tom Sukanen. It was his dream to sail the ship from Saskatchewan back to his native Finland. Sukanen, however, died before the voyage could be attempted. He is buried on the grounds near his ship.

In one of the village buildings are about 40 antique cars and trucks, most of which belong to local car collectors. Included with the vehicles is a large collection of vintage Canadian license plates. There is also a sizeable collection of antique farm equipment. Among the more permanent cars on display is a 1938 Ford V8 roadster, a 1938 Willys coupe and a Model A Ford converted into a snowmobile. Other buildings in the complex include a community hall, a fire house, a barber shop, a service station, a blacksmith shop, a post office, a carriage house and a town office. The museum has a gift and souvenir shop with many interesting items.

WESTERN DEVELOPMENT MUSEUM'S HISTORY OF TRANSPORTATION

50 Diefenbaker Dr. (Jct. of the TransCanada Hwy. & Hwy. 2)
MOOSE JAW, SK S6H 4N8
Phone: 306-693-5989
Hours: *April to Dec. 25* Tues.–Sun. 9–5. Admission charged.

This is a large museum tracing the history of the development of transportation in western Canada. There are displays of horse-drawn vehicles, trains, vintage cars, airplanes, riverboats, streetcars and snowmobiles. More than 40 cars and trucks are on display including a locally-built 1902 Holsman. Other displays include aircraft and memorabilia from Canada's armed forces aerobiotic team, an observatory and a Snowbird Gallery. There is also a miniature steam-powered train which visitors can ride on weekends. The museum has a gift shop offering merchandise related to the themes of the museum.

End of Moose Jaw area ◄

WESTERN DEVELOPMENT MUSEUM'S HERITAGE FARM AND VILLAGE

At the Jct. of Hwys. 16 and 40
NORTH BATTLEFORD, SK
S9A 2Y1 (80 miles northwest of Saskatoon)
Phone: 306-445-8033
Hours: *May through Sept.* daily 9–5, *rest of year* W–Sun. 12:30–4:30. Admission charged.

This is a reconstructed village showing life as it was in the pioneer days of western Canada during the 1920s. In the village are stores, homes, businesses, a school house, a grain elevator and an 80-acre working farm that is worked as it was in the 1920s. There are also displays of agricultural equipment and several antique automobiles.

WESTERN DEVELOPMENT MUSEUM'S 1910 BOOMTOWN

2610 Lorne Av. South
SASKATOON, SK S7J 0S6
Phone: 306-931-1910
Hours: *April–Dec.* daily 9–5, *rest of year* Tues.–Sun. 9–5. Admission charged.

This is a reconstructed village of about 30 buildings showing life as it was on a Saskatchewan prairie during the boomtown era around 1910 when new settlers were thronging into the province in large numbers. Among the numerous displays and exhibits are several vintage cars and trucks and an automotive library containing several thousand documents and is open to the public. There are also displays of wagons, buggies and farm machinery,

SASKATCHEWAN

an interesting museum store and a restaurant. Each summer, during the last week in June, the museum has a festival called "Pion-Era" in which their cars are displayed along with much of their vintage farming equipment.

WESTERN DEVELOPMENT MUSEUM'S STORY OF THE PEOPLE

Hwy. 16 West
YORKTOWN, SK S3N 2V6
(110 miles northeast of Regina)
Phone: 306-783-8361
Hours: *May 1 through mid-Sept.* daily 9–6. Admission charged.

This Western Development Museum focuses on the roots of the people who settled western Canada. Depicted in displays are the customs, homes, clothing, tools, musical instruments, crafts, etc. of the early settlers whose nationalities included Ukrainians, English, Germans, Icelanders, Swedes, Doukhobors, Americans and others. Additional exhibits include a trapper's cabin, a tea room, a music room, a 1930s kitchen, farm machinery and several vintage automobiles. There is a museum store and each summer during the first weekend in August the museum holds the "Threashermen's Show and Seniors' Festival" at which their antique cars are displayed and some of their vintage farm equipment is put into operation.

YUKON TERRITORY

YUKON TRANSPORTATION MUSEUM
Alaska Hwy. Km. post 1475.7
WHITEHORSE, YT
Phone: 867-668-4792
http://virtualguidebooks.com/Yukon
Hours: *Victoria Day through mid-Sept.* daily 10–6. Admission charged.

If you ever travel the Alaska Highway, here's a museum that is worth your while. It's just off the highway near the airport and highlights the many and various modes of transportation in this unique part of the world. There are several vintage automobiles and trucks on display along with railroad engines and cars, aircraft, military vehicles, boats, canoes, stage coaches and dog sleds. There is an informative exhibit telling of the construction of the Alaska Highway during World War II when it was of vital importance to our national defense. Another display highlights the history and activities of bush pilots which are so important in this part of the world. And still more, there is an extensive model train display and a number of attractive murals relating the history of the Yukon Territory.

INDEX

273

INDEX

INDEX

INDEX

INDEX